A Civil Republic

A Civil Republic

Beyond Capitalism and Nationalism

Severyn T. Bruyn

Kumarian
Press, Inc

A Civil Republic: Beyond Capitalism and Nationalism
Published in 2005 in the United States of America by Kumarian Press, Inc.,
1294 Blue Hills Avenue, Bloomfield, CT 06002 USA

The text of this book is set in 10/12 Palatino font.

Production and design by Publication Services
Proofread by Carol McGillivray

Printed by Transcontinental Printing G.P., Canada. Text printed with vegetable
oil-based ink.

⊚ The paper used in this publication meets the minimum requirements of the
American National Standard for Information Sciences—Permanence of Paper for
printed Library Materials, ANSI Z39.48-1984

Library of Congress Cataloging-in-Publication Data
Bruyn, Severyn Ten Haut, 1927-
  A civil republic : beyond capitalism and nationalism / Severyn T. Bruyn.
    p. cm.
  Summary:"Envisions a new model of governance: a civil republic, which com-
bines the human values of civil society and the market aspects of political econ-
omy, moving the world beyond conventions of capitalism and nationalism.
Written for scholars and practitioners of international relations, economics, polit-
ical science, business, international development, and international law"—
Provided by publisher.
  Includes bibliographical references and index.
  ISBN 1-56549-199-8 (pbk. : alk. paper)
  1. Civil society. 2. Globalization. 3. Capitalism. 4. International relations. 5.
International economic relations. 6. International organization. I. Title.
  JC337.B78 2005
    300—dc22
                        2004027485

14 13 12 11 10 09 08 07 06 05   10 9 8 7 6 5 4 3 2 1 First Printing 2005

Dedication

Elise Boulding

Author of eleven books and contributor to many more, she has been active in developing peace studies around the world. She is a former secretary-general, of the International Peace Research Association and is now professor emeritus at Dartmouth College. She and her husband, Kenneth Boulding, were active all their lives in conflict-resolution studies and led national groups working for world peace. She has been a long-time civic leader, lecturer, and editor of a newsletter providing news and networking opportunities to international peace teams. And she is a very dear friend of mine.

Acknowledgments

I want to thank Elise Boulding, an extraordinary leader in the field of world peace, for her personal support. I also want to thank steadfast colleagues in the Department of Sociology at Boston College who have supported my work over the decades; they have maintained a graduate program with the theme of Social Economy and Social Justice: Race, Gender, and Class in a Global Context. Students in that department working with Charles Derber alerted me to efforts that were being undertaken across the United States to stop overseas sweatshops that were unacceptable to them, a story found in Chapter 8. I also discussed the problems of global business represented in this book with colleagues in the joint degree program of the sociology department with the Carroll School of Management (*Leadership for Change*); this program trains top managers in business that face the issues covered in this book.

I benefited from panel discussions on the topics of this book. Boston College faculty members held a panel discussion on my last book (*A Civil Economy*) with numerous comments that informed this book. The panelists included Alan Wolfe (Political Science), David Rasmussen (Philosophy), Ali Banuazizi (Psychology), and Richard Tresh (Economics), and Stephen Pfohl (Sociology). The Coalition for a Strong United Nations organized a panel discussion on a draft for *A Civil Republic*. Among the panelists were Brian Aull (the Baha'i Community), Winston Langley (provost, University of Massachusetts, Boston, a professor of International Studies), and David Lewit (Alliance for Democracy), and their suggestions were also taken into account.

My gratitude goes to James Carey, CBS Professor of International Journalism at Columbia University, for his comments to me on problems in the mass media. As a former member of the board of directors of the Public Broadcasting System, a board member of Peabody Awards for Broadcasting, and author of *Television and the Press*, his advice was especially helpful to me.

The writings and research of Amitai Etzioni, former president of the American Sociological Association (ASA), clarified much of the path that I took; he supported my organizing an ASA workshop on social capital with Robert Putnam, Ron Burt, Viviana Zelizer, Carmen Sirianni, Charles Tilly, and Steve Waddell, thus providing more ideas for this book.

Richard Swedberg, a former student in the Boston College graduate program independently introduced a field of studies in economic sociology that became informative to me. This scientific orientation contributed to my writing the appendices found on my college Web site at http://www2.bc.edu/~bruyn.

Chris Kochansky contributed excellent editorial work on the draft manuscript. I want to thank Jim Lance at Kumarian for seeing the value in this work for publication.

My wife, Louise, is the most vital contributor of all, with all the faith and love that she has provided me in addition to reading, commenting upon, and personally supporting the writing of this book.

Contents

List of Boxes

Abbreviations/Acronyms

AAC&U, Association of American Colleges and Universities

AAHE, American Association for Higher Education

AAI, Aluminum Association Inc.

AASA, American Association of School Administrators

AASCU, American Association of School Administrators

AAU, Association of American Universities

ACE, American Council on Education

ACEHSA, Accrediting Commission for Education in Health Services Administration

ACLS, American Council of Learned Societies

AIA, American Institute of Architects

AICA, American Institute of Certified Accountants

AIP, Apparel Industry Partnership

AMA, American Medical Association

ANSI, American National Standards Institute

ASCO, American Society of Clinical Oncology

ASME, American Society of Mechanical Engineers

CAAHEP, Commission on Accreditation of Allied Health Education Programs

CCT, Civil Commission on Telecommunications

CDC, Community Development Corporation

CDD, Center for Digital Democracy

CEDAW, Convention on the Elimination of All Forms of Discrimination against Women

CEP, Council on Economic Priorities

CEPAA, Council on Economic Priorities Accreditation Agency

CEPH, Council on Education for Public Health

CERES, Coalition for Environmentally Responsible Economies

CHEA, Council for Higher Education Accreditation

CII, Council of Institutional Investors

CIPB, Citizens for Independent Public Broadcasting

CLC, Collegiate Licensing Company

CMI, Comité Maritime International

CSWE, Council on Social Work Education

CTF, Community Technology Fund

D&PL, Delta & Pine Land

EC, European Community

ECS, Education Commission of the States

FAIR, Fairness & Accuracy in Reporting

FLA, Fair Labor Association

FSC, Forest Stewardship Council

G-20, Group of Twenty

G-7, Group of Seven

GATS, General Agreement on Trade Services

GE, genetically engineered

GMO, genetically modified organism

HMO, health maintenance organization

HSN, Home Shopping Network

IAAE, International Association of Agricultural Economists

IAC, InterActiveCorp

IBO, international business organization

ICC, International Criminal Court

ICCR, Interfaith Council on Corporate Responsibility

IFG, International Forum on Globalization

IGF, insulin-like growth factor

IGO, intergovernmental organization

ILRF, International Labor Rights Fund

INGO, international nongovernmental organization

IPA, Independent Press Association

IPU, Interparliamentary Union of international business organizations

ISO, International Standards Organization

ITT, Illinois Institute of Technology

IUGG, International Union of Geodesy and Geophysics

IYF, International Youth Foundation

JCAHO, Joint Commission on Accreditation of Healthcare Organizations
LCHR, Lawyers Committee for Human Rights
LOS, Law of the Sea
MAP, Media Access Project
MEF, Media Education Foundation
MMS, Massachusetts Medical Society
NAB, National Association of Broadcasters
NAFTA, North American Free Trade Agreement
NAM, National Association of Manufacturers
NCA, North Central Association of Colleges and Schools
NCAA, National Collegiate Athletic Association
NEASC, New England Association of Schools and Colleges
NGO, nongovernmental organization
OPEC, Organization of Petroleum Exporting Countries
OSHA, Occupational Safety and Health Administration
PAC, political action committee
PBT, Public Board of Trustees
PBT, Public Broadcasting Trust
PCAOB, Public Company Accounting Oversight Board
PDB, Public Domain Board
POP, persistent organic pollutants
rBGH, recombinant bovine growth hormone
RFK, RFK Memorial Center for Human Rights
RTC, Research Technology Corporation
SAI, Social Accountability International
SEC, Securities and Exchange Commission
UNCTAD, United Nations Conference on Trade and Development
UNEP, UN Environmental Programme
UNITE, Union of Needletrades, Industrial, and Textile Employees
USAS, United Students Against Sweatshops
USDA, U.S. Department of Agriculture
WDM, wave division multiplexing
WI, Willamette Industries
WRC, Worker Rights Consortium
WTO, World Trade Association

Introduction

In his book *The Lexus and the Olive Tree,* Thomas Friedman, the foreign affairs columnist for the *New York Times,* defined globalization as "the inexorable integration of markets, nation states and technologies in a degree never witnessed before." And, he warned, over a year before September 11, 2001, "This process of globalization is also producing a powerful backlash from those brutalized or left behind by this new system."

For many citizens of the United States and its allies, the twin towers of the World Trade Center in New York City were a symbol of prosperity and freedom, but for others around the world they stood for arrogance and domination. The shock and terror, grief and anger provoked by their destruction—not just in this country but around the world—underscore the urgency of the topics we will address in this book.

While some would say that world trade is opening a path for free markets and democracy, it is also, undeniably, a struggle for power among nation-states and corporations whose interests grow ever more global. These markets are inexorably linked to issues of war and peace. In describing how markets and nations are moving on a single track, Friedman wrote,

> Managing globalization is a role from which America dare not shrink. It is our overarching national interest today, and the political party that understands that first, the one that comes up with the most coherent, credible and imaginative platform for pursuing it, is the party that will own the real bridge to the future.[1]

These are difficult times. There could be global calamities ahead. The state of the economy could worsen and be followed by a second great worldwide depression. Unchecked environmental pollution and exploitation could trigger a collapse of the world's interlocked ecosystems. Conflicts between governments and the spread of weapons of mass destruction could be followed by ever more horrifying terrorist attacks and even a World War III that would devastate the planet and its peoples.[2] All such terrible things could happen.

Could they be prevented? I think so. But preventing them would require a whole new system of governance in markets and states. This is what this book is about, strengthening and building upon existing structures to create a different type of governance for the economy and the nation, one that has links to similar efforts around the globe. I call that different type of governance a civil republic.

What is a civil republic? In the vision put forth in this book, a civil republic would be a society of federations that develops—by design and with government support—from local to global levels to bring core human values into the economy. This would require changes in public policies that would alter the direction of nations and specific market economies. It should lead toward a system of international law, a world court system, and a permanent multinational peace force. I will argue, it is the surest way for governments and civic leaders to prevent the disasters that loom above us.

Could such a thing be modeled and developed in the decades ahead? Why not? Many of the seeds for such a change were planted long ago. The Mayflower Compact that was signed on November 11, 1620, by 41 passengers who had arrived as colonists in the New World—heads of families, adult bachelors, and hired manservants—was a declaration that these men wanted to conduct their lives in a new way, under a new rule of civil law. Yes, they were intruders whose interests eventually clashed with those of the indigenous peoples they encountered. Yes, they were all male and propelled by self-interest as well as by a devotion to their ideals. But in agreeing to shape a type of government different from that of a European monarchy, and to safeguard religious freedom, they put forth a model for mutual self-governance that was new in the world.

The historian Daniel Boorstin describes this new kind of governance as having been born on a "fertile verge." "A verge is a place of encounter between 'something and something else,'" he wrote in 1989. "America was a land of verges—all sorts of verges, between kinds of landscape and seascape, between stages of civilization, between ways of thought and ways of life."[3] Far from the governments to which they still owed allegiance, the inhabitants of the all the European colonies in the North American Northeast grew used to a certain degree of self-determination. Like the signers of the Mayflower Compact, they began to develop their own extra-governmental institutions and associations for solving their own problems.

In 1776, the revolution of thirteen American colonies against the British Crown established a new form of government, a democratic republic based (in theory, at least) on the consent of the governed rather than the divine rights of kings or the authority of any one church. Above all, the new "Americans" were social inventors. Both before and after the American Revolution they created self-governing associations within this New World model. These associations—developed as churches, schools, colleges, clubs, and professions—sought to institutionalize their own goals and values, and to form relationships with each other for their mutual edification and benefit. In the late 1830s, Alexis de Tocqueville marveled at the propensity of Americans to form voluntary associations and identified this as a key characteristic of the new democracy. Writing a century and a half later, Daniel Boorstin agreed, calling these organizations "arenas of experiment and of progress" and "a new fountain of social creativity."[4]

Today, I would argue, we are living on a new, frightening but potentially fertile verge. Once again we are at the intersection of vastly different cultures and "ways of thought and ways of life." During most of human existence, political scientist Samuel Huntington writes, contacts between civilizations were intermittent or nonexistent. But today global politics has become "multipolar and multicivilizational."

> Peoples and nations are attempting to answer the most basic question humans can face: Who are we? And they are answering that question in the traditional way human beings have answered it, by reference to the things that mean most to them. People define themselves in terms of ancestry, religion, language history, values, customs, and institutions. They identify with cultural groups . . . and at the broadest level, civilizations. People use politics not just to advance their interests but also to define their identity.[5]

We face terrible challenges ahead, but I firmly believe that we can meet those challenges by drawing upon that "fountain of social creativity" to help us design a new civil republic.

"Can we start by building a global civil society?" asks Benjamin Barber, of Rutgers University.

> Until recently, one could look in vain for a global "we, the people" to be represented. That is now changing. There is another internationalism, a forming crystal around which a global polity can grow. Effective global governance to temper the excesses of the global market does not yet exist; however, international activism by nongovernmental organizations (NGOs) has made some surprising gains. People who care about public goods are working to recreate on a global scale the normal civic balance that exists within democratic nations.[6]

In this book we will discuss how the United States could begin to build a civil republic by advancing fresh links between the sectors of government, business, and the rest of society. This means creating higher levels of organization for markets, the nation, and eventually for the world at large.

We begin in Part 1 by asking, What's the problem? We take a look at what prominent business leaders and public commentators have to say about the multiple crises we face. They worry about the stock market, business ethics and the loss of core values, misguided government foreign policies and more. Some of them generalize. The problem is systemic, they say; it's the way nations are organized. They describe the frightening challenges before us as a set of problems created by the forces of the modern period: nationalism, capitalism, and globalization.

Then we'll turn to university scholars to see what they have to say about possible solutions. Academics see the problem in two frameworks: political economy and civil society. Political economists examine the organization of markets and states, asking how nations could improve their relations and their interlinked economies. The mainline of US government policy is based on this outlook. Civil society scholars, on the other hand, describe the problem as a decline in core values. They see churches building shopping malls, hospitals becoming businesses, and universities creating for-profit charters; they see professionals—accountants, lawyers, and physicians—supporting corporate interests more consistently than they support the values of honesty, justice, and public health. The scholars using these two frameworks do not see eye to eye. Our task is to bring the ideas and approaches represented in these frameworks closer together so that both can help us search for solutions.

In Part 2 we will look at the way nations organize a market economy from a new perspective. We start by re-defining markets and pose a question—how could markets develop differently? Other questions follow. Could capitalist markets become civil markets? Could a new market model be introduced into the global economy? Could new public policies offer a new constructive direction for globalization?

Parts 3 and 4 are about implementing this new model for markets and nations. They are about public policies that support the core values of society. They are about creating accreditation systems for industry and business, fashioning civil commissions that link associations in business and the Third Sector, and building a civil polity in the life of markets. They are about supporting civil investment, civil federations, and civil regimes on the world scene. They are about bringing accountability into the management of the economy, developing world law, and controlling global arms sales and weapons of mass destruction.

There is a lot here. Planners, scientists, scholars, educators, citizens, and community leaders must create markets that are internally safe and sound around the world. Third Sector associations must participate in markets as co-standard makers, monitors, and whistleblowers. The mass media must move from a private domain to a public domain. Local communities must achieve self-direction in global markets. As this "new market system" develops, it brings us to a civil republic.[7]

How does this happen? The three sectors—government, business, and the Third Sector—are very different. Their organizations are as far apart as states and churches, colleges and trade associations, global corporations and the United Nations. A new order of society must develop at the cross points of these sectors.

The plan is formidable and difficult to advance. It would require leaders with strength, courage, intelligence, and far-reaching vision, like the Americans who founded the United States in the eighteenth century—Washington, Jefferson, Adams, Franklin, Madison, and Monroe. These colonial leaders knew they had to overcome the power of a worldwide empire to create a new nation. As they fought their revolution and constructed the Constitution of the United States, they moved out of the medieval period.

I would argue that today we—all nations—need to move out of the modern period or perish. At the beginning of this new millennium, capitalism and nationalism are no longer workable. These "isms" lead only to injustice, ecosystem failures, economic depression, and the grounds for World War III. A new system of local to global governance is essential to counter the dangers of authoritarian governments, environmental collapse, and the use of weapons of mass destruction that could destroy humankind. Today America and nations around the world must create a civil revolution and a new republic. Here I offer a general outline and some specific proposals for how that could be done.

Notes

1. Thomas L. Friedman, *The Lexus and the Olive Tree* (NY: Anchor Books, 2000), 9, 437.
2. Terrorist groups and nation states are seeking weapons of mass destruction that can be moved easily through world markets. Deadly chemical weapons are attractive because they are simple to manufacture, easy to store and transport, and difficult for either governments or international inspectors to detect. Biological weapons can be equally elusive and lethal. Nuclear weapons are getting smaller for distribution and deployment. There is now a 58-pound nuclear "backpack" bomb that can be carried by one person.

    Historians have demonstrated that all countries eventually develop the latest weapons of war—from spears to long bows, from dynamite to guns and cannons—and none can control the sale of these arms once they have been created. While we can hope that the balance of power between nations will forestall the use of any of the more modern weapons of mass destruction, they may become available to terrorist organizations, and a terrorist attack using any of these weapons could destroy a whole city or even, at some point, a whole nation anywhere on earth.

3. Daniel Boorstin, *Hidden History* (NY: Vintage Books, 1989), xv.

4. Boorstin, *Hidden History, xv.*

5. Samuel P. Huntington, *The Clash of Civilizations and the Remaking of World Order* (NY: Simon & Schuster, 1996), 21.

6. Benjamin Barber, *The American Prospect,* Volume 11, Issue 20, September 11, 2000.

7. An extension of ideas in this book can be found in the Appendices on the Internet at http://www2.bc.edu/~bruyn.

Part One

The Problem
Capitalist Nations

1

Capitalism and Globalization
What's the Problem?

For much of the twentieth century, political leaders of the Western nations and the majority of their citizens saw the expansion of communism as the major threat to world peace and prosperity. That is no longer the case. Communism has collapsed or been transformed beyond recognition in all but a few countries (and arguably, even in those), and this turn of events has been and still is touted by many Western politicians as the victory of a capitalist market system over the tyranny of repressive economic controls. But the unfettered expansion of capitalism on a global scale has not, the evidence shows, brought that promised peace and prosperity to all.

Long before the attack on the World Trade Center and the war in Iraq, dissent had been mounting in the United States and around the world about the nature of globalization and the role that the United States has played in this seemingly unstoppable process. In the United States, people of all political persuasions have been deeply concerned about what they see as a decline in America's core values, and about whether current U.S. policies are imperialist and lead to war. Both of these concerns are seen by many—including business leaders, money managers, politicians, scientists, scholars, and civic leaders—as linked to the global expansion of capitalism without international law.

In what terms have such leaders cast these problems? In 1997, multi-billionaire George Soros published an article in the *Atlantic Monthly* entitled "The Capitalist Threat." Sounding like a revolutionary, he wrote, "Although I have made a fortune in the financial markets, I now fear that the untrammeled intensification of laissez-faire capitalism and the spread of market values into all areas of life is endangering our open and democratic society. The main enemy of the open society, I believe, is no longer the communist but the capitalist threat."

Soros's concerns echo those voiced by sociologist Henry Etzkowitz a decade earlier when he observed that all of society's major institutions were being affected by the convergence of capitalist markets with states. In the United States, for instance, the basic scientific research carried out in university settings is increasingly funded not by government and/or nonprofit entities acting in the public interest, but by corporations hoping to reap profits from that research. This "spiraling interaction," Etzkowitz pointed out, may promote the expansion of markets in the national interest, but it stifles rather than encourages the advancement of knowledge. As universities are getting more and more capital from business, they are losing their focus on their broader mission in society.[1] In this book, we will discuss this and other ways in which market values are intruding further and further into our lives.

Soros continued in his article,

> [Karl] Popper showed that fascism and communism had much in common, even though one constituted the extreme right and the other the extreme left, because both relied on the power of the state to repress the freedom of the individual. I want to extend his argument. I contend that an open society may also be threatened from the opposite direction—from excessive individualism. Too much competition and too little cooperation can cause intolerable inequities and instability. . . . Insofar as there is a dominant belief in our society today, it is a belief in the magic of the marketplace. The doctrine of laissez-faire capitalism holds that the common good is best served by the uninhibited pursuit of self-interest. Unless it is tempered by the recognition of a common interest that ought to take precedence over particular interests, our present system—which, however imperfect, qualifies as an open society—is liable to break down.[2]

Soros is not alone among US business leaders. Five years later, in 2002, Felix Rohatyn wrote in a similar vein about "The Betrayal of Capitalism." He had lauded capitalism in the past century, as he stated in his article in the *New York Review of Books*, but knows now that the system is not working. For Rohatyn, the collapse of markets overseas (e.g., the Asian market collapse), major disasters in banking (e.g., the savings and loans scandals), the costly collapse of hedge funds (e.g., Long Term Capital Management), corporate malfeasance at the highest levels (e.g., Enron), and dozens of other market-system problems all provide sufficient evidence that the system needs to be changed.[3]

The possibility that capitalist markets are destroying the earth's resources is also a major concern among those in a position to know what's happening on a global scale. Øystein Dahle, retired vice president of Esso for Norway and the North Sea, says, "socialism collapsed because it did not allow prices to tell the economic truth. Capitalism may collapse because it does not allow prices to tell the ecological truth."[4]

Physical and biological scientists see ample evidence of the destructive effects of global markets on the environment. They speak of forests decimated by market transactions, cut down at a rate of 16 million hectares per year. They testify that market decisions made by agricultural corporations and independent farmers in North America are resulting in the destruction of topsoil—at a rate of 6 billion tons per year. The private transactions of multinational firms cause fisheries to collapse in the world's oceans. The production and unregulated use of chemicals is resulting in high levels of toxins in the air, soil, and water—toxins that are dangerous not only to humankind directly but also to the ecosystems upon which all life depends.

The amount of sea ice in Arctic waters has been shrinking at an average rate of 14,000 square miles each year since 1978, but global warming remains a subject for debate, not action. Most recently, scientists have voiced their concern about how the market in biotechnology is already changing the DNA of species and might eventually affect the direction of human evolution. Even on a small scale, they warn, genetic manipulation could move in unpredictable ways, and certainly if markets alone drive research and use in this field, not all the results will serve the common good.[5]

The market system outpaces any efforts of individual national governments to restrain it, and even in the face of the possibility that human beings are causing serious climate change, there is no international governing system that can place meaningful controls on market-driven activities that have huge and long-lasting consequences. There are no enforcement agencies at the world level that can put limits on hazardous technologies or potentially dangerous production practices. As news keeps coming in about collapsing fisheries and shrinking forests, eroding soils and expanding deserts, rising carbon dioxide levels, melting glaciers, dying coral reefs, and species extinction, capitalist markets encourage people to *buy*—to believe that their well-being depends on more gadgets and bigger cars, on our possessions rather than our values. Even in political discourse, we are often addressed not as persons or citizens, but as "consumers."

Thomas Friedman, the *New York Times* columnist quoted in the introduction, talks with international leaders who see globalization as "the integration of capital, technology, and information across national borders, creating a single global market." We cannot understand the morning news or know where the world is going, he wrote in *The Lexus and the Olive Tree* (published in 2000), unless we understand this expanding system.

> [The globalization system] enables individuals, corporations, and nation-states to reach around the world farther, faster, deeper, and cheaper than ever before. . . . The driving idea behind globalization is free-market capitalism. The idea is that the more you let market forces rule and the more you open your economy to free trade and competition, the more efficient and flourishing your economy will be. Globalization means the spread of free-market capitalism to virtually every country in the world. Globalization also has its own set of economic rules that revolve around opening, deregulating and privatizing the economy. And globalization has its own dominant culture, which is homogenizing the life of nations around the world today.

In previous eras, Friedman says, this sort of "cultural homogenization" happened on a regional scale; he cites the Hellenization of the Near East and the Mediterranean world under the Greeks; the Turkification of Central Asia, North Africa, Europe, and the Middle East by the Ottomans; and the Russification of Eastern and Central Europe and parts of Eurasia under the Soviets. But today capitalism is homogenizing the whole world.

> Culturally speaking, globalization is largely, though not entirely, the spread of Americanization—from Big Macs to iMacs to Mickey Mouse—on a global scale. Globalization has its own defining technologies: computerization, miniaturization, digitization, satellite communications, fiber optics and the Internet. And these technologies helped to create the defining perspective of globalization. The United States can destroy you by dropping bombs and the Supermarkets can destroy you by downgrading your bonds. The United States is the dominant player in maintaining the globalization game board, but it is not alone in influencing the moves on that game board. This globalization game board today is a lot like a Ouija board—sometimes pieces are moved around by the obvious hand of the superpower, and sometimes they are moved around by hidden hands of the Supermarkets.[6]

As sociologist Immanuel Wallerstein pointed out five years earlier, behind what Friedman refers to as the Supermarkets and the dominant culture of globalization lies an effort to commodify—to bring into the marketplace and put a price upon—virtually all social transactions. The capitalist market system, he argues, has become incredibly far reaching as individuals and corporations seek to find profits in arenas of life that were once thought to be outside the realm of commerce.[7]

In 1991, Benjamin Barber, a scholar of democracy, describes two forces at work as determinants of our future—tribalism and globalism. In his way of looking at things, the "McWorld principle" represents capitalist markets and a process of homogenization through which a single commercial culture is transferred around the world, destroying cultural diversity. The "*jihad* principle" represents "retribalization," or "the threatened Lebanonization, of national states in which culture is pitted against culture, people against people, [and] tribe against tribe." Both of these forces threaten democracy, he argued in his book *Jihad vs. McWorld,* because even the most democratic of national governments have become captives of the capitalist system.[8]

This brings us full circle. The wrongdoings of the Enron Corporation were supported by the most prestigious accountants, lawyers, commercial and investment bankers, security analysts, and debt-rating agencies. The "shameful activities" of top executives were carried out within US securities regulations and the disclosure requirements of the government. The legal underpinnings of the business system make exploitation rewarding, whether it is the environment, workers, shareholders, or taxpayers that are being exploited. In short, national governments are also part of the problem because they let it all happen.

In the United States, the editors of business magazines reflect the views of many business leaders as they focus in on the specific systemic problems that plague a capitalist market structure.

During a recent wave of corporate scandals, for example, *Business Week* examined the theme "The Betrayed Investor" in a series of articles that argued that one elite "class of investors" has become a powerful"economic and political force"and that Wall Street, big corporations, major accountancy firms, and the government are mutually supportive in a system that deceives anyone who is not an insider, including the general public.[9] (None of this would have surprised the sociologist C. Wright Mills, who argued in *The Power Elite* and *The Causes of World War Three*—published a half century ago—that oligarchy had already won over democracy in the United States: "The political order, once a decentralized set of several dozen states . . . has become a centralized, executive establishment which has taken up into itself many powers previously scattered, and now enters into each and every cranny of the social structure.")[10]

Michael Mandel, chief economist at *Business Week,* announced the theme of his article in capital letters: "THE ECONOMY NEEDS A NEW MORALITY." Senior writer Gary Weiss, who has covered Wall Street scandals since 1986, titled his contribution "CONGRESS WILL HUFF AND PUFF AND DO LITTLE"; every few years, Weiss wrote, there are headlines about scandals, but there will be more financial catastrophes unless "the system" itself is changed. In a special report of May 6, 2002, *Business Week* reported on "The Crisis in Corporate Governance"; the subjects of this report included "excessive pay for CEOs," "weak leadership," "corrupt analysts," "complacent boards," and "questionable accounting."[11]

Business Week editors have focused in particular on the growing size and spread of corporations around the world. Wal-Mart Stores, for instance, had $245 billion in revenues in 2002, but its growing market dominance is linked to serious social problems. This "staunchly anti-union company, America's largest employer, is widely blamed for the sorry state of retail wages in America. On average, Wal-Mart sales clerks—'associates' in company parlance—pulled in $8.23 an hour, or $13,861 a year in 2001." The poverty line for a family of four in the United States in 2001 was $14,630. Wal-Mart, the editors also pointed out, plays a huge role in determining wages and working conditions not only in this country but also worldwide.[12]

Capitalism could not exist without the management of capital itself. What do thoughtful money managers, investment bankers, and business analysts think about the impact of globalization in the United States and around the world?

In the United States, many corporate lawyers and pension fund trustees are upset about a stock market that they believe is failing as a system. William Lerach, for example, is one of the corporate world's one hundred most influential lawyers, a partner in the law firm of Milberg Weiss Bershad Hynes & Lerach, LLP. He has filed hundreds of class-action lawsuits against large corporations, including Enron, and he speaks emphatically about the need for "system change" in corporate governance. He would require the rotation of independent auditors every three years for such powerful institutions. He would demand the installation of a corporate ethics officer with "real authority" and that independent reporting responsibility be given to the board. He would also demand rigorous controls that prevent "option flipping," insider trading, and various other forms of self-dealing by corporate officers, including a holding period on stock options that would prevent CEOs from cashing out in a falling market while other company shareholders are losing out.

Richard Moore, the treasurer for the State of North Carolina, agrees. He is sole fiduciary for over $60 billion in public monies and state investment. He oversees the pension funds of nearly 600,000 public sector employees, and is responsible for the management of the public debt of both the state government and local municipalities. He contends that without fundamental changes in the stock market system on Wall Street, he will "walk away"; that is, he and his professional colleagues will "pull out" of that market and look for other investment opportunities. An attractive option could be a new stock exchange established with stronger regulations.[13]

Most people think of the stock market as a place where "investments" are made, where people can take the risk of investing in new enterprises. This makes the market progressive and dynamic. But there's increasing evidence that this is a complete misconception of how today's stock market actually works. Only a tiny fraction of the money within the system is invested in new firms, the rest just keeps circling around among gamblers and speculators.

Business analyst Ralph Estes points out that in recent years only about one out of each hundred dollars trading on public markets actually reaches corporations. The rest goes instead to stockholders who are simply speculating on the market. Today's Wall Street, he argues, is like a Las Vegas casino: 99% of market money is speculative or just plain gambling. In other words, the stock market is not based on good economics.[14]

Marjorie Kelly, editor of *Business Ethics* magazine, agrees that the stock market is part of a deeply flawed system. As she sees it, "wealth inequality, corporate welfare, and industrial pollution" are symptoms of a sick economy, and its underlying sickness is the result of a system built to make profits for shareholders no matter what the cost to the public. In this capitalist system, the corporation is a piece of property owned by shareholders and its officers are responsible only to them. We need a new model, she argues, one of the corporation as part of a larger human context in which employees and communities are influential stakeholders as well.[15]

Furthermore, Kelly also argues, the stock market is losing money. She calculates "stock buybacks" into the equation and finds that the system is "totally counterproductive." ("Buybacks" occur when a company issues stocks and then later buys them back, often at a higher price.) Looking at the Federal Reserve figures for net new equity issues (new stock issues minus buybacks) each year, she found that for 1998 the figure was a negative $267 billion. This told her, she writes, that the stock market is actually less than 0% productive; in fact, it's losing money every year. [16]

Put another way, the stock market is a "negative source of funding" and this has been true for many decades. New equity sales are an example of this type of funding in fifteen of the nearly twenty years from 1981 to 2000. In looking back over these two decades, Kelly found no net stockholder money going into the market; it is all flowing out. The net outflows since 1981 for new equity issues was negative $540 billion.[17]

During those twenty years the largest bull market in history took place. But stockholders did not fund it. Instead, according to Kelly, "companies pumped massive amounts of money into [the market], to prop it up." That bubble has burst and trillions of dollars of value have evaporated while companies are left holding massive debt incurred on behalf of that evaporated value. Stock buybacks used up so much cash that companies had to borrow money to invest in their businesses. In other words, during this time of supposed prosperity, the debt of corporations in America grew substantially.[18] This is a "market system problem." Instead of capitalizing companies, the stock market is "de-capitalizing" them. The stock market produces a cash loss, as Kelly would say, stockholders are not investors, they are "extractors." Stockholders do not contribute wealth to the economy; they extract it.

Peter Peterson is chairman of the Federal Reserve Bank of New York and of his own investment firm, the Blackstone Group. He is a lifelong Republican who served as secretary of commerce in Richard Nixon's cabinet. He sees an economic and a moral crisis looming at the same time, and, in his view, the fiscal crisis is both domestic and foreign. "We are now facing a situation during a decade when we should have been saving for the Boomer revolution that's coming and the retirement costs. Instead of saving during that decade we're squandering it. The Concord Coalition, Goldman Sachs, [and] the Committee for Economic Development predict that over the next ten years we're going to be adding $5 trillion of deficits. So we have a domestic fiscal crisis."[19] Peterson claims that the United States has the lowest savings rate in the world and that we are now going to be "importing" something like $500 to $600 billion in foreign capital. In fact, he suggests, we have become addicted to foreign capital. At some point we're going to have to pay back the interest due on these loans, and in the meantime, foreigners end up owning a large part of the United States.

Furthermore, Peterson warns that, in the future, foreigners could lose confidence in the United States. The dollar could fall, the stock and bond markets might follow, and then interest rates would go way up. If these things were to happen, our already "mammoth" debt would also go up—astronomically. The foreign deficit is at 5% of the GDP, heading toward 6%. And the previous record high, during the Reagan years, was only 3.5%. So we have a dual crisis—the national deficit and the foreign deficit—in the making.

Peterson sees this phenomenon as especially troublesome when we know that ten years from now 77 million baby boomers will be retiring, and the entitlements we have promised them are not fully funded. According to his estimate, the unfunded liabilities for Social Security and Medicare amount to $25 trillion—a huge amount of public indebtedness that the general public simply does not know about. "The Trust Fund is one of the ultimate fiscal oxymorons of our time. . . . The Social Security Administration believes that my children and grandchildren will have to pay between 25 and 35 percent of payroll to fund these programs."[20]

Meanwhile, international leaders describe how global markets increase the likelihood of war through arms sales and the privatization of security forces. In developing nations, private security organizations are on the rise, including those loyal to regional warlords and corporate-sponsored forces, and the global firms that are seeking access to natural resources support the military dictatorships and authoritarian regimes.[21]

Governments and warlords have made billions of dollars on these markets, and small wars rage on because they are in fact part of corporations and governments doing business as usual. The UN Security Council, confronted by devastating conflicts in Sierra Leone, Angola, and Congo, has imposed embargoes on the diamond trade and military arms paid for with diamond money, and support has been growing to establish a standardized certification scheme for diamonds, but the UN has no enforcement power. Traders, governments, and bankers alike violate the sanctions with impunity. There is no law in commerce to address these issues.

The nonprofit Worldwatch Institute keeps an eye on these problems. Researcher Michael Renner states that oil and mining companies, trading firms, airlines and shipping companies, manufacturers, and banks carry some responsibility for the events that trigger the wars.

> This responsibility ranges from an active role (in which companies are directly and knowingly involved in illicit resource exploitation), to a silent complicity (in which firms do business with repressive regimes because of lucrative contracts), to a passive enabling role (in which few questions are asked by companies down the supply chain about the origin of raw materials or about money being laundered). . . . On a different front, lawsuits have been filed in the United States against a number of corporations, arguing that these companies have colluded with various governments in human rights violations aimed at suppressing opposition to a variety of resource extraction projects. Among the defendants are Shell (concerning events in Nigeria's Ogoniland), Rio Tinto (Bougainville), ExxonMobil (Aceh), and Unocal (Burma).[22]

And it is certainly no secret that US corporations influence US foreign policy directly and to an enormous degree. Long before the most recent war in Iraq began in March 2003, the Bush administration was planning to rebuild the country when fighting ceased. According to news accounts published that month, the US Agency for International Development had quietly asked six US companies to submit bids for a $900 million government contract to repair and reconstruct water systems, roads and bridges, and schools and hospitals in Iraq. The six companies—Bechtel Group Inc.; Fluor Corp.; Halliburton Co., subsidiary Kellogg, Brown & Root of the Louis Berger Group Inc.; Parsons Corp.; and Washington Group

International—contributed a combined $3.6 million in individual, PAC, and soft-money political donations between 1999 and 2002. Sixty-six percent of that total went to Republicans. Bechtel, the engineering corporation that employed former Defense Secretary Caspar Weinberger, former Secretary of State George Shultz, and other government officials before they took their government posts, gave $1.3 million in individual, PAC, and soft-money contributions over those three years.

Even as Bechtel prepared its bid for the postwar project, it was facing allegations that it had in fact also contributed to Iraq's military buildup nearly two decades ago. The *San Francisco Chronicle* reported on a document prepared for the United Nations by Iraq (uncovered and brought to public attention by a German journalist) that says Bechtel was among twenty-four US companies that supplied the country with weapons during the 1980s. Global firms follow the money. [23]

Wars are linked to the way markets are organized, which is why the leaders of many nongovernmental organizations (NGOs) support the idea of a permanent UN peacekeeping force and other measures to strengthen the role of the United Nations in world affairs.[24]

Business leaders worry about a lack of corporate ethics and talk about the need for a new morality. Civic leaders worry about the expansion of businesses into fields where they do not belong, as in science, the professions, religion, and education. Grassroots activists are concerned about consumerism and social scientists are troubled by the commercialization of culture. Political leaders are concerned about the spread of weapons of mass destruction. International leaders are apprehensive about the lack of a global governing system. So we have not one problem, but an array of problems that, taken together, seem overwhelming. If national governments seem powerless in the face of market forces, where can we make a start at reining them in?

In February of 2002, the World Economic Forum, attended by top government representatives and business leaders, ended its session by taking up the topic of globalization. Citing the new hope represented by the start of a new millennium, UN Secretary General Kofi Annan urged the delegates to study "the forces of anti-globalization, militant Islam, terrorism and poverty" and to pay attention to the "inhuman conditions under which much of the world lived. Business," he said, "cannot afford to be seen as the problem. The reality is that power and wealth in this world are very, very unequally shared, and that far too many people are condemned to lives of extreme poverty and degradation. . . . The perception, among many, is that this is the fault of globalization, and that globalization is driven by a global elite, composed of, at least represented by, the people who attend this gathering."[25]

Vaclav Havel, the former president of Czechoslovakia, has sounded similar warnings about the development of capitalist markets supported by nation-states without world law, but he has also pointed the way forward. The experience of two world wars, he stated in a speech reprinted in the *New York Review of Books* in 1999, should have brought us "the recognition that human beings are more important than states." In language similar to what we would use, he called for the development of civil society and new systems of governance. We must look at "the emotional role the state plays in our lives," Havel urged; our emotional allegiance to the state should be "redistributed among the other areas that shape our identity." Our emotional identities must "spread to the different levels of what we perceive to be our proper home and our natural world: our families, the companies we work for, the communities we live in, the organizations we belong to, and our region, our profession, our church, all the way to our continent and ultimately our earth, the planet we inhabit. All of these places are different environments in which our identities are formed and through which we live our lives."[26]

Havel's remarks call upon us to acknowledge values beyond those of the market and the state. These core values already exist in modern society, as do institutions and associations that seek to protect and defend them. They are part of what we mean when we speak of civil society, and it is the purpose of this book to present strategies for strengthening them in the process of globalization.

Globalization in its broad meaning has been going on since time immemorial, but it is a catchword today for the spread of capitalism and the struggle for power. We are saying that this struggle leads to the decline of civil society.[27]

The spread of capitalism is not new. Sociologist James Petras describes how Latin America's trade and external investment had greater significance in the fifteenth through nineteenth centuries than in the twentieth century. But the struggle for power between capitalist states that produces a decline in civil society has been in the public eye since the fall of communism. Capitalist nation-states are contesting in an age of technology that could lead down dangerous paths. The model of the capitalist nation is dangerous because it resists the development of the larger society and international law.

Capitalism emerged in the modern period with the concept of nationalism. But capitalism as a description of markets and the idea of nationalism as a totally "sovereign state" cannot be the future. Indeed these ideas of capitalist markets and nation-states are metamorphosing now. As we will suggest in this book, a new market system and a new international order is in the making.

Nation-states are beginning to develop higher forms of regional organization through international law. The more nations agree to the authority of the United Nations and regional organizations like NAFTA and the European Union, they move into new concepts of sovereignty. The final outcome is a different sense of autonomy for nations in a system of world governance and law.

The current agenda is about how capitalist markets develop around the globe and sovereign nations seek world power. But a new market system and a new system of global governance are the hidden agenda that we talk about in this book.

Notes

1. Henry Etzkowitz, "Interviews, University-Industry Relations Study" (Washington, DC: US National Science Foundation , 1986).
2. George Soros, "The Capitalist Threat," *Atlantic Monthly,* Volume 279, No. 2 (February 1997), 45–58.
3. Felix Rohatyn, "The Betrayal of Capitalism," *New York Review of Books,* 28 February 2002, 6.
4. Dahle is quoted by Lester Brown at a Worldwatch Briefing, Aspen, Colorado, 22 July 2001. See Lester R. Brown, *Eco-Economy* (NY: W.W. Norton, 2001), 23.
5. For an elaboration, see Severyn T. Bruyn, *A Civil Economy* (Ann Arbor: University of Michigan Press, 2000).
6. Thomas L. Friedman, *The Lexus and the Olive Tree: Understanding Globalization* (NY: Farrar, Straus and Giroux, 2000). On the Internet, see "What Is Globalization?" at http://www.lexusandtheolivetree.com/globalization.htm.
7. Immanuel Wallerstein, *Historical Capitalism, with Capitalist Civilization* (London: Verso, 1995).
8. Benjamin R. Barber, *Jihad vs McWorld* (New York: Times Books, 1995). See also Jeffrey C. Goldfarb, *The Cynical Society* (Chicago: University of Chicago Press, 1991).
9. "The Betrayed Investor," Cover Theme, *Business Week,* February 22, 2002, http://www.businessweek.com/magazine/toc/02_08/B3771magazine.htm.
10. C. Wright Mills, *The Causes of World War Three* (New York: Ballantine, 1958, 1960), 185–186.
11. See *Business Week,* 22 February 2002: Michael Mandel, "A New Economy Needs a New Morality," p. 114; Gary Weiss, "Congress Will Huff and Puff and . . . Do Little," p. 116. See also, *BusinessWeek,* "The Crisis in Corporate Governance," Special Report, 6 May 2002.
12. Wal-Mart's quest for profits on low-priced goods leads many manufacturing companies to move their factories overseas. In the United States, its labor costs are 20% lower than those of unionized commercial outlets, and it uses this "advantage" to force many local rivals, large and small, out of local markets. For every Wal-Mart Super Center that opens in the next five years, two other supermarkets will close. Because this chain often extracts tax breaks, economists believe that Wal-Mart's entry into a community does not result in any

net increase in jobs and tax revenues. Anthony Bianco and Wendy Zellner, "Is Wal-Mart Too Powerful?" *Business Week* (cover story), 4 October, 2003, p. 102ff.

13. The views of Learch and Moore were aired on Bill Moyers's PBS program *NOW* on 27 September 2002.

14. Ralph Estes, *Tyranny of the Bottom Line* (San Francisco: Berrett-Koehler, 1996). Reported in Marjorie Kelley, *The Divine Right of Capital* (San Francisco: Berrett-Koehler, 2001), 189.

15. See Kelly, *The Divine Right of Capital,* Introduction.

16. Kelley, ibid.,190.

17. Federal Reserve Flow of Funds Accounts of the United States, Annual Flows, where the Web site shows net new equity issues since 1946. Cited in Kelley, ibid., 34, 193.

18. Floyd Norris, "With Bull Market Under Siege, Some Worry About Its Legacy," *New York Times,* 18 March 182001. Cited in Kelly, ibid., 35.

19. Bill Moyers's *NOW* at http://www.pbs.org/now/transcript/transcript_ peterson.html. Broadcast 26 September 2003.

20. Ibid.

21. Global oil and mining corporations, for instance, rely on private security forces to guard their operations and facilities. Companies like Occidental Petroleum in Colombia, Shell in Nigeria, Talisman Energy in Sudan, and ExxonMobil and Freeport-McMoRan in Indonesia have subsidized or helped train and arm government security forces, or they have made equipment and facilities available to these governments. Global corporations that exploit natural resources are part of the mix of warlords and corrupt governments that help fuel wars. The massive proliferation of small arms in global markets, for example, plays a key role in domestic wars. Wars are carried out with light weapons because they are cheap, widely available, and easy to use and sell on the market. Markets are directly involved in the wars of Sierra Leone, Angola, Democratic Republic of the Congo, and Sudan. A small elite acquires the benefits for mining and logging, for oil in Colombia and Nigeria, timber and natural gas in Indonesia, and copper in Bougainville/Papua New Guinea.

22. Michael Renner, "The Anatomy of Resource Wars," Paper 162, Worldwatch Institute, October 2002, p. 58. This Worldwatch paper suggests that an estimated 8 million pistols, revolvers, rifles, and submachine guns were manufactured in 2000. (Renner, 60.)

23. Cheryl Fred, "Post War Profits," CapitalEye.org. http://www.capitaleye.org/inside.asp?ID=69.

24. The executive officers of CARE USA, for example, argue that the UN should commit resources to avert violent conflicts before they start. The UN should give more financial support for peacekeeping in its budget. Peter D. Bell and Guy Tousignant, "Getting Beyond New York: Reforming Peacekeeping in the Field," *World Political Journal,* 2001, http://www.globalpolicy.org/security/peacekpg/reform/2002/reform.htm.

25. Serge Schmenann, "Annan Cautions Business as World Forum Ends," *New York Times,* 5 February 2002.

26 This speech was reproduced in the *New York Review of Books,* 10 June 1999,
    http://www.nybooks.com/articles/article-preview?article_id=455.

27 Doug Henwood, a contributing editor to the *Nation* argues that instead of
    blaming globalization for economic ills, why not take it over? Doug Henwood,
    "Beyond Globophobia, *The Nation,* Nov. 13, 2003, http://www.thenation.com/
    doc.mhtml?i=20031201&s=henwood.

2

Civil Society
What's This Central Idea?

The term "civil society" features prominently in the debate about global-ization but it has different meanings for people. So, our first task is to clar-ify those meanings.

Let us begin with the term "society." A society is not the same as a "nation" or "state." It is more than a political idea; it is more than a "civil government." It is about how people build a consensus around competing ways of life. It is about how social institutions and subcultures emerge in a social order, about how organizations battle and about how people de-velop their lives together. It is about how social systems are constructed and markets change in this process of conflict and consensus.

The idea of a "*civil* society" has three meanings. First, civil society is a concept about institutional change in the modern period, i.e. about the creation of democratic governments and capitalist markets. Second, it is about the *Third Sector,* which is made up of non-governmental associa-tions that are not in business. Third, it is about the whole *voluntary sector,* excluding government but including both business and the Third Sector.

We will look at these three meanings in some detail because they are important to our argument. They help explain how a new society develops within a capitalist nation.

Civil Society is a Philosophical Idea (1600–Present)

As feudalism waned in the sixteenth century, the word "civil" became popular in everyday speech. People talked about how they had progressed from a primitive society to a more advanced (civil) way of life. They spoke about the importance of manners at home and decorum in public. "Civil" came to refer to "more class" and a more advanced social order than had existed in feudal times. Philosophers sought to describe the changes that were transforming European nations and Western culture.[1]

Thomas Hobbes (1588–1679) was among the first philosophers to use the word "civil" in reference to government. In order to live at peace with one another, he argued, human beings surrender their natural liberty and exchange it for civil liberty by means of a "social contract." After that social contract is established,"[t]he multitude so united in one person is called a COMMONWEALTH; in Latin, CIVITAS. This is the generation [origin] of that great Leviathan, or rather, to speak more reverently, of that mortal god to which we owe, under the immortal God, our peace and defence." By "Leviathan" Hobbes meant the commonwealth or state that is brought into being "by covenant of every one to every one" and requires a social agreement; the civil liberty it allows is the freedom to do whatever the law of the state does not prohibit. [2]

John Locke (1632–1704) broadened Hobbes's concept of the social contract and began the notion of civil society. Rather than identifying the notion with a state or government, he connected it with a social order. It was about the way in which people create consensus and develop rules and customs to live together. Included in this understanding of the social contract were non-governmental groups like the family and the church as well as the state. Locke called this realm "civil society" and saw it as being dependent on agreements among people and many kinds of organizations, not just between people and their governments. In fact, in a civil society people *authorized* government.[3] And this was a revolutionary idea.

As the concept of civil society spread across Europe, other theorists contributed their own various perspectives. The Baron de Montesquieu (1689–1755) went out of his way to distinguish "society" from "government"; like Locke, he saw society, with its own governing powers (i.e., its own customs and rules), as co-existing with the state and its laws. Adam Ferguson (1723–1816) wrote of "the formation of associations" within this social order as a means by which the conflicts between groups of people become resolved apart from government, through "social politics"; in 1767 he proposed that "the end of civil society is the happiness of all individuals."[4] Jean-Jacques Rousseau (1712–1778) explicitly linked the idea of society with the economic order, and in *A Discourse on Political Economy* he made a distinction between a "public economy" and a "private economy." Adam Smith (1723–1790) connected the idea of liberty within civil society with the new system of commerce in which markets demonstrated the power of self-regulation. All of these ideas placed civil society in contrast to feudal society.

And eventually, of course, they sparked revolutions. The idea of a "civil commonwealth" conceived by Hobbes threatened the authority of the monarchy, and Locke's idea of a "civil society" legitimized the English Revolution of 1688. In drafting the Declaration of Independence, the document that so eloquently set forth the justification for the American Revolution in 1776, Thomas Jefferson drew upon Locke in particular. By refusing due deference to the consent and welfare of those it governed, the Declaration announced, the restored British monarchy, in the person of King George III, had become despotic and tyrannical, and therefore the people of the thirteen colonies had the right to "dissolve the bands which have connected them" to the Crown in order to institute a new government that could defend their natural and God-given rights to "Life, Liberty, and the pursuit of Happiness."[5]

All of these ideas were certainly present in the minds of the leaders of the French Revolution in 1789, and, as further developed in the works of Thomas Paine, the first ten amendments to the U.S. Constitution (ratified in 1791 and known as the Bill of Rights), and France's Declaration of the Rights of Man and Citizen, they spread across Europe. But as new nations struggled to reorganize with new political principles, some philosophers saw civil society identified with markets. These markets were difficult to reconcile with the higher values of a good society.

In grappling with this problem, Georg Wilhelm Friedrich Hegel (1770–1831) said that civil society included every facet of life "except the government," describing it as a repository of public freedom while the state remained the final source of moral authority. Karl Marx (1818–1883) criticized Hegel's concept of government and civil society because it carried an acceptance of exploitative (uncivil) markets. These capitalist markets, in his view, were based on greed and self-interest; they contributed to the inequalities between classes and caused governments to become corrupt, and this would become the basis for a new revolution.

Indeed, new revolutions in the twentieth century created communist states, whose leaders offered an alternative vision to the civil society that had arisen in a capitalist world; they promised the abolishment of private property and state control of economic affairs in the interests of all citizens. It would lead to the elimination of class differences and to justice and equity for all. But by the end of the century these regimes had failed in the main, and with the collapse of communism in the Soviet Union and Eastern Europe, the older idea of "civil society" was revived. It became a source of hope and a basis for thinking about a new civil order. [6]

Civil society in this historical perspective evolves in three parts: democratic government, capitalist markets, and a Third Sector composed of neither government nor markets. Civil society advocates who accept this tri-sector notion emphasize ideals that have developed during the modern period. They would say that the "attributes" of civil society include representative government, freedom of religion, respect and protection of private life, the maintenance of public safety, and the right to free association that underlies the Third Sector.[7]

Civil Society Is the Third Sector

The Third Sector became visible in the mid-twentieth century. Some would argue that it offers an alternative or counterweight to the greed of the market and the indifference and inefficiencies of government bureaucracy.

The Third Sector is not government and not business. It is called variously the nonprofit sector, the independent sector, and the voluntary sector—and during the past half-century it has quietly been expanding both in the United States and worldwide.[8] It is in this broad context that Lester Salamon and Helmut Anheier have offered this definition:

> [Civil society is] the plethora of private, nonprofit, and nongovernmental organizations that have emerged in recent decades in virtually every corner of the world to provide vehicles through which citizens can exercise individual initiative in the private pursuit of public purposes. If representative government was the great social invention of the eighteenth century, and bureaucracy—both public and private—of the nineteenth, it is organized, private, voluntary activity, the proliferation of civil society organizations, that may turn out, despite earlier origins, to represent the great social innovation of the twentieth century.[9]

Brian O'Connell, a Tufts University professor and the founding president of an organization devoted to promoting the efforts of "charitable, educational, religious, health, and social welfare organizations," would agree. Emphasizing the separation between government and the Third Sector, he says that a civil society is one in which "the people are ultimately in charge."[10] This statement is a bit fuzzy, of course, but it reflects an ideal held by many, even as some scholars and observers remain critical of the realities, pointing out that many Third Sector organizations do in fact have strong ties to business and government.[11]

The Institute for Development Research also attempts to separate civil society from government and business, and it describes the Third Sector's distinctive institutions in terms of their values.

> The institutions of civil society are concerned with the expression and preservation of core community values and beliefs. Civil society includes

nongovernmental organizations, people's movements, citizens' groups, consumer associations, religious institutions, women's organizations, and indigenous people's associations. Civil society organizations may be grassroots organizations directly serving individuals of their community, or networks of grassroots organizations like federations.[12]

The "preservation of core community values" is another slightly fuzzy ideal, but the list of the kinds of nongovernmental organizations IDR would include in its definition of civil society makes the point that the values being referred to are not those of either business or government; indeed it suggests that "community values" may sometimes conflict with those of the other two sectors.[13]

Benjamin Barber, whose *Jihad vs. McWorld* we quoted in Chapter 1, defines civil society as *mediating between the state and business sectors,* offering people space for activity that is both voluntary and public. Put another way, Barber's argument is that civil society unites the virtue of the private sector (liberty) with the virtue of the government sector, that is, a concern for the public good.

> Civil society is a societal dwelling place that is neither a capitol building nor a shopping mall. It shares with the private sector the gift of liberty; it is voluntary and is constituted by freely associated individuals and groups. But unlike the private sector it aims at common ground and consensual, integrative, and collaborative action. Civil society is thus public without being coercive, voluntary without being private. . . . We do not need a novel civic architecture to recreate civil society. Rather, we need to reconceptualize and reposition existing institutions. Schools, foundations, community movements, the media, and other civil associations need to reclaim their public voice and political legitimacy against those who would write them off as hypocritical special interests.[14]

As we shall see throughout this book, the concerns that underlie this discussion are by no means limited to those who think about them from a leftist perspective. The conservative commentator William F. Buckley, Jr., for instance, has written, "The conservative movement perceives connections between the individual and the community beyond those that relate either to the state or the marketplace." Buckley goes on, "It was this essentially conservative insight that the liberal John Stuart Mill expressed when he wrote that 'though society is not founded on a contract . . . everyone who receives the protection of society owes a return for the benefit, and the fact of living in a society renders it indispensable that each should be bound to observe a certain line of conduct for the rest.'"[15]

In sum, these scholars, writers, and activists separate civil society from government (capitol) and business (capital). And they are in some agreement about the values and ideals that distinguish a Third Sector (civil society) from both business and government.

Civil Society is the Voluntary Sector

Other theorists insist that "civil society" is the voluntary sector, which includes business and the Third Sector, excluding only government.

Sociologist Edward Shils, for example, wrote that civil society "lies beyond the boundaries of the family and the clan and beyond the locality; it lies short of the state." But in that space between those boundaries lies both markets and civic settings "established for the purpose of public discourse." Civil society, he argued, is "an autonomous realm in which people are "engaged in acts of self-determination," safeguarded against the arbitrary and oppressive pressures of both the state and the "organic primordial community."[16]

Discussing this third perspective on civil society in more specific terms, political economist Francis Fukuyama defines it broadly as

> a complex welter of intermediate institutions, including businesses, voluntary associations, educational institutions, clubs, unions, media, charities, and churches. . . . [A] thriving civil society depends upon a people's habits, customs, and ethics-attributes that can be shaped only indirectly through conscious political action and must otherwise be nourished through an increased awareness and respect for culture.[17]

Fukuyama, then, explicitly includes business in civil society, and he argues that markets are positive forces for the development of a moral order. The early Scottish philosophers of the Enlightenment, he writes, all hoped that the destructive energies of a warrior culture (lords, barons, monarchs) would be channeled into the safer pursuits of a commercial society, with "a corresponding softening of manners." Human beings do not act like rational "utility maximizers" in the narrow sense, he contends; rather they invest economic activity with "the moral values of their broader social life." While the left-wing version of civil society may be about mobilizing a grassroots movement to stop Wal-Mart or lobby Congress, the right-wing version is about how civic groups, including those created by business leaders, are antidotes to big government. [18]

European leaders also argue that business should be included in civil society because business has the purpose of developing society. The Ministry of Social Affairs in Denmark, for example, put out a statement entitled *A New Partnership for Social Cohesion* in 1997. It goes a bit beyond most definitions of civil society in that it puts forth the idea of cooperation between government and business, but the point here is that it contains a vision of business as part of—rather than separate from—people's efforts for the common good.

> Business is increasingly accepting a joint responsibility for social development. This is very much in the interest of businesses, and an increasing number of business executives simply consider it the right thing to do.
>
> For governments, this new business paradigm holds an important promise for the future; the business of business is no longer just business but the development of a sustainable society. The question is whether a supportive new business-government paradigm can be developed as well. A new paradigm where governments enter a qualitative new role of supporting social processes that more effectively meet the social challenges: a new partnership for social cohesion.[19]

How does this all add up? *Philosophers* see "civil society" as evolving during the modern period with three sectors: a democratic government, free (capitalist) markets, and a Third Sector of voluntary organizations. *Development theorists* see civil society as the Third Sector alone, not markets or governments. *Business scholars* see civil society as the whole private sector apart from government, which includes both business and civic associations.

While these three perspectives differ markedly, it will be our project to bring them together. They all explain the development of society inside the nation.

Recent Critiques of Civil Society in the United States

Is, as de Tocqueville wrote in the 1830s, the propensity for voluntary association in the United States the key to its unparalleled ability to make democracy work? And if, as Salamon and Anheier point out, a "plethora of private, nonprofit, and nongovernmental organizations" have come into being around the world in the last few decades, why does Benjamin Barber speak of a need to "recreate civil society," to "reconceptualize and reposition" its institutions and "reclaim" its public voice?

Political scientist Robert Putnam is one of many scholars who have been concerned about a decline of civil society in the United States. In his book *Bowling Alone*, which attracted some attention in the mass media, he writes of a lack of "civic engagement" and a loss in the quality of human relations, in what he calls "social capital." Social capital encompasses those values found through "interpersonal networks"; it is the inclination that arises for people to do things for each other and includes a whole variety of benefits that flow from trust, reciprocity, cooperation, and the sharing of information.[20]

Putnam believes that these qualities are disappearing and that the problem is serious.

> Trust has been down under Democrats and under Republicans, in periods of prosperity as well as in periods of economic hard times. And it is not only distrust of government that has grown, and certainly not just the federal government. It is also a distrust of state and local government, a distrust and lack of appreciation, lack of approval, of the performance of most of the institutions in our society. Trust in business is down, trust in churches is down, trust in medicine is down. Trust in—I am sorry to have to say this—trust in universities is down. We have this feeling that none of our institutions is working as well as it did twenty or thirty years ago. The degree of this decline in confidence in public institutions is greater in the United States than in any of the advanced industrial democracies, at least to my knowledge.[21]

Bowling Alone ended with the hope that new forms of social connection might be invented to revive American communities. Putnam's recent book *Better Together,* written with civic activist Lewis Feldstein, is about the compelling ways in which renewal is taking place today. Putnam sees hardworking, committed people reweaving the social fabric all across America suggesting directions for the twenty-first century.[22]

Jean Bethke Elshtain, professor of social and political ethics at the University of Chicago, also describes the decline in "social capital formation" in terms of a loss of trust in others, in public institutions, and in the organization of society as a whole. Elshtain asks broadly how people could reestablish trust in each other, and in answering her own question she points to research that shows that when families and neighborhoods are intact, the social bonding that occurs within them has a positive long-range effects; for example, rates of drug and alcohol abuse, crime, and teen-age pregnancy diminish.[23]

For Elshtain, then, a key part of the solution to the civil society dilemma is for civic activists to strengthen family life and neighborhood organizations. Many would agree, and recent years have seen an increase in the number of community-based nonprofits as well as increased interest in community-based programs on the part of major philanthropic organizations.

Other social scientists, however, are more cynical about the basis for revitalizing civil society.

Sociologist Theda Skocpol is among those who argue that Americans have changed their *style* of civic and political association in the last third of the twentieth century. The civic world that was once centered in locally rooted "membership associations" with links to larger, nationally active networks, she writes, is now "a relic."

> Today, Americans volunteer for causes and projects, but only rarely as ongoing members. They send checks to service and advocacy groups run by professionals, often funded by foundations or professional fundraisers. Prime-time airways echo with debates among their spokespersons: the National Abortion Rights Action League debates the National Right to Life Committee; the Concord Coalition takes on the American Association of Retired Persons; and the Environmental Defense Fund counters business groups. Entertained or bemused, disengaged viewers watch as polarized advocates debate.[24]

The early American association-builders took it for granted that the best way to gain national influence was to knit together national, state, and local groups, which met regularly and "engaged in a degree of representative governance." Today, Skocpal says, this kind of individual involvement has largely been replaced by an expanding universe of "professionalized" institutions.[25]

Ambitious "civic entrepreneurs," Skocpal insists, do not build strong local and democratic bases for their organizations. In the early 1970s, for instance, when John Gardner launched Common Cause as a "national citizens lobby" demanding governmental reforms, he obtained start-up contributions from wealthy friends, contacted reporters in the national media, and purchased mailing lists to solicit masses of members not as active participants but as givers of modest monetary contributions. This is how most associations develop today: patron grants, direct mail techniques, and the capacity to convey images and messages through the mass media, have changed the realities of "organization building and maintenance."

In sum, the old civic America has been replaced by "memberless organizations," which are highly professional and oligarchical. They are staff-heavy and focused on lobbying, research, and media projects. They are managed from the top with few opportunities for member leverage from below. This top-heavy civic world is about "doing for" rather than "doing with," which then distorts national politics and public policymaking. The vital links in the nation's voluntary associations have frayed, Skocpol says, and "there is no going back to the old civic world we have lost."[26]

What is missing in these assessments of civil society and its decline?

First, these scholars do not include all non-governmental associations in their analysis. They emphasize Third Sector associations and look at neighborhoods and interpersonal relations. They examine old-line volun- tary associations like the Elks, the American Legion, and the League of Women Voters, but, as we shall see, they leave out trade associations, sci- ence associations, educational associations, and professional associations.

Second, we know that even in the most democratic of organizations there will be a tendency toward oligarchy and professionalism. Direct, un- alloyed democracy is notoriously inefficient; in order to get things done, people need leadership and expertise.

Oligarchy and hierarchy may be inevitable but in civil planning they have a different purpose. The purpose of leaders at the top of a corporate hierarchy during the nineteenth and early twentieth century was to con- trol the work process in ways that led to the domination of workers. The purpose of corporate leaders in the twenty-first century is to develop au- thority in lower ranks and to cultivate self-authority, to increase the level of responsibility and self-direction among those at the bottom. Civil plan- ning promotes greater equity and more channels of communication. The key to the development of civil society is new syntheses of social and eco- nomic values and the formation of civil associations.[27]

A Larger View of Civil Society

Focusing for the moment on the United States, let's take a look at a defi- nition of civil society that encompasses larger realms of the private sector.

The *educational* order includes associations whose members are vari- ously individuals, schools, colleges, and universities. The *religious* order includes associations whose members are individuals, churches, syna- gogues, temples, and mosques. The *professional* order comprises associa- tions whose members are lawyers, physicians, accountants, engineers, librarians, nurses, and architects, as well as hundreds of other associations whose members are schooled in other areas of professional expertise. The *intellectual* order includes the arts and sciences—its members are physi- cists, chemists, and biologists; political scientists, economists, and sociol- ogists; artists, musicians, and writers.

In addition, voluntary associations are created around specific move- ments with social concerns. The proliferation of social concerns around gender, ethnicity, race and the environment have replaced the abolitionist, temperance, suffrage, and March of Dimes movements. The list goes on but the point here is that all of these Third Sector organizations are linked to the development of society and its markets.

The second point is that the *business* order too has thousands of non- profit (non-governmental) associations. The members of these associa- tions are organized in production, distribution, and wholesale and retail sales. Many scholars do not view them as part of civil society. They include them as part of the "problem of globalization." We think of them as part of the solution.

There has always been a tension in the United States between business and the "core values" of society. A "free market" economy was organized around the ownership of property while the rest of the society was organized around values like democracy, equality, and justice. Nearly a hundred years ago, the historian Charles Beard documented how this tension influenced the framing of the US Constitution. Beard's hypothesis that property and economic self-interest was a compelling motivation is convincing today.[28] Today this tension persists between business and Third Sector orders of society, guardians of different interests and values. It is this tension that should be part of a theory of civil development, part of a public debate on the associations of America.

Every association in American society is linked with the economy. This is why reversing the "decline" of civil society means creating a new civil order in the economy.

Democracy vs. Oligarchy

In any kind of collective human endeavor, a different kind of tension exists between democracy and oligarchy. Theda Skocpol puts down civic organizations as having lost their democratic bases, but her critique could apply equally to political parties, governments, and trade associations.

After World War II, the German sociologist Robert Michel argued that the great error of socialists was their optimism—that is, their belief in the possibility of creating a classless society. Michel sought to prove that if socialists ever achieved parliamentary power, socialism in its ideal form could not succeed. The organization that would be essential to socialism's success would also be the greatest barrier to its implementation. In any democratic organization, leadership is essential, which itself contains powers and advantages because of "the nature of organization" itself. Whoever says "organization," he wrote, also says "oligarchy."[29]

But it's not all that simple. In studying the labor movement, sociologist Seymour Lipset discovered differences in degrees of oligarchy and democracy within trade unions. A union that expresses strong democracy (notably, the International Typographical Union) demands "rotating leadership," has "competing internal newspapers," competing internal parties, and keeps salaries relatively low for elected leaders. When such mechanisms are created inside unions, they become more democratic and less oligarchic.[30]

In other words, while there is always a degree of oligarchy within an organization, there are also social mechanisms that can increase democracy.

Hence civic-minded leaders might increase the level of democracy in both Third Sector and trade associations by organizational strategies.

But something else is important here. Civic scholars know that a nation state alone cannot govern a society. Thousands of associations govern a society along with the state, and the influence of the marketplace is felt in all arenas. And this is where our framework begins.

The Development of Civil Society

People know about business development. They know about market development, financial development, and educational development. They know about religious development. They know about professional development. But they do not know about *societal development,* that is, the development of civil society.

What do I mean by the development of civil society? I mean a complex mixing of values that happens on those verges where people in different organizations solve problems together. Societal development is about the creative blending of diverse values that happens through the action of citizens across unlike sectors of society. It happens, for instance, when the officials of government see that efficiency and productivity (core values of business) are important for reducing the inertia of bureaucracy. It happens when business leaders see "justice" and "democracy" (core values of government) as important to the trade association and then implement these principles along with profit-making. It happens through the interaction of dissimilar associations where people live and work. This is the Fertile Verge today.

Societal development happens throughout the whole fabric of a nation. It involves the entire web of life of a populace. It includes new blends of values—economic, political, governmental, educational, artistic, recreational, religious, scientific, and professional. It includes new-sprung structures of voluntary organizations and government. It includes fresh ways that people organize power in private (profit and nonprofit) corporations and allied associations. In other words, it includes the "core values" and structures of the entire society, not just those of politics and business.

What are the core values of American society? Francis Fukuyama defines core values as a "society's stock of shared values," which serves as "the prerequisite for all forms of group endeavor that take place in a modern society, from running a corner grocery store, to lobbying Congress, to raising children."[31] We see them embedded in government (justice, democracy, fairness, safety, and welfare), and in business (productivity, wealth, and efficiency). But we also see those that arise from other aspects of our lives-family and community (love, affection, trust, and caring), education and the arts (knowledge, truth, and beauty), and spiritual life (sacrifice, faith, and devotion). All these values are important to society as a whole.

But—here's the dilemma that faces us now—when one set of values overrides all others, the results may be disastrous. The commentators in Chapter 1 were saying just this: the imperatives of the marketplace—competition, productivity, efficiency, and profit—are overwhelming all others, and the result is the destruction of communities, cultures, and the environment itself.

As we've noted, Third Sector analysts do not usually include business and markets in their definition of civil society. Business scholars, on the other hand, include these markets and praise them but they do not connect them with causing problems in society. We intend to make these connections.

All three sectors of society—government, business, and the Third Sector—are involved in the economy, and all three play a critical role in the development of society. What is needed, I believe, is a new framework in which non-governmental (trade) associations in business and the Third Sector, plan development together, not just separately. We need government policies that encourage nonprofit associations to exert a greater influence upon business, commerce and the marketplace.

This outlook calls for the creation of a new market system. People in different sectors of society—with such unlike cultures as those of industries and universities—must link their work for the common good. (See Chapter 8.) The task for each sector of society—business, government, and the Third Sector—is to remain separate with their core values and independent associations while combining their purposes at a higher level of organization. The catchwords in civil development are combination (synthesis) and reformation in higher planes of organization.

In a civil (combined) framework, new standards for making economic decisions would not be determined by government alone, but would more significantly develop inside markets. Nonprofit associations would step forward more prominently to guide the direction of commerce. This view of development then addresses the problem of globalization. A new civic engagement in the private domain produces a type of republic that we have never seen before, a social contract that goes beyond the vision of the past, beyond John Locke and Adam Smith, indeed, beyond the vision of Karl Marx and John Maynard Keynes. We will be looking at how local-to-global organizations create contracts in very different fields of endeavor. As we shall see, this contract builds between unlike institutions (e.g. universities and industries, mass media and churches, etc.). If that contract happens properly, a mutual agreement on core values should produce a civil polity in the economy. A civil polity, by planning, then develops in markets that are as different as retail goods, steel, science, and education.

When this happens with public standards, the action adds substantive values to the economy, a proper mixing of Third Sector values with business values. In the long-range picture, we see the potential for developing a civil republic—a society of federations.

But the question is, Can this proposed civic reformation really happen? Could anything happen when—as we see in the next chapter—"a decline in core values" is the compelling feature of American society?

Let's take a closer look at that alleged decline before we look at how civil development might stop it.

Notes

1. The Swiss sociologist Norbert Elias studied the concept of "civility" as it emerged in the life of common people in Europe in the seventeenth and eighteenth centuries as a trend to control the functions and appetites of the body, and restrain aggressive instincts. See Norbert Elias, *The Civilizing Process* (Oxford: Blackwell, 1994). The word "civil," from the same Latin root, has several related meanings, including "of or relating to citizens," "established by law," and "of, relating to, or involving the general public, their activities, needs, or ways." *Merriam Webster's Collegiate Dictionary,* tenth ed.

2. The title of Hobbes's *Leviathan* was drawn from the biblical book of Job and refers to a power higher than people and lower than God. For Hobbes, it is synonymous with a Commonwealth or a State. Thomas Hobbes, *Leviathan* (Chicago: Encyclopaedia Britannica, 1952). Quotes in text, pp. 88, 100.

3. John Locke, "Concerning Civil Government," in Robert Hutchins, ed., *Great Books of the Western World* (Chicago: Encyclopedia Britannica, Inc., 1937), 74.

4. The quote in text is from Ferguson's *An Essay on the History of Civil Society.* For more on this essay, see http://socserv2.socsci.mcmaster.ca/~econ/ugcm/3ll3/ferguson/civil1.

5. Historians have noted the connection of the American Revolution and the writing of the Constitution of the United States with the formulations of Montesquieu and Locke. They say that some of Jefferson's phrases are exact quotations from Locke. And in virtually the same voice, James Madison said "It is essential to such a government (a democratic republic) that it be *derived from the great body of the society,* not from an inconsiderable proportion, or a favored class of it [my italics]." See Andrew McLaughlin, *Foundations of American Constitutionalism* (Greenwich, Conn.:Fawcett 1961; o.d.1932), 116; Adrienne Koch and William Peden, *The Life and Selected Writings of Thomas Jefferson,* (N.Y.: Random House, 1993 (o.d. 1944), 576, 656; and James Madison, *The Federalist* (1788, No. 9).

6. Marxists have also contributed to this effort. For instance, the Italian Marxist philosopher Antonio Gramsci (1891–1937) also developed a concept of civil society that differentiated it from the economy and the state. In Gramsci's version, culture played an important role in providing society's cohesion and continuity.

7. For more attributes, see Brian O'Connell, *Civil Society* (Hanover and London: The New England Press, 1999) p.12

8. Societies are developing voluntary associations around the world. In the United States, these associations began blooming in an unprecedented fashion from the 1960s to the 1990s. In 1958, there were approximately 6,500 associations; this total grew to some 10,700 national associations in 1970, to 14,726 in 1980, and by 1990 the number was almost 23,000. (*Encyclopedia of Associations*, Gale Research [1959–1999], cited in "Advocates without Members: The Recent Transformation of American Civic Life," by Theda Skocpal, in Theda Skocpal and Morris P. Fiorina, editors, *Civic Engagement and American Democracy* (New York: Russell Sage Foundation,1999), 470.

9. Lester Salamon and Helmut Anheier, "The Civil Society Sector," in Society, Vol. 34, No. 2 (Jan/Feb 1997), 60.

10. The organization referred to in the text is called The Independent Sector, and currently has its own website under that name. See also O'Connell, *Civil Society,* 12.

11. Many Third Sector organizations are closely related to business, often illegally. See the *Boston Globe,* 9 November 2002, A1, 10.

12. Steve Waddell and L. David Brown, "Fostering Intersectoral Partnering: A Guide to Promoting Cooperation Among Government, Business, and Civil Society Actors," IDR Reports (Institute for Development Research, 44 Farnsworth St., Boston, MA 02210–1211).

13. On core values in community life, see Amitai Etzioni, ed., *The Essential Communitarian Reader* (Rowman & Littlefield, 1998) and Robert N. Bellah, ed., *Habits of the Heart: Individualism and Commitment in American Life* (University of California Press, 1996).

14. Benjamin Barber, "The Search for Civil Society," *The New Democrat,* Vol. 7, No. 2, (March/April 1995).

15. William F. Buckley, Jr., *Gratitude: Reflections on What We Owe to Our Country* (NY: Random House, 1990), 18.

16. Edward Shils, "The Virtues of Civil Society," *Government and Opposition,* 26: 3.

17. Francis Fukuyama, *Trust* (New York: The Free Press, 1995), 4–5, 360.

18. Francis Fukuyama, *The Great Disruption: Human Nature and the Reconstitution of Social Order* (NY: Free Press, 1999). In this broad sense, civic-minded business leaders set their goal to advance the common good. See Joel Makover, *Beyond the Bottom Line* (N.Y.: Simon & Schuster, 1994), 26.

19. Ministry of Social Affairs, Denmark, *New Partnership for Social Cohesion* (Copenhagen, 1997).

20. Robert Putnam's argument for the development of civil society begins with his study of regional governments in modern Italy. In *Making Democracy Work: Civil Traditions in Modern Italy* (Princeton: Princeton University Press, 1993), Putnam attributed the superior effectiveness of northern Italy's regional governments to the dense "networks of civic engagement" fostered by "civil associations" of all kinds. Putnam's research in Italy showed a strong correlation between the effectiveness of a provincial government and the extent to which people participated in voluntary organizations and community affairs. (For a commentary, see Michael Walzer, "The Civil Society Argument," in Chantal

Mouffe, ed., *Dimensions of Radical Democracy: Pluralism, Citizenship, Community* [London: Verso, 1992].) In his book *Bowling Alone* (New York: Simon & Schuster, 2000), Putnam presents evidence that in the United States between 1980 and 1993 there had been a 40% decline in the number of persons who bowled as part of organized leagues, and that such declines had occurred equally in other fields of "civic engagement."

21. Robert Putnam, in an address given as part of the John L. Manion lecture series, Canadian Centre for Management Development, 22 February 22 1996, Ontario, Canada.

22. People are building communities in cities like Philadelphia, San Francisco, Chicago, Los Angeles suburbs, small Mississippi and Wisconsin towns, and in quiet rural areas. Robert Putnam, et al., *Better Together: Restoring the American Community* (NY: Simon Schuster, 2004).

23. Elshtain quotes Hannah Arendt on how authority "has vanished from the modern world. Since we can no longer fall back upon authentic and indisputable experiences common to all, the very term has become clouded by controversy and confusion." (Hannah Arendt, "What Is Authority?" *Between Past and Future* [Baltimore: Penguin, 1980], 91; quoted in Jean Bethke Elshtain, "Democratic Authority," *The Hedgehog Review*, Spring 2000, 26.) Other civil society advocates argue that the twentieth century is a record of societies that were "totaled into the state," from the Soviet Union to China, from the satellite countries of Eastern Europe to Indochina, as in Vietnam, Laos, Cambodia, and North Korea, and across Latin America to countries in Africa. It is impossible to reckon the full meaning of such catastrophes as Auschwitz, the Gulag, and the "killing fields" of Cambodia. A group of researchers tried to calculate how 85 million people died around the world and countless numbers were tortured while imprisoned, but words cannot tell the story. See Stéphanie Courtois, Nicolas Werth, Jean-Louis Panné, Andrzej Paczkowski, Karel Bartosek, and Jean-Louis Margolin, *The Black Book of Communism: Crimes, Terror, Repression* (Cambridge: Harvard University Press, 1999).

24. Theda Skocpol, "Associations Without Members," *American Prospect*, vol. 10, no. 45 (July/August 1999).

25. There was a golden era of national membership federations, Skocpol writes, but that civic base has disappeared. The old-line membership federations began to fade during "the long 1960s," stretching from the mid-1950s through the mid-1970s. The upheavals of the 1960s could have left behind a different civic world, one in which new associations would develop, but, she says, that did not happen. Instead, the 1960s, 1970s, and 1980s brought "professionalization." (Ibid.)

26. Ibid.

27. For a discussion on hierarchy and the evolution of management, see William E. Halal, *The New Management: Democracy and Enterprise as Transforming Organizations* (San Francisco, Berrett-Koehler, 2000).

28. Charles Beard's book was the first to question the motivations of American's "founding fathers" in drafting the Constitution. (Charles A. Beard, *An Economic Interpretation of the Constitution of the United States* [New York, 1913; 1941].)

29. For Robert Michel, all "differentiation of functions in large-scale organizations" implies specialization and expertise. What results is a class of professional politicians. These experts increasingly resemble the top officers of the organization. Hence the political organization becomes increasingly hierarchical and bureaucratic. What began as an egalitarian movement ends up as a system of leaders and followers, a "minority of the directors over a majority of the directed." In effect, increasing organization destroys internal democracy. The members (citizens) rely on their leaders' expertise, thus making it harder to remove them from office. Furthermore, Michels argues that decentralization cannot prevent oligarchic tendencies from taking place. An organization may be saved from "the gigantic oligarchy only to fall into the hands of smaller oligarchies," each of which is no less powerful within it's own sphere. Thus, the oligarchy remains. (Robert Michels, *Political Parties*. Glencoe, Illinois: The Free Press, 1949.)

30. Seymour Martin Lipset, *Union Democracy: The Internal Politics of the International Typographical Union* (Glencoe, Illinois: Free Press, 1956).

31. Fukuyama, *The Great Disruption*, 14.

3

The Decline of Civil Society
Where Are We Going?

> *Although tyranny, because it needs no consent, may successfully rule*
> *over foreign peoples, it can stay in power only if it destroys first of all*
> *the national institutions of its own people.*
> —Hannah Arendt, *The Origins of Totalitarianism*

We do not have any unified scientific basis to say that there is a general decline in the core values of American society—or that this happens when business attributes expand into the whole society—but there is plenty of reportage and scholarly evidence to support both of these as hypotheses.

The culture of business is grounded in attributes like profit making, efficiency, productivity, and competition. These attributes exist in other sectors of society as well, but with lower priority. The question is whether the priorities of business will come—or have already come—to direct the nation. Is the growth of business overriding all other values and goals of US society? And how does this affect the culture and values of other nations through globalization? The answers to these questions are important because the United States is a major power in the world, central to advancing globalization, but, at the same time—even after its invasions of Afghanistan and Iraq—America is depicted as a "civil society" and a model for developing countries.

Note that a certain degree of business influence on government and on the Third Sector (which comprises philanthropy and the nonprofit sector) is good, as part of the development of society. Indeed, as we shall see, a "mutual influence" is important because leaders in all sectors of society have much to learn from each other.[1]

Our question is whether business is moving—or has moved—too deeply into the life of the Third Sector and government. Certainly people in other countries around the world—the Middle East, Latin America, Africa, India, and China—whereas they may appreciate and desire the opportunities that business offers them, see major problems with the relentless expansion of markets. As we have seen, many critics here at home would agree. They ask, "Is the U.S. a civil society? Or, is it a capitalist society?"

Setting the issue of globalization aside for the moment, we will focus on the United States itself, taking look at how business and the values of the marketplace are affecting the fields of religion, recreation, health care, scientific and medical research, higher education, the professions, and government. This is important because we need to get a grasp on what is happening before we can look at alternatives.

Religion and Business

All religious institutions are connected with markets because they deal with business and engage in economic exchange. A church makes business decisions not only when it pays for supplies and services, but also, in a major way, when it purchases buildings and property or banks or invests its assets. The Trinity Episcopal Church, to cite just one example, was engaging in business when it bought the Standard & Poor's Building and eighteen other major commercial buildings in New York City.[2]

So how do we know when their involvement in business at this level distorts the core values of the religious institutions? Critics contend that one way this happens is when the quest for money leads religious leaders to take improper advantage of their tax-exempt status. For example, a consortium of churches took such an advantage when it purchased the Billman Hotel in Dayton, Ohio. Member churches bought the hotel and rented it back to its original owner to receive a net annual income without cost of maintenance, and the consortium eventually sold the building back again to the owner for a tax-free capital gain. This was a scam to make money for the member churches—a clear example of how religious organizations sometimes seek to exploit a market opportunity for profit.[3]

Religious organizations—churches, temples, mosques, and synagogues—are all deeply linked to markets. They own property and financial assets; they maximize capital dividends, interest, profit from subsidiaries, and rents on property. But legally and culturally these organizations are not businesses. They are nonprofit organizations understood to be serving different values. When religious organizations put too much emphasis on capital accumulation, they may lose credibility and undermine their purpose and their core values. This decline is difficult to measure and prove, but I would argue that it could be traced.

In addition to participating in market transactions, many religious organizations have begun to utilize market techniques to expand their influence. For example, some denominations now employ marketing firms to win new members, and critics say that in doing so they are looking for "customers" rather than promoting their core values.

As part of this trend, churches are building chapels inside shopping malls, and even building their own entertainment centers. Willow Creek Community Church, outside Chicago, offers shortened services for its 27,000 members, services that supply practical advice in settings that are reminiscent of the sets of late-night television talk shows. The church supports aerobics classes, bowling alleys, and multimedia Bible classes in which the snappiness of presentation rivals that of MTV. It has constructed several "mega-buildings" to serve large congregations, each with a 4,500-seat auditorium. It has two huge gymnasiums and a two-story atrium with tables in the middle and fast-food counters along the side. And it's interesting to note that, in addition to modeling itself after many of the most commercial aspects of consumer society, Willow Creek displays no religious symbols. One can only assume that its leaders feared that such symbols might make people uncomfortable or might make them realize they are not, in fact, at a mall or place of entertainment.[4]

This type of church expansion has appeared all over the country. In Houston, the Second Baptist Church has over 20,000 members and a staff of 500. It consulted with Walt Disney World on marketing and now uses a "vigorous entertainment schedule." Southeast Christian, in Louisville, Kentucky, is a "megachurch" that some observers have referred to as a "full-service 24/7 village." It offers the conveniences of secular life around a spiritual center, a place where people can eat, shop, go to school, bank, work out, scale a rock-climbing wall, and pray, all without leaving the grounds. In Glendale, Arizona, the 12,000-member Community Church of Joy has a school, a conference center, a bookstore, and a mortuary on its 187-acre property. It has begun a $100-million campaign to build a housing development, a hotel, a convention center, a skate park, and a water-slide park.[5]

At the Brentwood Baptist Church in Houston, a McDonald's restaurant opened in May 2002, complete with a drive-in window and small golden arches. Members say that the new McDonald's on their property is not just an investment for the congregation (the church put $100,000 into the business franchise) but a way to create jobs and generate money for scholarships and community programs. McDonald's gets its standard 4% from sales. Church members say that they want to offer the congregation a good reason to linger on church grounds. Brentwood Baptist offers a fuller range of family options, which serve a confusing mix of political, religious, and economic interests. Along with its choir and Bible study classes, it has housing for AIDS patients, adult computer classes, a children's theater, and a credit union. The church also offers its congregation of approximately 2,000 more than 80 evening activities—more excuses to "stick around."[6]

Dr. Randall Ballmer, a professor of American religion at Barnard College, says that "full-service churches" make it possible to be close to religious life from morning to night, cradle to grave. They shelter congregants from "a broader society that seems unsafe, unpredictable and out of control, underscored by school shootings and terrorism." But other scholars worry about round-the-clock ("24/7") churches. Wade Clark Roof, a professor of religion and society at the University of California at Santa Barbara, says that full-service churches are "the religious version of the gated community. . . . You lose the dialogue with the larger culture." Scott Thumma, a sociologist of religion at the Hartford Institute sees them as "a parallel universe that's Christianized." Marci Hamilton, a professor of constitutional law at Benjamin Cardozo Law School in New York, says that church growth—the expansion of megachurches, and, in some cases, of megasynagogues and massive Mormon temples—has become a contentious issue in nearby neighborhoods, whose residents are upset about "intensity of use." These full-service religious centers virtually never sleep, drawing cars, crowds, and even bright spotlights at all hours and on any day.[7]

John Vaughn, founder of Church Growth Today, tracks the growth of churches and says that, in 1970, there were 10 megachurches; in 1990 there were 250; and today there are 740. The average number of worshippers in these churches is 3,646, up 4% from 2002, according to Vaughn. The average net income of megachurches is estimated at $4.8 million by that same survey. These churches provide a transcript of the weekly sermons and a Web site, and they sell products, such as books and CDs. They encourage members to post prayers and donate online. Indeed, there is also a publicly traded company, Kingdom Ventures, whose sole mission is to help faith-based organizations get bigger.[8]

In another, perhaps parallel development, some of today's business leaders have brought certain concerns once thought to be the province of religion into the workplace. For some years, for instance, "spirituality" has had a place in some corporate development programs. Xerox, for example, has had its employees participate in spiritual "vision quests" to revolutionize product development. A peak moment in one such quest came when a dozen Xerox engineers, on a "spiritual journey" in northern New Mexico, saw a fading Xerox-paper carton bobbing in a swamp of old motor oil at the bottom of a pit. They vowed to build a machine that would never end up polluting another dump. This was understood to be a spiritual moment.[9]

Across the United States, major executives meet for prayer breakfasts and spiritual conferences supported by ministers and priests. In Minneapolis, 150 CEOs lunch monthly at an elite private club to hear other CEOs interpret business solutions from the Bible. In Silicon Valley, a group of religious-minded high-tech CEOs, including the founders of Circus Logic, Cascade Communications, and BioGenex, connect technology to spirituality. Top executives from Raytheon and Aetna International speak of the benefits of meditation.

Social scientists do not yet have the instruments to evaluate these links between religion and business, but I think it would be safe to say that it is not the higher religious values—faith in humankind and a sense of higher purposes at work to stop war—that are being strengthened.

Recreation and Business

Until the twentieth century, physical recreation was an informal activity involving fitness, fun, sportsmanship, the amusement of spectators, and (sometimes) civic consciousness. Certainly entrepreneurs staged horse races, boxing matches, and other contests, reaping profits by charging admission and from concessions, and money changed hands as people gambled on the outcomes of these events, but sports had not yet become big business. For most people, recreation was casual, for pleasure and merriment, with rules of impartiality and a focus on good will and festivity. Athletic coaches in public schools and private universities said, "It's not whether you win or lose, it's how you play the game." Engaging in athletics was considered to be a health-promoting and character-building activity, and young people were taught to win with grace and lose with strength and character.

Today universities have recruiters looking in high schools around the country for "million-dollar" athletes, especially football and basketball players. At the top of the collegiate sports pyramid, football bowl games return millions of dollars in profit. High school and university administrators now struggle to maintain the integrity of their sports programs against the attraction of big-dollar investments.

The purpose of the National Collegiate Athletic Association (NCAA) has been to maintain intercollegiate athletics as an integral part of educational programs. Its goals have been to keep the athlete an integral part of the student body and maintain a clear distinction between intercollegiate athletics and professional sports. But this distinction becomes ever more foggy as the NCAA itself becomes a business. The NCAA has organized its own marketing division, promotes its own line of licensed clothing, has its own corporate sponsorships, its own real estate subsidiary, and its own Learjet. In many ways, the NCAA behaves like a business. It negotiated with the city of Indianapolis, for example, to build a new headquarters there, providing an estimated $50 million in subsidies, and it left behind 300 employees without jobs when it abandoned its old headquarters in Kansas City.

The lure of big business and the revenues it can generate have attracted both the NCAA and universities across the country. Notre Dame University signed a seven-year, $45-billion contract with NBC to televise its regular season football games. The major conferences have a $700-million, seven-year contract with ABC to televise the football bowl championship series. The NCAA has $1.725-billion eight-year contract with CBS to broadcast its annual men's basketball tournament. The NCAA's budget, surpassing $270 million in 1997/1998, has been growing at an annual rate of 15% since 1982.[10] Is the NCAA (as a nonprofit association of colleges and universities) part of the Third Sector? Or is it a business?

Meanwhile, professional sports have become so intertwined with profit making and the marketplace—taking in revenues not only from ticket sales and concessions but also from licensing everything from broadcast rights to bobble-head dolls—that the question of whether sports are businesses or part of the Third Sector seems moot.

Professional golf, for instance, is a "corporate Mecca," not only producing its own revenues but also providing a venue for corporate self-promotion and profit making. To advance the interests of his own company, the president of John Hancock Mutual Life Insurance Co., David D'Allessandro, cultivates a "sports marketing strategy," which includes sponsoring the Olympics and the Boston Marathon. He acknowledges the importance of entertaining big-time clients at all major sports events, particularly events like golf's Ryder Cup, a series of matches between national teams whose Web site is sponsored by IBM. If Hancock did not attend the Ryder Cup, Hancock's president says, "It would reach beyond a breach of etiquette and run into the category of business stupidity." The earnings from the Ryder Cup tournament held in Brookline, Massachusetts, come from television rights ($13 million), corporate tents ($16 million), corporate tables ($15 million), merchandising ($8 million), ticket sales ($5 million), food and beverages ($ 3 million), and program advertising ($2 million)—altogether, a total of about $63 million.[11]

In his 1995 book *When Corporations Rule the World*, global analyst David Korten noted that even apart from their contracts with teams or earnings from competitions, some athletes' earnings from product endorsements have become the size of the budgets of small nations. The $20 million that Nike paid basketball star Michael Jordan to endorse its shoes was more than the entire annual payroll of all the Indonesian factory workers who make those shoes.

Some professional athletes become CEOs as they link up with business. In January of 2000, the *Boston Globe* reported the following.

> Professional golfer Greg Norman agreed to a wide-ranging deal with Fairhaven-based Achushnet Co., in which he will do more than just play with its Titleist golf clubs and balls. He'll distribute them, too. The deal offered Norman a chance to expand his role as the exclusive distributor in Australia for Cobra Gold Equipment, part of the Achusnet family. Norman has been affiliated with Cobra since 1990. [Now] Great White Shark Enterprises will be able to add the popular Titleist and Foot-Joy brands to its distribution operations in Australia. Terms of the deal were not disclosed.[12]

Finally, the commercialization of sports venues themselves is yet another way in which business is moving into sports. Look at football in Boston. In 2000, the New England Patriots sold the naming rights for their new stadium to CMGI, an Internet firm that is in the business, among others, of the "name game." The newly completed facility is now known as Gillette Stadium. Fans leave their cars at the Taurus New England Ford Dealers parking lot, walk through the Ubid stadium gate (Ubid is an Internet auction firm connected with CMGI), and meet friends under the McDonald's golden arches near the end zone. The front gate is named after the FleetBoston Financial Corp., and the luxury clubhouse after Fidelity Investment. Virtually everything at the stadium has a business name.

The corporation CMGI reportedly paid $100 million-plus for the stadium's name. McDonald's paid $21 million for the right to sell its food at the stadium and was, by contract, allowed to install its trademark arches near the end zone. The New England Ford Dealers acquired naming rights to the 10 parking lots that circle the 68,000-seat stadium. To find their cars, patrons will need to remember the row number and Ford model.

The naming of stadiums after businesses began in the 1980s and has spread to public museums and parks, art centers, and high school football fields. In Boston, the new incarnation of the venerable Boston Garden is now the FleetCenter, at a cost of $30 million for naming rights. In Foxborough, the football stadium's hometown, the board of selectmen objected when the team announced plans to name the clubhouse access road Fidelity.com Way. A Fidelity spokesman announced the company would respect their wishes and drop the name, but residents later decided to cash in on the opportunity by authorizing the selectmen to sell business advertising on a town-owned water tower built for the stadium.[13]

A sports fan once asked Wayne Gretzky, the all-star hockey player, how he could play so well. His answer was, "I skate to where the puck is going to be and not where it is." In a manner of speaking, when it comes to sports—and many other sectors of society—business "skates" to where the money will be.

Business, Medicine, and Health Care

Health care is moving from the Third Sector, with families and nonprofit institutions as caregivers, to becoming more and more a business. Our definition here is a broad one, including not only medicine but also medical research and the care of children, of the elderly, and of adults with mental and physical disabilities.

Most people feel that health is the most precious possession they have, and that the medical profession and hospitals have a public purpose. But as public health links with business, will this purpose be served? Some of the core functions of the family are increasingly being given over to corporations. Let's take a look at the some of these trends.

Can the values of public health be sustained when turned over to the for-profit sector? Should health maintenance organizations (HMOs)—originally designed to coordinate patient care and focus on disease prevention—be organized as businesses? Today, between 60 and 80% of HMOs nationwide are chartered as businesses. Private investors run them to make a profit. Most researchers agree that investor-owned HMOs spend more dollars on advertising, administrators' salaries, and profits for stockholders than do nonprofits engaged in the same effort. This means, of course, that less money is spent on patient care.[14]

So whereas health care professionals may have much to learn from business, the expansion of market values into this realm may undermine rather than strengthen it. In his book *Everything for Sale*, economist Robert Kuttner tells us in detail why markets are a danger to health care, and then he sums up the problem in terms of the difference between two cultures.

> To discipline opportunistic market behavior in healthcare, society cannot rely entirely on market incentives, since the market is so structurally imperfect to begin with. Much of the recent history of health policy in the United States has been a hapless effort to bring "market efficiency" and "pro-competitive reform" to a sector that is inherently extra-market. Not surprisingly, most have backfired.[15]

The changing purpose and charters of hospitals provides another example of the problem. Hospitals have the public purpose of promoting health and providing medical care to all members of society. Government and charitable hospitals have represented that purpose within the non-profit sector, but huge rises in the cost of health care have put them under tremendous financial pressure. (It's relevant that for-profit companies manufacture pharmaceuticals as well as medical devices ranging from bedpans to X-ray machines and beyond.) In addition, they also face competition—and the threat of takeover—from for-profit institutions, which are on the rise. Kuttner points out that with the acquisition of a nonprofit hospital by a for-profit company, there is a windfall conversion of social assets to market ones. The entrepreneur is arbitraging between two kinds of markets—one of them a "social market," in which norms of service limit opportunism, the other a conventional and profit-maximizing one. When such takeovers occur, Kuttner says, the entrepreneur pockets the difference at the expense of the hospital's social objectives.[16]

The question today is how hospitals, increasingly chartered as a private business, can remain true to their public purpose. How can a competitive business—or a nonprofit enterprise that must cope with markets and competition—be designed so that it fulfills a public good as its primary mission?

The hospital is like a microcosm of society in that it needs to have a proper mix of society's core values, especially those associated with government (equity, safety, and public welfare), family life (love and caring), and professional life (skill, integrity, and expertise). Hospitals also need to be well managed, of course, so business values like efficiency and productivity need to be part of that mix as well. But as hospital corporations have become more and more intricately involved with markets, these latter values tend to override all others. Observers say this leads to a loss of care-oriented management and a decline in professional standards.[17] Meanwhile, the pressures of the marketplace are felt in every aspect of a hospital: administration, surgery, outpatient care, marketing, insurance, and the medical profession itself.

Physicians, for example, have become increasingly dependent upon advice from business representatives on the latest medicines and surgical devices. Corporate representatives bring their wares for display at physicians' offices. They extend free samples for doctors to offer patients. They are given special access to hospitals and are often present at surgical operations to give counsel to doctors on the use of the devices they sell. Such visits to doctors' offices and operating rooms are "business as usual" in virtually every US hospital. Local hospital officials say that permitting doctors and surgeons to interact with sales representatives in this way speeds up their physicians' mastery of new tools and techniques, and that these interactions also provide companies with valuable feedback on how to improve their products.

These things may be true, but a recent incident in a Boston-area hospital points to another side of this equation. One summer day in 2002, David C. Arndt, M.D., walked out of a surgical procedure to run to the bank and deposit a check, leaving his patient on the operating table for 35 minutes. The state medical board suspended Dr. Arndt's medical license and imposed a penalty on the hospital as well (for initially concealing what had happened from the patient). The critical point is this: *the business representative who was providing advice on the operation drove the doctor to the bank.* This is obviously a bizarre case. But the interpersonal relationships between physicians and business reps can be very close, and, as many have pointed out, this can reduce the autonomy of the profession and erode its values.[18]

Indeed, those values are under assault on many fronts. The Massachusetts Medical Society (MMS) gains millions of dollars in revenues from its *New England Journal of Medicine,* which has a circulation of 230,000 and has been one of the most respected of all medical journals. But when MMS upgraded its online services and began to forge marketing deals with firms like BarnesandNoble.com, moral issues heated up. Some physicians saw such marketing deals as tarnishing the publication's name and lamented the fact that it was becoming associated with commercial products. Others saw the practice as part of an "inevitable progressive future." In the end, the MMS chose to fire the journal's top editor, Jerome Kassirer, when he balked at using the publication's prestige to sell products unrelated to medicine. Dr. Kassirer, who had been editor-in-chief of the *New England Journal of Medicine* for eight years, was discharged for protesting "the intrusion of business interests."[19]

Is this a sign of business moving ever more deeply into the profession of medicine? Many critics would say so, and Robert Kuttner goes further. As he sees it, monetary interests have captured the profession as a whole, and he describes how in protecting its own self-interest the profession is failing to shore up core values in health care. The American Medical Association, for instance, has long opposed any national health insurance plan as an "interference" with the doctor-patient relationship; in the meantime, doctors' average earnings have outstripped the consumer price index throughout the postwar era, which has added to the total cost of health care.

One question here is whether most Americans already define the professions (we'll discuss others below) as a "means for making money" rather than by their other, nobler purposes. Another concerns how a capitalist system tends to impose a market-oriented organization on all kinds of human activities.

Scientific breakthroughs during World War II made blood transfusion safer and more universally available as an important, often life-saving, medical technique. And for a time the donation of blood was a voluntary activity. The offer of blood to a relative (or perhaps a friend or neighbor) was a gift, a bonding between people who cared. Even after blood banks were established to extend that gift to strangers one might never meet, blood was neither bought nor sold. The giver had no expectation of money as a reward.

But between 1956 and 1968 the demand for blood increased, due in part to the introduction of new surgical techniques. In Britain, the need for blood was met by a corresponding rise in voluntary donations. But in the United States, shortages were overcome by organizing commercial blood banks. Now, with a "market for blood" and payment to some (still not all) donors, there are fewer givers in the United States.

Does the commodification of blood lessen a sense of family and community values? Does it contribute to a loss of goodwill? Do financial payments curb the inspiring force of generosity and social concern? Professor Richard Titmuss thinks so. He argues that gifts of blood are an expression of personal concern and self-sacrifice. They invoke a sense of one's humanity. But the market now devalues this gift and diminishes a sense of responsibility for the fate of others.[20]

Now notice where the change has taken place—in the Third Sector. In the United States today, the Red Cross and two other nonprofit organizations dominate the $2-billion market in whole blood, and a pint of it now goes for about $100. It is not "business" per se that has benefited from and advanced the commercialization of blood, but business values have seeped into one of the most personal and compassionate acts—the giving of life through the gift of one's own blood. Although these organizations, supposedly not motivated by profit, now dominate the market in blood, it is they who have brought business values into an arena of charity and giving, and who are therefore linked to the corresponding decline in availability of this life-giving substance.

Focusing on another, much larger realm once considered the province of voluntary action on the part of families and communities, sociologist Evelyn Nakano Glenn addresses the growing commodification and "defamilization" of the care of children and the elderly. She sees potential danger in a changing climate in which, for a host of reasons, family members are increasingly being replaced by paid caregivers—resulting in a loss in family and community values.[21] Here we'll use day care for children as our example.

Childcare is moving from the Third Sector—family, neighbors, and religious institutions within communities—to the business sector. Some for-profit day care centers "do good and do well" at the same time. They train aides and teachers well; they provide low adult/child ratios, sound nutrition, pleasant surroundings, and interesting activities for children. These are the necessary components of quality day care—for nonprofit and for-profit centers alike—but maintaining all of them at once while charging fees that families can afford is a challenge. And as costs go up (in particular staff salaries), a tug-of-war between costs and care-oriented priorities has priced many working-poor and middle-class parents out of private day care.

For example, when Bright Horizons (a nationwide day care chain) faced a national shortage of preschool teachers, it sought to raise pay and benefits and to "reach out" to family childcare providers who had previously worked in their homes, but this raised costs to a level that was simply too much for low-income families. To cite another example, the Children's Center in Lexington, Massachusetts, charges $1,192 per month for a full-time toddler. The center offers a teacher-to-toddler ratio of two to seven. This low ratio is part of good care, but only the wealthy can afford it.[22]

What does this mean for children and the core values of society? If it is a core value in our society to take good care of all children, then this value is undermined when many Americans cannot afford either to stay home with their children or pay for quality care. Some civic and religious leaders argue that with the rise in single-parent families and in the number of families in which both parents must work to make ends meet, the care of children has become a commodity. Belief in the inestimable worth of children, they contend, is losing to the culture of markets.

Science and Medical Research

Medical researchers and scientists have long claimed high standards and values in their work, including honesty, truth, integrity, and open sharing of research data. At the National Academy of Sciences headquarters in Washington, D.C., a bronze statue of Albert Einstein is emblazoned with this statement attributed to him:

> *The right to search for truth implies also a duty; one must not conceal any part of what one has recognized to be true.*

What has happened to this core value as scientists and medical groups move into the private sector and engage in commerce?

Increasingly, people with different agendas in two sectors—medicine and business—now collaborate to make money in the market. Medical scientists are employed directly by for-profit firms with negotiated rights (or none at all) over any discoveries they might make; some work in academic settings on projects that have been funded by private enterprise; some are principals of for-profit research enterprises. Scientists working under contract are forbidden or disinclined to disclose to the public what they have discovered alone in their laboratories—at least until the company in question has approved and/or legal patent protections have been obtained. This conflicts with the tradition and ethical code that says that scientists should share what they have found. It also has a stifling effect on the development of research in the nonprofit sector as well.

By tradition, nonprofit organizations release research abstracts to members in advance of scientific conferences, so attendees can be prepared for discussions and choose which sessions to attend. But business investors now get hold of this information for their own purposes (as we shall see below). They also follow academic programs very closely and provide funding for some. After all, talented researchers and new inventions and discoveries can make big profits.

Scientists whose work is either directly or indirectly funded by business routinely sign agreements requiring them to keep both their research methods and results secret for a certain period of time. Confidentiality is necessary to prevent competitors from pilfering ideas, but is this "science at its best"? What constitutes a reasonable period of secrecy? I am concerned about the influence of the business practice of secrecy over the free flow of information and peer review inherent in good research.

The National Institutes of Health recommends that universities allow corporate sponsors to prohibit publication of their findings for the length of time necessary to apply for a patent. But lengthier delays are becoming standard. The University of California at Berkeley's contract with Novartis, for example, allows the company to postpone publication of findings for up to four months. A survey of 210 life-science companies, conducted in 1994 by researchers at Massachusetts General Hospital, found that 58% of companies sponsoring academic research require delays of more than six months before publication.[23]

According to a recent study led by doctors at Massachusetts General Hospital and published in the *Journal of the American Medical Association,* nearly 50% of geneticists surveyed at major US academic institutions said problems had arisen from this conflict of interest. In the past three years, "another faculty member had denied them at least one request for information." This was a "startling figure," the study's authors wrote, because today it is much easier to share and transfer information quickly on the Internet. Seventy-three percent of those surveyed said that that data withholding slowed progress in their field, and about half said that this failure to share information had had adverse effects on their own research.[24]

On April 11, 2001, shares in Genentech mysteriously dropped $5.37 (or 12.5%), wiping out $2.8 billion in market value. The same day, shares in another California biotechnology company, Tularik, fell 5%, or 79 cents, while the stock of Cambridge's Millenium Pharmaceuticals and New York's ImClone Systems rose for no apparent reason. No public news releases explained these movements in stock prices. What is going on here?

The only common denominator was that each of these for-profit companies was known to be planning to present results from studies of their new cancer drugs at the annual meeting of the American Society of Clinical Oncology (ASCO)—and that abstracts of those studies had been posted that day on a password-protected portion of ASCO's Internet website. The firms in question were bound by the group's rules not to comment on the results of their studies before the formal presentations to be given at ASCO's annual meeting, scheduled for May 18-21, and the general public could not have had access to the data until that time.

Only physicians and other health care professionals in oncology are admitted into ASCO, and, although nonmembers can attend its meetings, only cancer researchers and physicians are given the right to see the abstracts in advance. In this case, however, because people using member IDs and passwords accessed the abstracts online, that data found its way almost immediately to certain analysts and investors, giving them an economic advantage in the market and fueling a flurry of rumors and trading.[25]

The Securities and Exchange Commission (SEC) cannot solve this problem. The SEC Fair Disclosure policy prohibits business companies from disclosing material information to insiders who might exploit it before public announcements are made, but nonprofit medical groups are not subject to this rule.

The growing intrusion of commerce into science on campus presents legal and ethical issues. Duke University has a patent for medicine to treat Alzheimer's disease. The research that produced it was undertaken for the public good, but this patent is now licensed to Glaxo, a business firm. How will the availability and cost of this medicine be different under business rather than academic ownership? The range of fields in which university-business patents have been negotiated has grown at an alarming rate—and these patents focus primarily on profit, not the common good.

Since 1978, Michigan State University has collected more than $160 million in royalties on the sale of drugs known generically as cisplatin and carboplatin. Michigan made a deal with a technology-licensing organization known today as Research Technology Corporation (RTC). This corporation helps commercialize inventions for more than 100 other universities. Michigan State has fought legal battles with RTC for a greater share of the profits gained from the two drugs that were invented at its own facilities. Their focus on profits rather than on the science or its implications for the public seems far more congruent with the values of a business than those of a university.[26]

In August 2000, the US Department of Health and Human Services hosted a conference to get advice on scientific conflicts of interest. Conference participants concluded that scientific research has become so commercialized in the last decade that existing safeguards are failing to protect patients and that academic integrity is suffering. Conference speakers reported that scientific experiments, once funded mainly by the federal government and conducted openly in academic settings, are now done in the private sector, under a cloak of secrecy. Even the fraction of research still conducted at academic medical centers is tainted, many said, because these centers and their scientists have a financial stake in the outcome. Jane Henney, commissioner of the Food and Drug Administration stated flatly, "profits drive this business." Dr. Greg Koski, the newly named director of the federal Office for Human Research Protection said, "Conflicts of interest are very real, very serious and a threat to our entire endeavor. . . . Public trust has eroded."

The conference speakers described business tactics that included cash payments to doctors who recruit their patients into experiments. They spoke of an increasing bias in the design and reporting of studies to favor the projects' funders. One speaker cited a study showing that when drug companies funded experiments, the results favored their new drugs 89 of the time, compared with only 61% when studies were funded by independent sources.[27]

This is a tangled web, indeed, and although the theme of this chapter is about civil society in the Third Sector, government itself also partners with business in scientific endeavors, to the possible detriment, some would argue, of the public good. Many environmentalists and consumer advocates argue, for instance, that the government regularly supports businesses that make products harmful to the environment and consumers. Two examples they cite come from the field of genetic engineering.

Recombinant bovine growth hormone (rBGH) is a genetically engineered artificial hormone that tricks a cow's body into producing more milk than it otherwise would. Scientists argue that rBGH, developed by the Monsanto Corporation, has serious health implications for both cows and people. Milk from cows treated with rBGH often becomes contaminated with pus from udder infections (and with antibiotics administered to stem those infections) and with high levels of insulin-like growth factor (IGF), which has been linked to human breast and gastrointestinal cancers. Nevertheless, the federal government approved the use of rBGH in 1993, to the outrage of farmers and consumers alike. The Canadian government banned it, noting that the United States is the only "developed country" permitting the use of this hormone.[28]

The genetic modification of crops—once hailed as part of a "green revolution" that increased the yield of farmers worldwide—today offers a second example of what many argue is the misuse of genetic engineering with government support. Over a billion farmers in Africa, Asia, and Latin America have traditionally depended on farm-saved seeds as their primary source for the following year's planting, and exchanging seed with other farmers has helped ensure that the crops they grow are genetically diverse and adapted to their own environments. But they also buy seed from agricultural marketers, and this is where they have recently become vulnerable to the collaborative action of business and government.

In 1999, a patent was granted on genetic technology, developed jointly by the US Department of Agriculture (USDA) and Delta & Pine Land (D&PL), a subsidiary of Monsanto, that can be used to modify plants so that they produce sterile seeds and therefore cannot reproduce naturally.

These trends raise disturbing questions. What is the purpose of medical and scientific research? Who decides what types of research are for the common good? Are markets in charge of science? Should they be? How can science be organized for the common good?

Higher Education and Business

The purpose of a general education is to cultivate the mind, to strengthen the public quest for knowledge, and to teach a new generation about the current state of knowledge in society. A good liberal arts university trains students in citizenship, teaches natural and human history, and explores the values, principles, structures, and norms that have shaped society and the course of civilization. Traditionally, the goal of a university is not to identify with any single sector of society, such as religion, government, or business, but rather to promote understanding of history and culture, and to transmit complex forms of knowledge.

But today there are signs pointing to changes in the "climate" of general education, changes associated with business rather than cultural or intellectual values.

One such sign is that business executives are creating new accredited, degree-granting, for-profit universities. Higher education is developing a commercial market, and these institutions are competing very well on business terms. The for-profit University of Phoenix, for example, had profits of $33 million in 1997 and a price/earnings ratio of 50 in 1999. Other for-profit universities include DeVry Inc., with 48,000 students; ITT, with 26,000 students; Education Management, with 19,000 students; and Strayer Education, Inc., with more than 10,000 students. These for-profit universities are attractive stocks on NASDAQ, rivaling many Internet companies.

In July 2002, the *Chronicle of Higher Education* reported on a study of the Education Commission of the States (ECS) that sought to develop a clearer picture of what was happening in this rapidly growing sector of for-profit postsecondary education. Among the findings of the ECS study were the following.

1. Between 1988 and 1998, enrollment in for-profit degree-granting institutions grew by 59% to roughly 365,000 students.
2. The for-profit sector's emphasis on career-oriented, hands-on, and customer-focused programs, services, and institutions appeals to new types of students. Working adults and parents with family responsibilities are drawn to these schools by accelerated programs, flexible schedules, and convenient locations.
3. The program design of for-profit institutions is driven by employer needs and student interests. Success is measured by retention of students, degree completion, job placement, and employer satisfaction with graduates' performance.[29]

The Education Commission of the States found that, at first, traditional colleges and universities distanced themselves from the for-profit sector, but today more and more of them are embracing the same kinds of entrepreneurial, customer-focused approaches that have proven so successful on the for-profit side.

The vast majority of the students in the United States attend public or private nonprofit ("charitable") institutions, but by spring 2004, a rapid double-digit growth in enrollments was taking place in private for-profit institutions. Of the 9,485 postsecondary institutions in the United States today, about 47% are organized as for-profit institutions.[30]

Traditional universities are struggling with soaring costs and plunging taxpayer subsidies, but the 10 largest (publicly listed) for-profits have already taken more than a half-million students. In the year ending August 31, 2003, earnings of Apollo Group Inc., surged 53% to $247 million, as revenues jumped by a third, to $1.3 billion. This has given Apollo a market value of $11.4 billion—equal to the endowment of Yale University, the nation's second-wealthiest college. Add the hundreds of smaller players, and the overall for-profit enrollment jumped by 6.2% in November 2003, or five times the pace at conventional colleges. According to Boston market researcher Eduventures Inc. this development pushes the private industry's revenues to $13 billion, up 65% since 1999.[31]

Some observers argue that for-profit institutions are so cost effective that state universities could be in line for privatization. Organizational efficiencies, they maintain, can lower the cost of higher education for everyone. In the meantime, for-profit schools compete with existing public and nonprofit universities and colleges by keeping their costs low and offering students a degree for less money. They do this by investing little or nothing in faculty, research, libraries, or campuses. In order to compete, full-scale nonprofits could be forced down that same low-cost road, lowering academic standards and losing the richness in culture and broad-based support of learning that still does exist on traditional campuses. Whereas this competition may provide some increased efficiencies and benefits to students, the ultimate nonmonetary costs may very well outweigh the benefits.

This movement to create profit-oriented universities is now worldwide. It is strong, competitive, and carries serious implications for the future. Gordon C. Winston, an economics professor at Williams College, observes:

> The schools least able to withstand for-profit competition, clearly, are concentrated in the private sector, more than four out of five are private. . . . Two alternatives appear. One is that the nonprofit school might fight back, making significant changes in what it does and how it does business, either by reducing costs or by altering its product and organization to meet the competition. If you can't beat'em. . . . That might mean altering the school's relationship with its faculty using fewer full-time tenured faculty and more part-time tenured faculty and more part-time adjuncts and, if Phoenix is a guide, reducing faculty discretion over both what is taught and how it's taught.[32]

The newer universities are becoming multinational corporations as their business increases around the world. Sylvan Learning Systems, a company known for its tutoring and testing programs, is creating a network of private, for-profit universities overseas. Joseph D. Duffey, former president of American University, past chancellor of the University of Massachusetts, and current director of the U.S. Information Agency, manages the international venture. Sylvan Learning Systems plans to begin its expansion in Spain, where it has an exclusive option to buy an existing for-profit institution, the European University of Madrid, which has 7,200 students in 20 undergraduate and graduate programs in dentistry, law, language translation, and the liberal arts. Sylvan has offered to pay about $51 million, including the assumption of about $22.5 million in debt, which is 54% of the university's total indebtedness.[33]

At the beginning of the twentieth century, social economist Thorstein Veblen expressed concern about how business leaders were being placed on university boards, rather than scholars and educators.[34] But today the whole university—whether traditional or for-profit—is becoming a business.

A whole new team of players has come onto the field. In the past, a relatively small number of people have studied and earned degrees through "distance learning"—correspondence courses of varying degrees of academic rigor, some offered by well-respected institutions, some little more than scams. More recently, the Internet, says Michael P. Lambert, executive director of the Distance Education and Training Council, has given new forms of life to this sort of educational commerce. One form is stand-alone e-colleges and e-universities, whose Web sites mimic the appearance of those of traditional institutions, displaying a college or university seal and a message from the president, providing links to catalogues of courses and on-line applications, and advertising themselves as accredited. Indeed, such institutions are accredited, but most often by agencies that they themselves set up, and critics contend that their enrollees are not receiving an education that is in any way substantial or consistent with sound academic standards. But even as the critics argue that the deficiencies of such learning programs require a nationwide response from educational associations and the US Department of Education, the commercial impetus for creating such programs is growing around the world, attracting untold thousands of student applicants. The new e-universities are now in global markets.

Supporters argue that higher education can be supplied in cyberspace without the added cost of land, office buildings, libraries, and other physical facilities. The promise in this trend is the expansion of American education and heightened interest in learning. But the commercialization of education in cyberspace could result in losing those features that are most central to our current system of higher education: face-to-face learning between students and faculty, a broad-based exposure to new ideas and experiences on campus, learning grounded in big questions and ideas rather than simply how to make more money, and resources ranging from libraries and art galleries to research labs and concert halls. Is the trade-off worth it?

A major trend among established universities today, perhaps in response to these kinds of competition, is the increased offering of "post-baccalaureate certificates" and "occupation-oriented course sequences," which focus on special competencies designed for a market sector. Such course programs are different from those leading to a master's or doctoral degree in an established field of knowledge. In particular, class attendance, seat time, homework, and grades do not count to establish eligibility for certification, only demonstrated performance on an exam.

Will these low-cost, efficient business models drive out the traditional model? If so, what would be lost? Will the growth of for-profit educational alternatives stimulate a better quality of higher learning in America, or lead to its decline? William Sullivan, a public policy scholar, observes that

> to an increasing degree, higher education is understood as an "industry" in which "firms" compete for "customers." For their part, most of these consumers understand education as a means by which they can better their chances for socioeconomic success, in a highly competitive market society. Education, that is, is generally assumed to be a primarily private good. What is missing in most of contemporary awareness is the notion of education as training for citizens committed to involving themselves in the larger public life.[35]

Robert Zemsky, director of the Institute for Research at the University of Pennsylvania, says that while a hierarchy has always existed in private education, disparities in institutional wealth have become more obvious and more pronounced. "Very wealthy" institutions can withstand competition and/or a boom-and-bust cycle, but others (below the $1-billion mark) will not weather economic disturbances so easily. It is better, he concludes, to be wealthy.[36]

In response, some nonprofit universities are creating for-profit subsidiaries in order to be more "efficient" and compete more deliberately in the market. Columbia University, the University of Maryland, and Cornell University are developing distance-learning programs through for-profit subsidiaries. Although such for-profit subsidiaries are a growing practice, some faculties resist the idea. At Cornell, for example, the faculty voiced their concern about the loss of local control and the liberal tradition, and, in response, Dean Robert J. Cooke organized a universitywide faculty forum to discuss the new subsidiary, called *e-Cornell* and billed as the first "centralized effort" to move into distance-education courses. "This is only one piece of a larger approach," said Mary J. Sansalone, the university's vice provost. "There will definitely be other models. . . . But we are faced with a big challenge as many outside third parties eager for profits come in and try to sign up faculty. This [for-profit endeavor] allows us to protect the Cornell name and get the best return."[37]

New profit-making schemes in universities are called "revenue streams," and they include revenues derived from scientific research done in their laboratories. Florida State University, Montana State University, and Montana Tech each hold patents on inventions for producing Taxo, a drug derived from Pacific yew trees. Taxo produces about $1.3 billion each year for Bristol-Meyers. Those sales, in turn, translate into major economic revenues for the universities in question; Florida State collected about $29 million in royalties from Bristol-Meyers in fiscal 1997 and $45 million in fiscal 1998. [38]

Stanford University receives millions of dollars in royalties on projects ranging from genetic engineering to synthesized music, and it has decided to package a brand name so that it can continue to profit from faculty inventions. Since patents expire but brand names live on to make more profits, Stanford has developed a partnership with Yamaha (the Japanese electronics corporation) to establish a brand name-Sondius-XG. Stanford and Yamaha have agreed to pool more than 400 patents and patent applications and will license them as a package along with rights to the Sondius-XG trademark. The two "companies" will share the royalties. Sondius-XG will market to companies that make karaoke machines, electronic musical instruments, and video and computer games.

College and university officials do not want to talk publicly about the $1-billion-plus annual royalties that their institutions and inventors make from patents, but in some cases they have sued students and faculty who make money they believe belongs to their institutions. This more aggressive approach comes as more universities are placing emphasis on commercializing inventions made by people working, wholly or in part, under their auspices.

Although the average salary of a college or university faculty member is about $56,000, many professors in fields such as computer science, business management, mathematics, and the physical sciences have become wealthy from endeavors made possible, at least in part, by work supported by their institutions through various arrangements. At Stanford University, a third of the 45 professors in the computer-science department are millionaires. Professor Eric Brewer, who is 33 years old and has earned tenure at the University of California at Berkeley, claims a net worth of $800 million. Mathematics Professor F. Thomson Leighton, of the Massachusetts Institute of Technology, has earnings of more than $2 billion, at least on paper, with his Akamai Technologies venture. Most of the academics that hit the Internet jackpot did not quit their university jobs; they generally remain at their universities, but they stay involved in private ventures, taking more time off from teaching than the average faculty member while they continue to cash in on the "new economy."[39]

Other faculty members, entering the marketplace in a more modest way, are selling their lectures on the Internet, or, by putting them on videotapes and CD-ROMs, making their courses, in effect, commodities. This is arguably a good thing for the advancement of learning, but it does not provide the same experience as taking the same course on campus from a professor. The student has lost the context of a campus community and its resources, interactions with others studying the same material, and the soul of a teacher present to work with his or her students.

Universities often support their faculty's new business interests. When it was reported that a psychiatry professor at Brown University earned more than $500,000 in consulting fees from pharmaceutical companies whose drugs he touted in articles and lectures, Brown officials said he had not violated their policies. At Boston University's School of Medicine, officials did not find a conflict of interest in the fact that one of their deans owns 1.4 million shares of a private Internet company that the school will use to offer doctors online versions of its medical courses. Harvard Medical School has often enforced strict conflict-of-interest policies but is now giving more leeway for researchers to profit from their work. Harvard used to prohibit faculty from devoting more than 20% of their time to outside work or holding more than $20,000 worth of stock in a company that funds research at the university, but it is now reviewing that policy and relaxing its rules.

In addition, colleges and universities are "outsourcing" their own traditional functions, contracting businesses to manage, for example, dormitories, dining services, parking facilities, and bookstores. At the University of Pennsylvania, officials boast of a 15-year deal with Barnes & Noble, which pays the university a percentage of sales to manage its store, with a guaranteed minimum annual profit of $1.3 million for the university. Independent university bookstores, once a bastion of intellectual life, have become a vanishing breed. The University of Notre Dame's bookstore was "very profitable," its defenders maintain, before Notre Dame turned over its management to the Follett Education Group about five years ago. But profitability is still an issue. It is not profitable enough from the university's point of view. The question is whether the values of learning or sales volume should determine which books are readily available to students and scholars. At Hunter College of the City University of New York, the outsourcing to Barnes & Noble drew fire from faculty who argued that they saw a "different culture" emerging at the college. The norms and values of Hunter, they said, clash with those of this for-profit company.[40]

Some schools pursue profit even more directly. Boston University, for example, has become engaged in venture capital through the school's Community Technology Fund (CTF), which has been quietly investing the university's money since 1975, when cofounder Matthew Burns took $2 million from Boston Univesity's endowment to invest in such ventures as Amos Hostetter's Continental Cablevision. Today the fund is a modest $55 million, but its profile has been rising following a string of successful investments and early-stage tech deals; according to rankings by PricewaterhouseCoopers, CTF jumped from relative obscurity to being one of the 20 most active backers of Boston-area start-ups.[41]

The purpose of a college or university in the liberal tradition is not to advance business interests or fit into the market system. Yet profit making, marketing strategies, competition, and a business orientation seem to be flourishing on campuses in this country and worldwide. Do these signs of a shift toward a market culture indicate a decline in the core values of education? How much will business and government determine the direction of research in the future? Will "profit" and "the national interest"—rather than the quest for knowledge and the common good—determine the direction of American education?

Business and the Professions

During the first half of the twentieth century, the number of professionals quadrupled in the United States. In 1973, sociologist Daniel Bell predicted that a "postindustrial society" would develop through the expansion of the sciences and the professions. We are now in that future.[42]

In the meantime, how far have the professions moved into business? Sociologist Elliott Krause argues that the guild system of the Middle Ages led to a nonprofit ethos in the professions, such as law, medicine, and engineering, and in the academic disciplines that prepared people for them. But today, he says, the professions have converted to a business mentality and a market orientation, and he describes in detail how capitalism captured them. He takes on each major profession, one at a time.

Regarding the profession of law, for example, Krause argues that it has always been a party to economic advantage, but it has also stood for ideals not in accord with markets or states. It has carried ideals of justice and fairness that go beyond political or corporate self-interest. Today, however, "lawyers as a profession help to preserve the present US system of overwhelmingly capitalist domination over state policy." The profession on the whole, he asserts now supports capitalist markets.[43] About engineers, he writes:

> Professions, in theory, are supposed to have codes of ethics. Not so in engineering. One thing that engineers almost never do, given their values, is to complain when they work on projects that maximize profits through cutting back of safety. Whether the area is nuclear engineering or the O-ring seals on the space shuttle, whistle blowing on the company will lead to being fired, and usually also to being ostracized by other companies working in the same field. The moral is not lost on US engineers; do not question the safety aspects of your work if you want to remain employed. The codes of ethics of engineering societies are mere pieces of paper, and the officers of the associations who have drafted the codes are practically all in corporate management.[44]

Whether or not one sees a significant change in the character of the professions depends upon one's perspective. The social economist

Thorstein Veblen would have said that the legal profession was without any moral grounding to begin with. He argued that law should not be taught as part of higher education: "In point of substantial merit the law school belongs in the modern university no more than a school of fencing or dancing." Veblen thought that all the "liberal professions" had a "trained incapacity" to understand or apply their own core values. They were simply part of the power structure.[45]

In the insular world of private business, who cares about high ideals? But the disregard of the profession's ideals has begun to apply to the Third Sector. Take the arena of nonprofit foundations. A Minnesota lawyer finds a legal way to boost his annual fee as a foundation trustee 10-fold—to $206,000—after the last member of the founding family dies. A New Jersey attorney reports that he works full time for one foundation and 30 hours for a second, and still has time to bill a third for legal fees. And a prominent Boston attorney helps direct millions of dollars in donations to his alma mater from a foundation his firm administers.

Lawyers advise thousands of private foundations that funnel billions of dollars to charities every year. They join foundation boards and their advice is eagerly sought in this litigious society. They charge enormous fees for uncomplicated tasks that trustees in the past performed for no compensation.[46]

Many critics would agree that the major professions no longer follow what had been their high ideals, such as justice or truth. Rather, they serve whatever corporation or system of power they are a part of—and their own interests.

Krause sees the professions as latent monopolies. Government courts have curtailed some of their monopolistic tendencies under the Sherman Antitrust Act, but it is difficult today to get a ruling against a professional organization in court. Krause contends that lawyers, who preside as judges on the highest courts, are sympathetic to the professions, and that they make decisions that permit the latter to be monopolistic, claiming that "constitutional principles" are involved. Professional organizations, which control certification and licensing, are given the freedom to set their own admission fees (excluding those who cannot afford to pay), for example, and the right to maintain exclusive claims on certain (expensive) tasks and services. They can deny the opportunity of legal work to others who are qualified to perform it at a lesser cost.[47]

In spite of these criticisms, the best legal scholars believe that the professions continue to carry society's highest values, and that although they are snarled in markets, they stand apart from them. The legal profession in particular, they argue, still has the capacity to advance its own core values—justice, equity, fairness, order, impartiality, objectivity, and probity—for the common good; these core values may be in decline but they remain at the heart of the profession.

Government and Business

Government lies outside the Third Sector, but this chapter would not be complete without a few words on the subject. Sociologist Theda Skocpol is one of many who contend that public life is so dominated by business today that the United States is a democracy in name only. The problem as she and others see it is not simply the role of big money in electoral politics. We have a system, she argues, in which centrally organized interest and advocacy groups clash among themselves in state and national centers of power, and thus the interests of the average citizen are completely overlooked in the battle between well-represented elites. In effect, she argues, the power elite in business have taken over government.[48]

Civil government was founded on "self-rule" based on principles like democracy, liberty, justice, and the common welfare. But critics are saying that that government today has lost those principles. Legislative and public policy, they contend, is formulated in "business councils" outside the government.[49]

In her book *Pigs at the Trough,* political commentator and erstwhile gubernatorial candidate Arianna Huffington writes of the "unholy alliance" of CEOs, politicians, lobbyists, and Wall Street bankers who have shown complete disregard for investors and employees, let alone the public good. The economic game is rigged, she says, between CEOs and politicians. The rise of a "callous and avaricious mind-set" is wildly out of whack with the core values of the average American, in Huffington's view, and WorldCom, Enron, Adelphia, Tyco, AOL, Xerox, Merrill Lynch, and other recent scandals are just the "tip of the tip" of the corruption iceberg.[50]

Sociologist William Domhoff describes how business controls government in several ways, both direct and indirect. First, campaign donations from business play a critical role because candidates require financial support to be elected. Second, the officials nominated to top office from both parties are drawn mainly from business. Third, business writes government laws through its nonprofit think tanks. Fourth, exclusive clubs and wealthy pressure groups shape public opinion. In his 1996 book *Who Rules America?,* Domhoff reviews in great detail how deeply the government is embedded in the capitalist system.[51]

An additional sting here is that the US government bestows upon the business sector about $77 billion in tax breaks. In other words, it subsidizes those very markets that citizens must then pay taxes to regulate, and many argue that this amounts to a double tax that favors business at public expense. [52]

Small governments around the world could lose with the globalization of markets. Big corporations exercise an influence on big government but civil society advocates are concerned now about the loss of local rule in global markets. In one instance in the United States, a business firm convinced citizens in a small town to take over its name. Halfway, a town of 360 in the eastern mountains of Oregon changed its name to "Half.com" in a publicity arrangement with a Philadelphia Internet business of the same name. Ranching and mining were in a decline in Halfway, so when the owner of this start-up business came to town with an offer of $75,000, local citizens paid attention. Changing their name gave them computers for the elementary school, as well as the promise of new jobs in an Internet call center as the business grows. Half.com describes itself as a "one-on-one auction site" but the integrity of government is challenged.[53]

Small towns are no matches for manufacturers like General Electric and big retailers like Wal-Mart, Target, and Home Depot. Global corporations can easily destroy local firms in competition. This may look like "normal competition" but it can result in the loss of local autonomy, the loss of medical benefits to employees, and a lowering of local wages. A global corporation can colonize a small town and then threaten the community by going overseas. When the corporation moves overseas, the town loses its tax base and its schools.[54]

Finally, national governments today cannot control global markets as they do domestic markets. Global firms transcend the power of market regulation by any single nation. Big business corporations in the developed nations routinely move domestic factories overseas to countries that do not have the power, or the motivation, to regulate them. They establish headquarters abroad where financial accounting becomes invisible. They buy and sell on a worldwide Internet outside any nation's ability to monitor what is happening. And firms join global cartels that serve the interests of their home governments in ways that reduce the desire of those governments to control their exploitation of the environment worldwide.

Corporate scientists develop thousands of new chemicals annually and compose transferable genetic materials in ways impossible to supervise or regulate in world markets. Some domestic firms allow themselves to be purchased by foreign corporations in ways that place them outside home controls. Others buy a majority of stock in foreign subsidiaries in authoritarian states that do not have solid government controls. The many-sided ways in which capitalist markets produce problems and evade government control is too detailed for us to review here, but there is a long list of books to read on this issue.[55]

In sum, the question is whether the US government has the power to regulate business. In this country, the standard solution to problems created by the market has been to institute government controls and regulations, but the federal government is completely intertwined with the very markets that it would regulate. As a result, it provides subsidies for lobbied markets, asks executives to head agencies that would regulate their own industry, and places top business leaders in top government positions. Some would argue that this has ever been the case, but many would respond that business forces have more power over government than ever before and that globalization has made the consequent problems even more difficult to address.

Conclusion

There is a growing influence of business on the field of education. There is a growing influence of business on the fields of science. There is a growing influence of business on religious establishments, health care institutions, recreational organizations, professional associations, and government.

Governments support "economic development," not "societal development." Economists measure business development, not the development of society.

The public is aware of the problem at certain levels and questions, What's happened to family values? Why are doctors going after big money rather than public health? Why are universities building big endowments and not lowering tuition rates? Why are lawyers working for big business rather than for the public good?

A framework for thinking about "political economy" that accepts capitalist markets as part of public policy is part of the problem. A framework for thinking about "civil society" that does not provide alternatives to the capitalist market is another part. How could these two frameworks connect in a way that would allow each to change and come closer together? Could public policies advance the interests and values of civil society, not just those of markets and states? The search for a new market economy and a civil republic will be our task for the rest of the book.

Notes

1. Business learns from government and the Third Sector and vice versa. During this past century, business leaders developed values that were not once considered part of its domain. It developed safety in the work place as it negotiated

contracts with labor unions. It advanced programs in human relations, organized pension systems, created departments for environmental protection, and made other changes in corporate life. And how did this social development take place? Changes can be attributed to the influence of government *and the Third Sector.* Some economists would contend that the market has already become more humane, generous, welfare-oriented, and democratic as it has developed in the context of society.

2. We are looking at institutional religion, not religion as a "way of life." On the corruption of religious values in society, see Harvey Cox, *The Seduction of the Spirit* (New York: Simon & Schuster, 1973), 14.

3. For many other cases like this one, see Martin Larsen and C. Stanley Lowell, *Praise the Lord for Tax Exemption* (Washington, D.C.: Robert Luce, 1969).

4. Gustav Niebuhr, "Where Shopping-Mall Culture Gets a Big Dose of Religion," *New York Times,* 16 April 1995, A1, 14. Paul Goldberger said in reference to this case, "Add a McDonald's arch and it could be the food court in a nearby shopping mall." (Paul Goldberger, "The Gospel of the Church Architecture, Revised," *New York Times,* April 1995.)

5. For more on megachurches, see Hartford Institute for Religion Research, http://hirr.hartsem.edu/org/faith_megachurches.html.

6. Patricia Leigh Brown, "Megachurches as Minitowns," *New York Times,* 9 May 2002. The Fellowship Church in Grapevine, Texas, offers a 40,000-square-foot youth center with a climbing wall and video arcade. It is creating a lake to encourage father-son bass fishing. The Prestonwood Baptist Church in Plano, Texas, has a youth center so elaborate that some have called it Preston World. It has 15 ballfields, a 1950s-style diner, and a fitness center, as well as classrooms and a 7,000-seat sanctuary. It is adding a $19-million school, to include a coffee shop, food court, student ministry center, youth building, an outdoor prayer walk, a chapel, and an indoor commons—all modeled on the theme of Main Street, USA. "We're not a large church," said Mike Basta, the executive pastor. "We're a small town." See also, http://www.selfknowledge.org/resources/press/nyt_brown.htm.

7. For all quotes see, Patricia Leigh Brown, "Megachurches as Minitowns," *New York Times,* 9 May 2002.

8. Kingdom Ventures disclosed that it has received a subpoena from the Securities and Exchange Commission relating to its stock transactions. The company operates 12 subsidiaries and claims to work with 10,000 churches on everything from fundraising to event planning (it provides speakers and artists for events) to upgrading technology by helping sell new audio and visual equipment and sound systems. World Changers Ministries operates a music studio, publishing house, and computer graphic design suite and owns its own record label. The Potter's House has a record label and a daily talk show. Lakewood Church, which recently leased the Compaq Center, former home of the NBA's Houston Rockets, has a four-record deal and spends $12 million annually on television airtime. Luisa Kroll, "Christian Capitalism: Megachurches, Megabusinesses," 09.17.03 2003. Forbes.com.

9. The result was the design and production of Xerox's hottest seller, the 265DC, as a 97% recyclable machine. Other senior executives from companies as diverse

as Ford, Nike, and Harley-Davidson made pilgrimages to Rochester to learn about this "sprinkling of the sacred" at the workplace. (Ibid., 152.)

10. Andrew Zimbalist, *Unpaid Professionals: Commercialism and Conflict in Big-Time College Sports* (Princeton, New Jersey: Princeton University Press, 1999).

11. Gregg Kupa, "Getting Down to Business," *Boston Globe,* 21 September 1999, F8. The D'Allesandro quotation is drawn from Bob Duffy, "Ryder Had Faith in His Idea," *The Boston Globe,* 22 September 1999, G8.

12. AP, Business Briefs, "Norman Cuts Achushnet Deal," *Boston Globe,* 22 January 2000, Cl.

13. Robert Peer, "Pats Take 'Name Game' to Higher Level," *Boston Globe,* 27 May 2002, 1, 10.

14. At the same time, nonprofit HMOs can be inefficient and poorly managed, and many have failed financially. The nonprofit Harvard Pilgrim Healthcare Plan, for example, was taken over by regulators after losing at least $177 million. In 1999, 21 health plans across the country were taken over by state regulators. "Health/Science," *Boston Globe,* 31 January 2000. Liz Kowalczyk, "Fate of Health Plans Taken Over Last Year Bodes Ill for HMO," *Boston Globe,* 19 February 2000, C1, C2.

15. Robert Kuttner, *Everything for Sale* (New York: A.A. Knopf, 1998), 111. Kuttner describes how the causes for problems in health care go deep into the capitalist system.

16. Kuttner, *Everything for Sale,* 128.

17. For a look at one case of a nonprofit hospital in New York, see Jennifer Steinhauer, "Death in Surgery Reveals Troubled Practice and Lax Hospital," *New York Times,* 15 November 1998, 37.

18. Raja Mishra, "Case Puts Focus on the Role of Drug Firm Representatives," *Boston Globe,* 10 August 2002, B1.

19. Larry Tye, "Medical Journal's Top Editor Is Fired," *Boston Globe,* 26 July 1999, A1.

20. Richard Titmuss, *The Gift Relationship* (London: Allen & Unwin, 1970).

21. Glenn says the sheer demand to care for the elderly, plus the inability of families to provide good care for their children, is part of the story. The transfer of "caring" from private households into the business sector, she says, inserts "third parties" into the caring relationship. The economic incentives to "commodify" care are part of the problem. Evelyn Nakano Glenn, "Creating a Caring Society," in *Contemporary Sociology,* Vol. 29, No.1 (January 2000), p.84 ff.

22. Diane E. Lewis, "Day Care Catch-22 driving up costs," *Boston Globe,* 20 February 2000, G9.

23. Eyal Press and Jennefier Washburn, "Secrecy and Science," *Atlantic Monthly,* March 2000. Theme article, "The Kept University."

24. Nicholas Thompson, "Scientists Say Sharing of Key Data Has Slowed," *Boston Globe,* 5 March 2002, C1.

25. Naomi Aoki, "When Science and Finance Collide," *Boston Globe,* 24 April 2002, F1–4.

26. The drugs were developed from inventions licensed to Bristol-Myers Squibb. Michigan signed its patent management agreement with Research Corporation, a charitable foundation created in 1912. By 1987, however, Research Corporation had determined that it could not accomplish its business

goals under its charitable umbrella. Under the Tax Reform Act of 1986, the organization created a new entity, Research Corporation Technologies (RTC), an independent, nonprofit company that pays taxes and has no shareholders. See Goldie Blumenstyk, "How One University Pursued Profit from Science—and Won," *Chronicle for Higher Education,* 12 February 1999, A39–A40.

27. Alice Dembner, "Research Integrity Declines," *Boston Globe,* 22 August 2000, E1, E2.

28. Martin Tietel and Kimberly Wilson, *Genetically Engineered Food: Changing the Nature of Nature* (Rochester, Vermont: Park Street Press, 1999), 34.

29. "For-Profit Colleges and Universities: No Longer Outside the Mainstream of Higher Education," *The Chronicle of Higher Education,* 19 July 2002, A22, A23. The report on which this article was based, "Meeting Needs and Making Profits," is available on the ECS Web site at www.ecs.org.

30. Guilbert C. Hentschke "U.S. For-Profit Postsecondary Institutions—Departure or Extension?" *International Higher Education,* Spring 2004. Center for International Higher Education, Boston College.

31. What has happened here? Basically, the new for-profits have taken the ethos of the traditional trade school into higher education. For example, Katharine Gibbs, the 100-year-old secretarial school, has exploded from 2,000 students to 15,000 since Career Education bought it in 1997. Gibbs now offers degrees in "business and technology" to a student population that is 40% male, versus 2% before the change.

32. Gordon Winston, "For-Profit Higher Education," *Change,* Vol. 31, No. 1 (January/February 2000), 13 ff.

33. Kit Lively and Glodie Blumentsyk, "Sylvan Learning Systems to Start a Network of For-Profit Universities Overseas," *Chronicle of Higher Education,* 29 January 1999, A43–44.

34. Thorstein Veblen, *The Higher Learning in America* (New York: B. W. Huebsch, 1918).

35. William M. Sullivan, "Higher Education and Civic Deliberation," *Kettering Review,* Vol. 18, No. 1 (Spring 2000), 24.

36. See Joyce Mercer, "As Elite Universities Increase Spending, Many Others Strive to Keep Pace," *Chronicle of Higher Education,* 9 October 1998, 45–47.

37. Sarah Carr, "Cornell Creates a For-Profit Subsidiary to Market Distance-Education Programs," *Chronicle of Higher Education,* 24 March 2000, A-47.

38. Goldie Blumenstyk, "Universities Try to Keep Inventions From Going 'Out the Back Door'," *Chronicle of Higher Education,* 17 May 2002, A-33.

39. Robin Wilson, "They May Not Wear Armani to Class, But Some Professors Are Filthy Rich," *Chronicle of Higher Education,* 3 March 2000, A-16.

40. Students at Guilford College also protested vigorously when their administration negotiated a takeover of their bookstore by the Follett Education Group. "It's like beach erosion," says Brian Cartier, chief staff officer for the National Association of College Stores. The number of bookstores managed by colleges and universities or student associations and local cooperatives has been steadily declining. See John Pulley, "Whose Bookstore Is It, Anyway?" See *Chronicle of Higher Education,* 4 February 2000, 41.

41. Venture Capital, Boston University Community Technology Fund, http://www.bu.edu/ctf

42. Daniel Bell, in *The Coming Post-Industrial Society* (New York: Basic Books, 1973).
43. Elliott Krause says that the professions have become identified with business. Professionals (for example, doctors, lawyers, and engineers) have become highly paid functionaries of business, making money rather than seeking justice and the public good. The professions also become monopolies. Associations of lawyers, doctors, architects, accountants, educators, and others draw tight boundaries around their membership and certified authority. Some professions impose rigid rules for membership, increase their fees to unfair levels, and become exclusive clubs. And governments cannot regulate professional monopolies as easily as they can a business monopoly. See Elliott Krause, *Death of the Guilds: Professions, States, and the Advance of Capitalism, 1930 to the Present* (New Haven: Yale University Press, 1997).
44. Ibid, 65. Thomas Haskel says that there is a crucial difference between medieval guilds and today's professions. The guilds were monopolies, which suppressed both competition and self-assertion of their individual members. See Thomas Haskell, "The New Aristocracy," *The New York Review of Books*, Vol. XLIV, Number 19 (1997), 47–53.
45. Thorstein Veblen, *Higher Learning in America* (New York: Transaction, 1993 [orig. pub.1918]).
46. For more details on a spotlight team survey, see Beth Healey, Francie Latour, Socha Pfeiffer, and Michael Reszendes, and editor Walter Robinson, "Foundation lawyers enjoy privileged position, *The Boston Globe*, December 17, 2003, p. A1.
47. The United States has over 800,000 lawyers. A large part of legal work today is done regularly on behalf of business for very high fees. Do lawyers now have more interest in money than in justice?
48. Theda Skocpal, "Toward a Popular Progressive Politics," *The Good Society*, Vol. 7, No. 2 (1999), 22.
49. How much does the market system influence government? Does "the political economy" (states and markets) represent the cardinal structure of modern society? These questions are too abstract for easy answers, but James O'Connor conducted a study on the subject at the California State University, San Jose. His thesis (in the Marxist tradition) is that the growth of the state sector (and state spending) is "functioning increasingly as the basis for the growth of the monopoly sector and total production." He argued, "the growth of state spending and state programs is the result of the growth of the monopoly industries. In other words, the growth of the state is both a cause and effect of the expansion of monopoly capital." See James O'Connor, *The Fiscal Crisis of the State* (New York: St. Martin's Press, 1973), 8.
50. Arianna Huffington, *Pigs at the Trough: How Corporate Greed and Political Corruption are Undermining America* (New York: Crown Publishing Group, 2003).
51. Business is equally influential in both Democratic and Republican governments. See William Domhoff, *Who Rules America?* (London: Mayfield , 1996).
52. Domhoff is convinced that this irony continues because of the all-pervasive influence of business throughout society. He describes how 154 Business

Council members (in *Who's Who in America*) held 730 directorships in 36 different foundations and 125 trusteeships with 84 universities.

53. Fouad Ajami, "E-gads!" *The New Republic,* February 21, 2000, p.6.

54. How can this power of "global corporations over small towns" be treated? We answer that question in Chapter 6 with different options.

55. One might start with Herman E. Daly and John B. Cobb, Jr., For the Common Good (Boston: Beacon Press, 1989) and end with William Greider, *The Soul of Capitalism: Opening Paths to a Moral Economy* (NY: Simon and Schuster, 2003).

Part 2

The Solution
Civil Markets

4

Two Models
Could a New Market Develop?

I do suggest that given the decayed condition of representative democracy the political system must itself undergo a profound reformation before government will be trusted again as the reliable voice speaking for society's nobler aspirations. Since I am increasingly skeptical that regular politics will reform itself, I suspect the best route to restoring our democracy might begin elsewhere, confronting the undemocratic qualities embedded in the economic system which are in fact a principal source of democracy's decline.
—William Greider, *The Soul of Capitalism,* 2003

We have seen how a decline in core values can happen with the expansion of capitalist markets into nearly every realm of society. And we have noted that some scholars fear that the worldwide extension of a capitalist economy is eroding the foundations of democracy everywhere. An unfettered global expansion in capitalist production and the profit-driven distribution of natural resources, they point out, is linked with environmental destruction, fascism, and terrorism.

Now we look at the possibility that a different type of market could stop this decline and help us avoid the catastrophes that loom on the horizon. In this chapter we will explore how government, business, and civic leaders could develop a *civil* market system, one that would not destroy the core values of society but cultivate and strengthen them.

In feudal times, when monarchs ruled, they were supported by a myth called the "divine right of kings." In modern times, when corporations rule, they are supported by a myth called "natural rights," extended in the nineteenth century beyond individuals to corporations and written into law. Today corporations have a power not unlike that of the "divine right of kings," supported by law and ideas of high abstraction.[1]

This chapter considers these abstract ideas, which have complexities we cannot explore fully but are nonetheless important to review before we begin thinking about specific proposals for a different market system, one that could lead to a civil republic.

A Conceptual Framework

Two scholarly outlooks comprise the bases for defining the problem of market globalization. They are *civil society* and *political economy.* We have looked at the idea of civil society in Chapter 2; here we'll consider what's meant by the phrase "political economy." Both frameworks are needed in modeling the development of markets.

Traditionally, studies in political economy focus on markets and nations. Research includes such fields as monetary and fiscal policy, labor economics, government planning and economic development, micro- and macroeconomic theory, international trade and finance, industrial organization, and economic thought. All these sub-fields of political economy are important for the advancement of knowledge but they do not speak to the problems of markets in a society struggling to preserve civic values.

Political economists—Marxist, liberal, or conservative—differ in their views, but they all believe that government is central to solving problems in the economy. This is not exactly the position held by students of civil society.[2]

As we noted in Chapter 2, the concept of "civil society" developed centuries ago and refers to a social order within which people find consensus. A society is about rules and institutions that make it possible for people to live together. It has an economy and is part of a nation, but larger sets of values define it. It is more than a government and more than an economy and different from a "state."

Great scholars work within these two frameworks, but they become isolated in their research and thinking. Students of civil society do not usually study the economy and economists do not usually study social and cultural development. Could their isolation from one another be part of the problem? Could ending that isolation be part of the solution?

Could scientists working separately in these two frameworks think together on the issues of globalization? Could their combined visions help prevent the calamities many have forecast? How could the values of "the economy" be brought into better alignment with those of civil society?

It is beyond our capacity to bring these two frameworks together, but we will point in that direction. We will view the political economy and civil society together as part of a nation but also part of a system of global markets. An economy that is growing worldwide should remain connected to the concept of civil society.

Sociologists make the connection of an economy with society. Max Weber, for example, saw how social phenomena have an impact on economic phenomena. A market exists, he said, wherever there is competition for economic opportunities of exchange. His study of *The Protestant Ethic* showed how social institutions and cultural values shape a market economy. There are many institutions and patterns of interaction that determine how people develop a market. Markets are invested with social meaning.[3]

Neil Fligstein saw markets as "organizational fields" in which people "orient their actions to one another." In this perspective, we can see the market is connected with all organizations of society—governments, schools, sports, churches and synagogues, science organizations, etc. And the market invokes all kinds of social processes that go beyond the subject of mainstream economics.[4]

For our purposes—envisioning a civil market—we will begin by thinking of economic values as the main attributes of capitalist markets. These include efficiency, productivity, profit making, competition, and calculable utilities. They stand in contrast to core values in civil society, for example, love, truth, faith, and beauty. A core value of society is not measurable in terms of efficiency, productivity, profitability, or a market price.[5]

In Chapter 3, we described how core values embodied in Third Sector organizations have become part of the market and given a price. Blood is marketed. Childcare is marketed. Hospitals are marketed. Colleges are marketed. Critics of the system argue that substantive (inestimable) values in these organizations could be lost. Market calculations are entering into all orders of life—education, religion, family life, and the professions.

Fredric Jameson, a critic of capitalism, argues for a change in thinking about the capitalist economy. He sees capitalism as developing in stages through history, moving from an early market form, to a monopoly and imperial form, and into its current multinational form. He pursues the "unforgiving character of capitalism" as it continues its "destructive path" in each stage, but he also wants to advance research on how it could be transformed, and he encourages us to invent models and alternatives and utopias that can then be criticized and refined. He wants to keep both criticism and hope alive.[6]

In that spirit, we will propose a set of ideas for a new system of markets. As we shall see, it is utopian in one sense but in another sense it provides a basis for scientific studies and public planning. The model outlined below and explored in the rest of this book presents capitalist markets as one type of exchange. I call the alternative a "civil market," and it is no more than a compilation of attributes that stand in contrast with—and might serve as counterweights to—those of capitalist markets. As we shall see, the attributes are "latent" in markets today.

These latent attributes, I will argue, are ready to be developed. They serve as a guide for public policy and a basis for scientific inquiry. The implementation of the ideas at the heart of this civil model, I believe, could, with careful planning, carry us beyond capitalism. A capitalist market could be transformed into a civil market if we design and implement a different order, not a utopia, but something that could actually develop in this 21st century.[7]

Capitalist Markets vs. Civil Markets

First, a caveat. All the words we use below to describe markets are part of common speech and used in shaping public policy, but they are also subtle and abstract, and their meanings are shaped in context. Policymakers do not normally think about changes of meaning in different contexts when they talk, for example, about "preserving freedom" in markets, but "freedom" is not a word like "table" or "tree," which have specific referents to which we can point and which we can see with our eyes.

When we put together a list of the attributes of a "capitalist market," for instance, we are talking about abstract concepts that operate like ideals. These concepts become a set of beliefs in policy, and perhaps even the underpinnings of an ideology for which people will fight and die. For our purposes, however, they can be viewed as theoretical ideas to be studied and researched.

So, we work in the middle of a myth. Capitalist markets are real but also an ideal type, part fiction: nowhere are "free markets" entirely free. Our exploration of a possible alternative, then, will begin with attributes that are also abstract, that is, part fiction. Each attribute we describe, therefore, will need to be defined with greater specificity as we proceed to discuss and compare the two models at greater length in subsequent chapters.

Here I will distinguish these two market systems side by side, as if they were or could be separate—first the capitalist model and then the proposed civil market model. Looking at the two models next to each other helps us see how they differ. But in truth, as we will see, elements of a civil market already exist (latent) within capitalist markets, and the challenge is to imagine how the new model could be applied to bring them to the fore. In order to do that, we need to add the idea of civil development.

As we shall see, "civil development" is not "market development" and it is not the same thing as "business development." As I propose to define the phrase, it refers to how a market can be structured to incorporate the core values of society. The challenge for civil planners will be to develop this model inside capitalist markets without losing their freedom and spontaneity, to explore how systems of economic exchange can be encouraged to encompass and serve noneconomic values such as health, safety, truth, compassion, and caring.[8]

The Market Models

As noted in Box 4.1, below, *capitalist markets* are systems of exchange that give priority to economic and financial values and correlative attributes, whereas *civil markets* are systems of exchange that give priority to social and cultural values and correlative attributes.[9]

The distinction between these different models (capitalist and civil) is similar to that drawn by Max Weber between two "types of rationality." The parallel is not perfect, but capitalist markets have kinship with Weber's *formal rationality*. Civil markets, on the other hand, have a kinship with Weber's concept of *substantive rationality*. Let's look at his definitions and at this distinction as it bears on the idea of civil development.[10]

Formal rationality is based on calculability, efficiency, quantification, prediction, and control. Substantive rationality, on the other hand, is based on values that are "ultimate" in nature, as in high principles of justice, goodness, truth, and beauty. The values of substantive rationality are not calculable in their full meaning. But through a process of civil development, markets could become more closely aligned with these core (substantive) values of society.[11]

In sum, we will focus on the culture and structure of markets. We will make a distinction between core social and cultural values, and economic values such as profit, efficiency, and productivity. And we will argue that both social-cultural and economic-financial values are vitally connected to the development of the economy and society.

Put another way, we propose that combining core (substantive) values with economic (formal) values will invoke *societal development*, not just business development—and that civil markets will emerge when these two sets of values can be linked and coupled for the common good.[12]

In Box 4.1, we lay out the attributes of our two theoretical market types. The right side of our table depicts the (ideal) characteristics of the capitalist market; those of the (ideal) civil market as it might eventually develop are represented on the right.[13] Here's the key. In developing from a capitalist market to a civil market, we would expect the attributes of the latter to develop inside the former. This would be civil development.

Civil development, as we shall see, could produce a synthesis of the attributes of both models, that is, a convergence of these different value orientations, which would in turn produce a new, integrative model.

Box 4.1. Two Ideal Markets: Attributes

Capitalist Markets (Manifest)	**Civil Markets (Latent)**
Goal: Greater Wealth	*Goal:* Common Good
Theory: Formal Rationality	*Theory:* Substantive Rationality
Values: Economic-Financial	*Values:* Social-Cultural
Domain: Private	*Domain:* Public
Core Principle: Freedom	*Core Principle:* Justice
Optimizing Principles	*Optimizing Principles*
Profit Making	Standard Making
Competition	Cooperation
Productivity	Accountability
Efficiency	Sustainability
Privacy	Transparency
Command management	Democratic (self) management
Corporations	Associations
Stockholders	Stakeholders

Capitalist markets in their ideal type are systems of exchange that emphasize economic values. Economic values are expressed in the quest for efficiency, productivity, and profit making. They are allied with the ideal of competition and the advancement of self-interest. All these values are embedded in the business sector. While the core principle of capitalist markets is "freedom," which could be considered a substantive value, the culture of business is characterized primarily by formal rationality, and success is measured in terms of profits.

Corporations in these markets compete for profit and contend for power. They are organized to produce and distribute goods and services and to advance economic returns. The overall goal of capitalist markets is to create wealth, not to provide for the common good or serve the principle of justice. They are managed as a private system, as opposed to being managed by government.

Civil markets, on the other hand, are systems of exchange that emphasize core values and public standards. They are "economically oriented" (prudent) but not "economically determined" (profit-driven). Their values are located in the entire society, and today most notably advanced in the Third Sector.[14]

Here is where the integrative model comes in. We would propose that core values could become more strongly linked with economic values through civil planning. Economic values (e.g., productivity and efficiency) would have their place in civil development, but non-market values (e.g., cooperation and transparency) would be cultivated as well. Civil markets as envisioned in our model are provident but their values are linked directly with the life of society.

How does this link between the two models take place?

Core values are brought into markets when people make imaginative connections with non-market associations, transcending the dominant capitalist values. As we shall see, inventive associations with Third Sector organizations can bring together all those who have a stake in a given transaction. This can be encouraged to happen as part of the normal operations of "the market."[15]

The key is in government planning that will support stakeholders in defining who they are, how they are affected by a market sector, and how they can influence market decisions. "Transparency," for example, has a commonsense meaning in our civil market model, but stakeholders must learn to define it more precisely in terms of contracts and agreements. (Transparency for stakeholders in the stock market is very different from transparency as it is defined in the biotech market.) A first step, then, is for stakeholders and government planners to specify what is meant by the attributes in each model, so governments and civil society groups that engage in civil planning will have their special definitions to make.[16]

Planners will also have paradoxes to solve. The attributes that are paired in these different models—"cooperation" and "competition," for instance—appear to be separate, even opposites, but in reality they coexist in every market as latent or manifest. Both their differences and their connections need to be seen by development planners.

In real life, competition is highly valued (and manifest) in the capitalist model, but cooperation is also there, latent, less visible. In capitalist markets, cooperation is often seen to be a dysfunction, as in a "collusion" among competitors, but cooperation must also be cultivated to make markets operate effectively. For instance, as we shall see, cooperation is basic to the organization of trade and professional associations and can work for the common good.[17]

The US Justice Department defines competition in capitalist markets in degrees of "corporate concentration"—precision statistics are used to define a market with only a few firms as an oligopoly, for instance—but it does not define degrees of "cooperation" because there is no rationale for that attribute in the capitalist model. In civil market planning, however, the department would study and measure cooperation as it works in the public interest.

When we see these paired attributes (e.g., cooperation/competition or private/public) to be complementary rather then in opposition, we can see the possibility of what I will call an associative economy, which evolves as the latent dimensions of the capitalist market are strengthened. This associative aspect of capitalist markets—which already is latent—is the forerunner of the ready-to-emerge (integrated) civil market system.

Civil planners could thus develop this (latent) aspect of the economy by applying the principle of cooperation, a central attribute of the civil market model. The capitalist economy is already partly "associative" through the cooperation of conflicting groups, like labor vs. management in a negotiated contract, competitors vs. competitors in a trade association, profit vs. nonprofit corporations in a civic partnership. But civil planners will now have to ask, How could *cooperation* become supported in new ways so that *competition* works for the common good?

A very important question indeed.

The answer is found in succeeding chapters but in a nutshell, it means building a higher purpose for competing organizations and a new level of governance among them. Finding a higher purpose among competitors in systems of mutual governance is exactly what created the United States as "the first new nation" and exactly what will build a civil republic.[18]

What do we mean?

The United States was founded in a new system of mutual (democratic) governance. It began with a group of loosely knit American colonies that were competing against one another in the eighteenth century. The colonies struggled against one another, yet, were able to put aside their differences, keeping their separate identities by organizing a federation with a higher purpose. And this same process of building new systems of governance created a civil society. How?

Competing business firms in the nineteenth century put aside their differences and created trade federations. They kept their corporate identities and advanced their higher cause for the industry together. (Adam Smith never saw this hidden hand but inter-organizational cooperation allowed markets to become relatively self-regulating.) Competing unions put aside their differences, kept their original identities and created a federation to advance their higher cause for justice together. Competing religious denominations put aside their differences, keeping essential doctrines, and created federations to advance their higher spiritual cause together. Competing colleges and universities put aside their differences, kept their school identities by creating federations to advance higher education together. These processes created a new society.

Inter-organizational cooperation is what created a democratic nation and a civil society. All these instances cited above brought about new federations and associations based on mutual (self) governance. This is the key to societal development.[19]

What happens? Competing organizations keep their identities by organizing a civil association to achieve a higher mission, a new combination and synthesis of beliefs with the new undertaking. A "synthesis" means preserving the original values that people hold dear and bringing them into a higher level of design and purpose. People develop a more elevated order of thinking in their new association. And this integration of conflicting and diverse interests can happen from local to national levels.

In this book we take a look at examples of how this happens—and can happen in the development of a civil economy.

As we shall discuss in greater detail in chapters 6 and 9, business and Third Sector associations develop standards to address issues like public safety and health, and economic values then adjust to these public standards. And increasingly, when market participants are in disagreement, they settle their differences by cooperating for their common good through mediation and arbitration. This reduces the need for government settlements. Professional associations and corporations engage in "conflict resolution" over workplace problems, sexual harassment, age discrimination, and workers' compensation, and mediators are often called in to settle disputes among rival firms and associations. I would argue that the advance of mediation and arbitration as a market mechanism is part of the development of this (latent) associative economy.

Latent vs. Manifest

This is important to follow. The market attributes listed in Box 4.1 can be found in every market as latent or manifest. For example, "cooperation" and "transparency" are not noted on the left side of Box 4.1 because they exist only as latent attributes; they are not part of the capitalist ideal. But they are listed under the civil model as manifest ideals, and civil planners would emphasize them. They should lead toward a civil market with a greater degree of stability and self-regulation.

To do this planners take the lead in creating higher-order associations. Planners will ask not only, How can we get more efficiency, competition, and productivity? but at the same time, How can we get more transparency for the common good? Government officials and civic leaders would emphasize transparency in such a planning process because they want customers to be fully informed and their goal would be an open (public) market in the private sector. In Chapter 5 we will discuss how this can be done through associations that include for-profit and nonprofit organizations.

Looking at another set of these models' attributes, "productivity" is heavily promoted in capitalist markets, while although "accountability" exists today in markets, it is mostly latent, called for whenever the public becomes aware of grievous corporate malfeasance but otherwise awaiting further development as a market attribute.

Civil market development means finding links between those manifest and latent attributes, a reconciliation of the divergent values expressed in our two models.[20]

"Efficiency" and "sustainability" (see Box 4.1) provide another example. While efficiency is promoted in business, sustainability is gaining popularity, and these attributes are not necessarily in opposition. A business firm may find sustainability and efficiency to be mutually enhancing, and choose to develop them together. What we are saying is that the advancement and coordination of the values in both of these models is vital to civil development.

In this connection, "indexes for sustainability" are beginning to be established in capitalist markets. The Dow Jones Sustainability Indexes, for instance, were created in 1999. These global indexes are measuring and tracking the financial performance of "the leading global sustainability-driven companies."[21] The fact that the staff at Dow Jones knows that corporations are finding a synergy between efficiency and sustainability is good news for civil market planners.

In sum, a civil market is recognized by the attributes of *cooperation, transparency,* and *standard making* and implemented in a *public domain* for the *common good.* These attributes can be developed, I argue, by linking (i.e., integrating and combining) them with capitalist attributes of *competition, privacy,* and *profit making* in a *private domain.* A market sector would achieve the designation "civil" at that point when capitalist attributes, while still present, no longer typify it, that is, when the civil attributes become primary or ascendant.

An emphasis on civil attributes in research, scholarship, and government planning, then, could change the culture of capitalist markets as the norms laid out in each of our two models develop in new systems of exchange. This change in the meaning of attributes is normal in the history of capitalism. For example, the overall goal of producing "greater wealth" in capitalist markets has changed quite a bit since capitalism began.

Let us look at this last point in relation to what we conceive of as an ongoing development process. The question emerges, Could greater wealth be redefined again, in relation to the common good?[22]

Changes in the Meaning of Wealth

The idea of seeking greater wealth for nations began around the time of Adam Smith, when wealth was defined in terms of material progress and more profit in small business and agriculture. By the mid-nineteenth century, however, the emphasis had shifted to include manufacturing and technology, and by the mid-twentieth century economists had added "services" to the definition of wealth for a nation.

In other words, economists have redefined "wealth" many times, without losing its former meaning to keep pace with the development of society, and by the end of the twentieth century the meaning of "wealth" had expanded to include education, expertise, and knowledge. The concept of human capital had grown to mean roughly "whatever it takes to make a living," and now it is possible to think of greater wealth as including the expansion of knowledge within society.[23]

So the terms used to explain markets evolve new meanings through stages of development in society. The old attributes of capitalist markets gain new meaning over time. What does this signify for the future?

In new stages of development, fresh definitions might be given to *productivity, efficiency, competition, property,* and *ownership* as they become defined for the common good. Old ("capitalist") terms could well find new meanings with the advance of *public standards, accountability,* and *sustainability* in markets. In other words, markets are social structures that carry meaning and over time develop in value to society.[24]

In sum, the market prototypes depicted in Box 4.1 have attributes that are listed as latent or manifest. The manifest attributes in the civil market (such as cooperation and transparency) are latent in the capitalist market, i.e., not so active or visible to the observer. But they could become manifest through new public policies. With the help of government planners, a market might develop from a capitalist ("economically determined") system to a civil ("economically oriented") system of exchange.[25]

Now we need to look at how nonprofit corporations and organizations can, and do, influence markets.

Nonprofit Corporations: Business and Third Sector

What is a nonprofit corporation? According to the U.S. Congress, there are many "classes" of nonprofit and tax-exempt corporations, too many to list in detail, but here, by way of illustration, are some or the kinds of organizations the nonprofit tax code specifies in its definition:

> Corporations, and any community chest, fund, or foundation, organized and operated exclusively for religious, charitable, scientific testing for public safety, literary, or educational purposes, or to foster national or international amateur sports competition [under certain conditions] . . . civic leagues or organizations not organized for profit but operated exclusively for the promotion of social welfare, or local associations of employees, the membership of which is limited to the employees of a designated person or persons in a particular municipality, and the net earnings of which are devoted exclusively to charitable, educational, or

recreational purposes. . . . Labor, agricultural, or horticultural organizations. . . . Business leagues, chambers of commerce, real-estate boards,
boards of trade. . . .[26]

As we can see from this list, trade associations are "nonprofits" and
operate inside both the business sector and the Third Sector. They are
technically outside the goal of profit making even though they lobby
Congress for business.

Close observation will reveal a strong intent among some trade
groups, like local chambers of commerce, to emphasize civil attributes,
such as local cooperation and public standards. In effect, some nonprofit
trade associations are lodged in between the two sets of model attributes
listed in Box 4.1.

A civil action planner would ask, Could nonprofit trade associations in
the business sector become part of a process of civil development? The answer is yes.

Standard Making and Market Sectors

There are thousands of market sectors, encompassing, for instance, agricultural chemicals, autos, batteries, bottled water, business equipment,
clothing, computers, confectionery, cosmetics, drugs, food and drink,
footwear, fresh produce, frozen food, furniture, and on and on.
Competitors in each market organize associations to serve their own interests and often the common good as well. Competitors cooperate
through trade associations to advance public standards, for instance, as
well as lobby Congress.

Standard making by trade associations most often serves a larger
good when it involves many thousands of competitors. The American
National Standards Institute (ANSI), for example, works for both business
and government. It sets standards in technology in the United States and
it also links with other standard-making bodies around the world. It stan-
dardizes products (like carpentry nails or computer chips) that are purchased by businesses, government, and the Third Sector.

Through the actions of associations that bridge market sectors, a certain common good thus develops in society as a whole. A sense of what is
good for all participants (buyers and sellers) in all markets then contributes to what we would call associative development. This is the latent
side of capitalist markets. Translating core values into public standards
(e.g., regarding public health and safety) in the private sector is part of the
agenda for civil development.

Third Sector nonprofits are also involved in standard making. Today
schools, churches, and professions set standards through their own non-

profit associations. Nonprofit corporations in the field of religion set standards for membership and for priests, rabbis, and ministers. Nonprofit professional corporations set standards for members like lawyers, physicians, nurses, librarians, architects, city planners and accountants.

Furthermore, Third Sector nonprofits have played a direct role in standard making in the private sector. Trade unions, for example, took that role early as they battled against private corporations that lacked standards for worker safety and health. A pattern of accountability was set up, settlements were made, and workplace standards and pension benefits were put into place. When the values of business and the values of the Third Sector conflict but are resolved by contract agreements, this is also civil development.

As we will discuss in greater detail in Part 3, Third Sector buyers and sellers include nonprofit universities, schools, churches, medical clinics, sports teams, and museums, which have power to insist that their values be expressed in public standards within the market.

Third Sector Markets

We do not usually think that Third Sector nonprofit corporations have markets like business but they do compete with economic incentives. Universities compete for students. Hospitals compete for technology. Libraries compete for rare books. Art museums compete for great paintings. Churches compete for parishioners. They compete for power, recognition, status, and money, just like businesses do.

Third Sector organizations, however, are different from business. They have their economic side (calculated monetary returns) but they also have core values that are contrary to business. That is, Third Sector corporations sustain (at best) substantive values in their market orientation.

Here are the key questions.

Could those core values in the Third Sector combine with business to develop a new market system? Could this blend lead toward a higher order of values in market life?

Linking the For-Profit and Non-Profit Sectors

In Chapter 3 we presented evidence that business could destroy core values in the Third Sector. (Max Weber feared that substantive rationality would lose to the advance of formal rationality.) Could the Third Sector stop the decline in values? Could those core values in the Third Sector influence business, rather than the other way around?[27]

We need to look at these questions.

Ethical Action: Today's Sector Interaction

There are different ways in which society's core values develop in markets and business. To begin with, people work and live in both business and the Third Sector at the same time. They make an adjustment between these different values to maintain their personal integrity. So, "ethical action" occurs constantly in business on a small scale. Business leaders organize Kiwanis and Rotary Clubs and work on the values they carry from their family and religious life into business. They go to a church or temple and bring spiritual concerns into business.[28]

There is also the gentle push from Third Sector organizations like churches and universities that invest their endowments in the stock market with attention to larger values. University schools of management bring business ethics into core curriculums and into the thinking of students who will carry them into management. There is also the effort of CEOs to develop corporate responsibility, contribute to social causes, offer money to Third Sector organizations, collaborate on the rehabilitation of slums, etc. So business and Third Sector leaders interact in many ways to advance what they see to be a common good.

More examples of this link between the Third Sector and business can be found in the appendices.[29] They include new types of "donations" (e.g., Microsoft provides software, and technical expertise to public libraries through the American Library Association), new types of "social marketing" (e.g., Denny's restaurant chain raises money for Save the Children's new urban programs), "operational transactions" (e.g., Pioneer Human Services provides jobs for its ex-offender clients by contracting with Boeing to make parts for aircraft) and "employee accountability systems" that develop by degrees (e.g., corporate ownership for unionized employees and warranties for organized consumers).[30]

These developments are important but the structure of capitalist markets remains the same. Granted, Third Sector organizations pass along core values to business; markets develop ethically, but the capitalist system remains unchanged.

What would be different in developing the civil market model?

This new strategy for development is to build *public accountability* systems in the private sector. This changes the market structure. Stakeholders would create contracts based on principles of transparency, cooperation, fairness, and justice. These principles become built into the market structure itself and monitored. This then becomes a new exchange system.[31]

This is the blueprint for civil development that we will propose and discuss in detail in later chapters, using existing examples as points of departure. In Chapter 5 we will describe the Joint Commission on Accreditation of Healthcare Organizations (JCAHO), a public domain organization with Third Sector stakeholders that establish, monitor, and ac-credit public standards in business. In Chapter 6 we will consider the New England Association of Schools and Colleges and its stakeholder-based agreements, standards, monitors, and authorities. In Chapter 7 we will propose the construction of a public accountability system for the mass media. In Chapter 8 we will discuss how Third Sector leaders are working to develop a system of public accountability in the apparel industry. In Chapter 9, we will describe international organizations (e.g., the Forest Stewardship Council) that develop public accountability (agreements, standards, monitors, and authorities) worldwide.

In these examples, we will see how the values of civil society become linked with economic values at a higher order of association. Markets would now have professional (neutral) monitoring and enforcement as part of their structure in addition to monitoring by governments. As we shall see, these would not be capitalist markets. They would be civil markets.

Civil Development Principles

Now it's time to lay out some notions about how civil development might unfold. Below are hypotheses for researchers and guidelines for govern-ment planners. They are different from the economic principles that guide public planning today.[32]

First, a caution. There is as yet no overall theory of civil markets that analyzes core values of our society—in particular, freedom, democracy, and justice—in the market. The all-encompassing value of freedom has certain iterations—personal choice, private transactions, "free entry," "free trade," voluntary association, "unforced options," and more—that are studied by economists, but economists do not ask themselves how democracy and justice work in the market.

So researchers and planners of civil markets would be guided by the propositions below, in Box 4.2. All of them should be given greater speci-ficity in planning because these assertions are abstract. They are drawn from Box 4.1 and they represent the start for a theory of societal develop-ment. They need to be tested as the schema for organizing a civil republic.

Box 4.3 is a model for civil society planners to put these ideals and propositions into practice. Planners would attempt to integrate the op-posing attributes listed in Box 4.1. Below is a statement of how these at-tributes might be brought together as a vision for planning. The propositions listed above in Box 4.2 and the vision outlined below is the basis for our discussion in Part 4. Here the vision is without details, but its general outline offers a basis for thinking about a market with a novel structure: new motives, norms, values, and goals.

Box 4.2. Propositions for Civil Development

I. Goals and Ideals

1. *Greater wealth* can be developed in the private sector for the *common good.*
2. *Formal rationality* can be linked with *substantive rationality* by public standards.
3. A *public domain* can be developed within the *private domain* of markets.
4. The principle of *justice* can be developed in markets with the principle of *freedom.*

II. Optimizing Principles[33]

1. Public *standard making* can be advanced with private *profit making* in markets.
2. *Stockholder* rights can be protected with the advancement of *stakeholder* rights.
3. *Public accountability systems* can develop without loss of *economic values.*
4. The principle of *sustainability* can develop with the principle of *efficiency.*
5. *Transparency* can increase while *privacy* rights are safeguarded.
6. Corporate *command* management can develop systems of *self-management.*
7. *Corporations* can develop public standards through *associations.*

III. Establishing Public Accountability

1. The core values of society can be defined as public standards in markets.[34]
2. Impartial monitors in the private sector can enforce public standards.[35]
3. Systems of procedural justice (e.g., due process and civil tribunals) can be developed in the private market through associations.[36]
4. Core values of justice (e.g., fairness, impartiality, and equity) can become developed in systems of accountability.[37]
5. Stakeholder representatives (e.g., fiduciaries and communities) can integrate public values with economic values.[38]

Box 4.2 continues

Box 4.2 continued

IV. Oligarchy and Democracy

 1. Self-management practices can develop (and oligarchy reduced)—in both business and Third Sector corporations.[39]
 2. Greater local responsibility and authority can develop in global markets.[40]
 3. Government can reduce its bureaucracy judiciously by increasing public accountability in the general economy.[41]

Box 4.3. The Vision: Imagining a New Market System

The goal of civil development planners is to increase wealth for the common good. The process involves joining economic values in the profit sector with substantive values in the larger society. The aim is to create a public domain within a private (voluntary) domain. This involves the advance of public accountability systems organized by stakeholders. The purpose is to foster core values like democracy, freedom, and justice together in the market system.

Competitors are encouraged to cooperate in setting public standards. This collaboration is achieved through systems of public accountability established by trade and Third Sector associations. Productivity and efficiency are respected while care is taken to advance financial accountability and sustainable use in the development of resources. In civil associations, market participants increase the transparency of their transactions (i.e., setting open standards and monitoring practices) while retaining appropriate levels of privacy for competition.

Key strategies are to overcome excessive oligarchy and to advance "self-management" in corporations. Civil development means decentralizing authority in large-scale organizations while keeping an appropriate higher authority to advance the common good. The higher authority of associations brings forward core values in the economy. An associative (civil) economy then develops through greater responsible authority taken by stakeholders in local to global associations.

This vision statement brings together the different attributes in Box 4.1, but notice how it produces a mood change about the meaning of a "market." The goal of wealth is now linked with the common good. The operational meaning of wealth and the common good can be expected to develop more specificity and evolve over time.

The meaning of the term "stakeholder" will also evolve. Today it refers to people who are affected by business and believe they have a role in shaping markets. CEOs respond to stakeholder concerns today and would hopefully develop a "socially responsive business." But this concept of stakeholder is a latent part of capitalist markets, not a well-known national concept, and not part of public planning.

As we shall see in the next chapters, stakeholders have begun to build new market structures. They have begun to translate society's core values into public standards and started to organize associations that fit a public domain. We will illustrate in chapters 5 through 8 how Third Sector associations become stakeholders and how public standards—transparency and accountability in particular—are created. The concept of stakeholders is central to how the civil market model might be extended into the global market, which we will examine in the last two chapters of the book.[42]

Conclusion

The myth about capitalist markets is powerful and very persuasive. But if global firms and capitalist markets continue their expansion, scientists will go into business and research will be done for private gain rather for the common good; scientists will refuse to let their procedures and data go public. Artists will work mainly on commercial projects; the field of aesthetics will descend into the culture of commerce. For-profit corporations will advance inside the Third Sector; the substantive values of education, religion, and the professions will continue their downward trend into a market tradition. In the United States, government will develop as a command bureaucracy and collude with business until it has lost its autonomy and integrity. It will no longer serve to uphold a republic "of the people, by the people, and for the people."

The picture we have set forth of a capitalist market is about an economy that links to business while the picture we propose for a civil market is about an economy that links to the entire society. The capitalist model will lead to government bureaucracy; the civil model will lead to a new republic.

Civil development will not be trouble-free. Some people will not want to give up privilege and will fight against the process. The outcome may not be all that is hoped for because conflict and negotiations occur. The challenge for civil planners will be to convince the public about how the change will benefit everyone.

As we shall see, the two models invoke different government policies. A *capitalist government* regulates markets from the outside. A *civil government* also regulates markets from the outside but emphasizes self-regulation from the inside, highlighting self-development, encouraging standards to develop within the market itself. It would cultivate public accountability and transparency from the market's interior structure. It would encourage market self-governance in collaboration with the Third Sector.

Business cannot regulate itself without the help of government and the Third Sector. Applying the new model will involve public planning that emphasizes a greater civic engagement between business and the Third Sector. Government planners would encourage self-determination (not elitism and oligarchy) in nonprofit associations. They would bring substantive values like justice and democracy into systems of economic exchange. They would ask civic leaders to build a new market system imbued with the values of a civil society.

Max Weber said that "formal rationality" (calculability) is a major theme in modern society but this worried him because it could become the master theme of society. Its opposite, "substantive rationality," could be lost. Weber never saw these two themes coming together in a creative way. Now we have proposed that new public policies should involve a synthesis—the creative resolution of differences—between these two types of rationality. We shall see in the next chapter that making the connections between these two themes can make a difference.[43]

Could this new market model combine with new policies in government to stop civil decline? Could the United States implement a new market and advance a civil republic? We will now explore those questions.

Notes

1. "Natural rights" is a moral theory that goes back many centuries and many writers have commented on its exploitation by corporations. See Richard L. Grossman and Frank T. Adams, "Taking Care of Business: Citizenship and the Charter of Incorporation," *Earth Island Journal,* spring 1993, p. 34 (The full version is available as a pamphlet from Charter, Ink., PO Box 806, Cambridge, MA 02140). The Fourth Amendment to the U.S. Constitution spells out the (natural) right of citizens to be "secure in their persons, houses, papers and effects against unreasonable searches" by government. When that amendment was ratified in 1791, however, no one imagined that it could be corporations, not just government, that would use their power to legally invade the privacy of citizens and, in effect, carry out unreasonable searches of the most intimate personal data. See also The Nader Page, http://www.nader.org/interest/062101.html.

2. I am drawing these current subjects from the *Journal of Political Economy* at the University of Chicago Press; see http://www.journals.uchicago.edu/JPE/brief.html. When first advanced by the French Physiocrats, the term "economy" was expanded beyond Aristotle's definition (of a household) to refer to the productive efforts of a community or a nation-state. This "classical" meaning refers

to natural laws governing the production and distribution of wealth. Contributors to classical political economy included Adam Smith, Ricardo, Malthus, Mill, and Marx. The classical model changed in the latter part of the nineteenth century to studies of marginal utility, and the historical and neo-classical approach represented by Jevons, Bohm-Bawerk, J. B Clark, Marshall, and others. By the 1930s, the Keynesian approach had swept the field and economics became the main focus of study. Social historians like Henri Pirenne, Karl Marx, Maurice Dobbs, Werner Sombart, Max Weber, and Karl Polanyi were critical of political economy as a field, but today they should be taken more seriously. See Severyn T. Bruyn, *A Future for the Economy* (Stanford: Stanford University Press, 1991), Chapter 1.

3. Max Weber, *Economy and Society: An Outline of Interpretive Sociology* (Berkeley: University of California Press, 1978, pp. 48-50.

4. Neil Fligstein, "Markets as Politics: A Political-Cultural approach to Market Institutions," *American Sociological Review.* 61:656-73.

5. Stephan Casler defines economic values. He sees economics as being concerned with the efficient allocation of scarce resources among competing uses. Economic principles represent values that guide strategies in business thinking, which include efficiency, scarcity, competition, and optimizing utilities. Stephen Casler, *Introduction to Economics* (New York: Harper Perennial,1992), p. 3. The principles of productivity, efficiency, and profit transmute into strategies for economic development. Economic values can be seen as core values when they are viewed as abstract concepts or high principles (e.g., the *idea* of efficiency), but they are not core values when they are taken as business strategies in the market. See Christopher Pass, et al., *The Harper Collins Dictionary of Economics* (New York: Harper Perennial, 1991), p. 541.

6. Jameson is a neo-Marxist who favors "dialectical criticism." Dialectical criticism holds that we should not examine abstract categories just for their own sake but study them for how they lead to practice and concrete inquiry. This kind of criticism means reflexive thinking and represents a different approach from that of G. W. F. Hegel and Karl Marx, who thought in terms of a "certain future." Fredric Jameson, *The Cultural Turn: Selected Writings on the Postmodern 1983–1998* (New York: Verso, 1998).

7. This outlook on the future is different from that expressed by Francis Fukuyama. In the summer of 1989, writing in the periodical *The National Interest,* Fukuyama spoke of the end of revolutions in grand terms, suggesting "the end of history" and "the evolution and the universalization of Western liberal democracy as the final form of human government." Subsequently, the journal published responses on this idea by Allan Bloom, Irving Kristol, Gertrude Himmelfarb, Samuel P. Huntington, and Daniel Patrick Moynihan. This notion of a civil market and its development does not conflict with Fukuyama's portrayal of the future insofar as he might see markets evolving, but it does suggest that capitalism should have a conclusion in time. Capitalist markets will "end" just like primitive markets and feudal markets ended. The question is not "whether" but "when" and "how."

8. "Core values" are discussed in detail in other books. Sociologist Amitai Etzioni, for example, outlines "basic values as social virtues" such as "life and health."

They become part of "a voluntary moral order and a strong measure of bounded individual and subgroup autonomy, held in careful equilibrium, the new golden rule." Amitai Etzioni, *The New Golden Rule* (New York: BasicBooks, 1996), p. 244.

9. We do not make definitive distinctions between these types of values—economic, financial, social, and cultural. We take these distinctions to be clear by their use, by their contrast in everyday speech and by common sense. All these "values" have technical meanings in economics and sociology but we use them in their common meanings and by their contrast with one another. Economic values are defined by the advance of productivity, efficiency, competition, and profit making. Financial values are defined in relation to advancing monetary returns. Social values are defined as they advance the general interests and well-being of people apart from monetary returns. Cultural values are qualities related to the substantive values of society.

10. Weber wrote, "The term 'formal rationality of economic action' will be used to designate the extent of quantitative calculation or accounting which is technically possible and which is actually applied. The 'substantive rationality,' on the other hand, is the degree to which the provisioning of given groups of persons (no matter how delimited) with goods is shaped by economically-oriented social action under some criterion (past, present, or potential) of ultimate values, regardless of the nature of these ends." See Richard Swedberg, *Max Weber: Essays in Economic Sociology* (Princeton: N.J.: Princeton University Press, 1999), p. 214. Weber defines the market in terms of its "formal rationality," i.e., a quantitative calculation "to prove the achievement of a definable goal." This calculating rationality stands in tension with "substantive rationality," which expresses values without a basis for calculation. Substantive rationality for our purposes includes core values in the expression of, say, "truth," and "beauty." These are not values proposed to typify the capitalist market.

11. Weber's fear was that "formal rationality" would become dominant in the entire society and "substantive rationality" would decline. While formal rationality is linked with capitalist markets, Weber saw it growing in other realms of modern society, as in science and bureaucratic organizations. He foresaw that the advance of this type of rationality could cause a decline in substantive values and limit the possibilities for creative social action. Weber wrote "a system of economic activity" will be called "formally rational according to the degree in which the provision for needs, which is essential to every rational economy, is capable of being expressed in numerical, calculable terms, and is so expressed...The concept of 'substantive rationality,' is full of ambiguities....There is an infinite number of possible value scales for this type of rationality, of which the socialist and communist standards constitute only one group." Ibid., p. 214. Our concern about the decline of core values is similar to Weber's concern about the decline in substantive values, but we do not apply his framework in this text. For Weber, economic action is concerned with the satisfaction of a desire for utilities. We do not take Weber's "utilities" and "desire" as central to our discussion. But we do look at how an excess desire for utilities and an emphasis on formal rationality could be a danger to civil society.

12. The separation of core values from economic values is important for analytical purposes but in public planning they would be seen as linked. As we shall see, civil development requires a link to be made between business values and Third Sector values. A "value" for our purposes, by the way, is high societal standard, like an ideal or a principle. It represents what people believe to be most important, like freedom and truth, what people believe is right and good. "Substantive values" are core values in that people hold them vital to society, not all measurable. They are "ideal" in the sense that they are not defined as "economic" or "financially sound" in business and the market. Substantive values are not part of the defined purpose of business or the economic tradition. Great feelings such as tenderness and love, and great concepts such as freedom, and justice are at the moral foundation of society. Economic values are what we expect in capitalist markets while core values are more likely in the Third Sector. Core values carry an "infinite number of possible value scales," as Weber would say.

13. The attributes in these two models should be seen as "sensitizing concepts," which orient us to a *general* meaning, not as an operational meaning. The sociologist Herbert Blumer describes sensitizing concepts as offering a general orientation to (rather than an exact definition of) "a phenomenon." Sensitizing concepts are not operational concepts but communicated "by means of exposition, which yields a meaningful picture, abetted by apt illustrations which enable one to grasp the reference in terms of one's own experience." Herbert Blumer, "What Is Wrong with Social Theory?" *American Sociological Review* 19 (February 1954), p. 9.

14. The terms in quotes are close to those of Max Weber but not exactly. Weber: "Action will be said to be 'economically oriented' so far as, according to its subjective meaning, it is concerned with the satisfaction of a desire for 'utilities' (*Nutleistungen*)." Max Weber, *The Theory of Social and Economic Organization* (New York: Free Press.1947) p. 158. By "economically oriented," we mean that even though civil markets are related to core values, they are still oriented to economic values, done with prudence. By "economically determined," social action takes place primarily for economic ends. See Richard Swedberg, ed., *Essays in Economic Sociology* (Princeton: N.J.: Princeton University Press, 1999), p. 200.

15. Notice that while both models are "ideal types," economic values (capitalism) dominate the US and world markets. The "civil market" is an ideal in a different sense. It exists minimally (latently) within capitalist markets, waiting to be cultivated. It is in the womb of capitalism, as Marx would say.

16. Transparency is a problem notable in all three sectors—business, government, and Third Sector. Ocean Spray is a farmers' cooperative with sales of $1.07 billion. Dissident farmers in this co-op have challenged the board on "transparency." They say the company became "secretive and unaccountable." Chris Reidy, "Ocean Spray Board Facing Challenge," *Boston Globe,* 8 March 2003, p. C1. There are heated debates about what should be transparent (or public) in each market.

    For example, the Massachusetts Pension Reserves Investment Trust (PRIT) refused to comply with an order from the secretary of state's office to disclose its "venture capital investment performance" to a private citizen who requested it. This pension fund made commitments to venture capitalist companies to keep their transactions private. This same concern about transparency plays out with university investments. The universities of Texas and California declined to reveal the returns of their venture investments on the basis of confidentiality. But a Texas attorney general forced the University of Texas to disclose its venture returns. At stake is the privacy that venture firms have enjoyed for decades. Venture capitalists are afraid that they won't be able to keep competitive matters private, such as fees and the specifics of how individual portfolio companies are faring. In a civil market plan, however, these transactions would come into "the public domain." See Beth Healy, "Pension Fund Rejects Order to Share Data," *Boston Globe,* 28 October 2002, C1, C3.

17. In our model, "cooperation" does not mean "collusion" but collaboration for a common good defined by stakeholders. This emphasis on cooperation is an attribute of civility in markets in which competition remains vibrant. I discuss the measurement of cooperation in my book *A Future for the American Economy* (Stanford, California: Stanford University Press, 1991), Chapter 8, "A Method of Measurement."

18. See Seymour Martin Lipset, *The First New Nation: The United States in Historical and Comparative Perspective* (New York: W.W. Norton, 1979/1973).

19. Trade competitors *cooperated* in the nineteenth century to defend themselves against government intervention and outside regulation, and against trade unions, but they also saw themselves destroying each other by fierce competition. Now, in a civil model, "cooperation" becomes an ideal for competitors to build higher associations for the common good of society. See *A Future for the American Economy,* Chapter 8.

20. Here the field of economic sociology represents the frontier of university studies. Sociologists examine the politics of markets, the development of corporate power, the meanings of markets, the values that govern economic exchanges, and the functions and dysfunctions of exchange systems in society. They are in a position to examine the degree to which a value is latent or manifest, dominant or subdominant, dormant or active, visible or invisible to people acting within markets.

21. Based on the cooperation of Dow Jones Indexes, STOXX Limited and SAM, these indexes provide asset managers with reliable and relatively objective benchmarks to manage sustainability portfolios. Dow Jones Sustainability Indexes, http://www.sustainability-index.com/djsi_pdf/news/PressReleases/DJSI_PressRelease_031017_UBS.pdf. Among corporations seeking to make the higher synthesis, see the Ecos Corporation. Its officers believe that "sustainable growth" can motivate people. Focusing on core values is "the most powerful way to initiate change in business." Ecos Corporation, http://www.ecoscorporation.com/about/beliefs_actions.htm.

22. The development of wealth as an idea shaping the market system in the future is suggestive of how under the best conditions the latent becomes manifest. Think of a novel or a play to understand this latent-manifest relation. Actors in the background slowly come forward into the foreground and are then seen in more depth and detail. As these background actors slowly move

forward they change their appearance and the original plot of the play changes. The goal of wealth making could develop from an exterior meaning in land and money to an interior condition of knowledge. There is much more to this theory of "latent and manifest" to be found in Appendix P. For example, Louis Althusser contrasts the manifest text with a latent text, which is the result of the lapses, distortions, silences and absences in the manifest text. The latent text is the "diary of the struggle" of a question yet to be posed and answered. Sigmund Freud describes the transformation of a latent dream into a manifest dream. Sigmund Freud. "The Dream-Work: 1916." *Introductory Lectures on Psychoanalysis.* By Sigmund Freud. Trans. James Strachey (Norton, 1966).

23. Adam Smith, *The Wealth of Nations* (1776). Note that "wealth" representing land and money has never disappeared. It was incorporated into the broader meaning of "services and human resources." So, the development of *material* wealth, which was allied with capitalism in the eighteenth century, now changes its meaning into *immaterial* (cultural) wealth. The latent meaning of this abstract idea of wealth comes to the foreground and changes the whole meaning of a market. For details on this shift in the meaning of wealth, see Bruyn, *A Future for the American Economy,* pp. 322-325.

24. Sociologist Charles Geisler and environmentalist Gail Daneker describe how the concept of property and ownership are changing now to include the Third Sector. Geisler and Daneker point out "public and private are, at best, clumsy pigeonholes that cramp our thinking. They blind us to many cultural alternatives to public and private ownership at home and abroad and to the active realm of third sector ownership." Charles Geiser and Gail Daneker, *Property and Values: Alternatives to Public and Private Ownership* (Washington, D.C.: Island Press, 2000), p. 283.

25. For more details on the latent and manifest aspects of the market, see Bruyn, *A Future for the American Economy,* Chapter 2.

26. This list is illustrative, drawn from the Internal Revenue Code on the Internet.

27. Could we see a creative synthesis of values between business and the Third Sector? Could the core values in universities, religious groups, and professional associations mix in within the capitalist market to reshape business, not the other way around? Could this action reverse the decline described in Chapter 3? Not easy. Henry Mattera of the Corporate Research Project cites two examples of failure: a Blue Cross / Blue Shield plan that converted itself into a for-profit insurance company, and a major industrial polluter that funneled money to a nonprofit think tank that publishes reports raising doubts about the environmental harm caused by that company. Henry Mattera, Corporate Research Project, "Researching the Non-profit Sector" http://www.goodjobsfirst.org/crp/oct00.htm.

28. Sociologist William Graham Sumner, who studied the evolution of human folkways and mores concluded that these quiet forces, developed over the course of human evolution, rendered useless any attempts at social reform. Sumner also wrote conservatively in *Folkways* (1907) about the tendency of institutions to borrow traits from each other; social institutions and folkways, he argued, grew to be more like one another through osmosis, a kind of mutual

assimilation of values that occurs through the interaction of people living near to one another. The "osmosis" that Sumner described between institutions, this inter-institutional action, has yet to be fully studied.

But this is not what we are talking about here. The first president of the American Sociological Association, Lester Ward (1906), had a different idea about how change takes place. He developed a theory of planned progress called telesis, in which people, through education and public development, could direct progress. Ward's classic outlook and that of his inveterate contemporary, William Graham Sumner, represent two contrasting modes of change. We see both these outlooks explaining the development of civil markets.

29. For these appendices see my website at http://www2.bc.edu/~bruyn.

30. The convergence of these trends is interesting. Corporate-Nonprofit Partnerships is an organization that wants to enhance both a nonprofit mission and business goals. Independent Sector, http://www.independentsector.org/mission_market. Also see Shirley Sagaw and Eli Segal, Common Interest, *Common Good: Creating Value through Business and Social Sector Partnerships* (Cambridge, Mass.: Harvard Business School, 2000).

31. For more on public accountability systems, see Bruyn, *A Civil Economy,* Chapters 2, 7, and 8.

32. Stephan Casler defines economic principles as concerned with the efficient allocation of scarce resources among competing uses. Economic principles represent values that guide strategies in business thinking, which include efficiency, scarcity, competition, and optimizing utilities. Stephen Casler, *Introduction to Economics* (New York: Harper Perennial,1992), p. 3. The principles of productivity, efficiency, and profit transmute into strategies for economic development.

33. Examples of how these principles are optimized together are given in Part 4.

34. See Chapter 6 and Chapter 10 for examples of how core values are converted to standards in accord with economic values. This is done through accountability systems in market sectors.

35. See Chapters 5–10. What is "impartial" or "accountable" is a judgment made among stakeholders.

36. See Chapters 5–10 for due process and civil commissions. On trade tribunals, see Bruyn, *A Future for the American Economy,* Chapter 8. A supposition: the lack of a theory of justice for the development of markets is one reason why government becomes a bureaucracy, attempting to regulate markets.

37. See Chapter 6 and 7 on these values in systems of accountability. When professional tribunals and market mechanisms of mediation are organized, the ideal of fairness becomes real. Fairness is then structured inside the market. Justice-related concepts such as "fair trade" are made operational; civil planners aim to "integrate" free trade with fair trade.

38. See Chapter 5 and Conclusion on social investment. See chapter 6 on the integration of values in communities.

39. For discussion on the development of self-management, see Bruyn, *A Future for the American Economy,* Chapter 3, and Carole Pateman, *Participation and Democratic Theory* (Cambridge: Cambridge University Press, 1970).

40. See Chapter 6 for illustrations of this "integration." Citizens in community corporations work with global corporations to advance the common good of their locality.
41. Self-regulation refers to the whole (business/Third Sector) economy. We show how this happens throughout the book, especially Part 4 and Conclusion. Appendix C proposes a theory of the "general economy."
42. On stakeholder involvement, see John Jackson, Roger Miller and Shawn Miller, *Business and Society Today* (New York: West Publishing Co., 1997), and Grover Starling, *The Changing Environment of Business* (Cincinnati, Ohio: South-Western College Publishing, 1996).
43. Note that the capitalist model is not devoid of substantive values. It is grounded on the core value of freedom, but other core values also interpenetrate markets. The new (civil) model is grounded in the values of freedom (e.g. options) and justice (e.g. fairness). Civil planners would seek a synthesis between such contrary values. Civil society advocates talk about "fair trade" coupling with "free trade." But government officials today do not aim to develop fair trade. Capitalist markets are viewed only as "free," "competitive" and "natural" without further thought. Nonetheless, concepts such as the "fair price" and the "just wage" did attract the attention of scholars during the Middle Ages. Edward J. O' Boyle, "Contributions of German and American Jesuits to Economics: The Last 100 Years," *Forum for Social Economics*, Vol. 31, Number 2 (Spring 2002).

5

A Theory of Development
How Is the New Model Applied?

We are beginning a mythic period of existence, rather like the age portrayed in the Bhagavad Gita, *the* Lord of the Rings, *and in other tales of darkness and light. We live in a time in which every living system is in decline, and the rate of decline is accelerating as our economy grows. The commercial processes that bring us the kind of lives we supposedly desire are destroying the Earth and the life we cherish. Given current corporate practices, not one wildlife reserve, wilderness, or indigenous culture will survive the global market economy.*

—Paul Hawken

Revolutionaries fought capitalism because they believed it was destroying the core values of society, but communist governments of the twentieth century proved to be worse, even more destructive to people than the "free market" system. With the collapse of all but a few remnant communist states, however, the values of the market are now moving deep into the life of society. We live in a capitalist society, not a civil society in the best and largest sense of that term.

Philosophers see nations evolving as civil societies throughout modern history. The modern period is marked by the development of a democratic government, a capitalist economic system, and a Third Sector. In this historic sense, they see society as a whole as continuing to change. We call the positive side of this process "societal development" and it includes all three sectors together.

But today we face the possibility of decline instead of development. In the United States, capitalist markets are shaping the field of education, challenging the core values of teachers and educators. Major players in these now global markets are shaping the field of government, challenging the core values of political parties and Congress, supplying major campaign funds, writing legislation, and determining the direction of public policies.

In this chapter we begin to examine how capitalist markets could be transformed into civil markets without violence. This new revolution would be civil and take place through the voluntary sector. The change agents are government officials who become rebels inside the system and civic leaders who become responsible radicals. They will need a certain amount of nerve to reverse the trend toward decline.

Responsible rebels and radicals will be needed in all orders of society—government, religion, business, recreation, education, art, science, and the professions. The problem is this: local and national leaders have a sense of the erosion of substantive values within society, but no overall picture of how to stop this process, let alone reverse it. They have no sense of what "societal development" might mean.

We have proposed a starting place by presenting a civil market model in Chapter 4, but in order for this idea to be useful we need a plan and theory for action. Could civil society and government leaders plan and develop a new market system?

This chapter is about how it begins to happen, about how latent attributes of the civil market model can be strengthened and brought to the fore. First, we will show how the economy is already linked with civil orders of society and how core values in these orders are translated into market standards. Second, we will look at how business standards are monitored and enforced by Third Sector associations. Third, we will look at how government-sponsored commissions might advance civil development.

Fourth, we will look at how Third Sector values can be brought into "financial markets." This is a big one. Financial markets are at the heart of capitalism. While governments have supported "capitalist investment" in the past, we argue that they should now support "social (civil) investment." This practice will change the purpose of capital allocation by synthesizing economic values with core values for the common good.

Finally, we will put forth a specific plan for civil development that would include a Council of Social Advisers in the federal government. It would provide Congress and the president of the United States with studies on what is happening in society, not just in business.

Nonprofit corporations are a key part of this vision for development. The aim is to bring business under the influence of nonprofits that carry core values into the market.

Civil Orders of Society: The Location of Core Values

Modern society is composed of different civil orders and ways of life. Each order has a different culture and its own associations that carry core values, rules, and norms. These "orders" are involved in what we call societal development. In our scheme, civic leaders in each association are potentially agents for positive change.[1]

Box 5.1, on page 98, is about the nature of these civil orders. It does not represent the full story, but it suggests how certain orders stand apart from each other. Other orders could be listed, such as science and art, but this listing is sufficient for our purposes.

In a sociological perspective, all of these orders are in the economy, and while they are all interdependent and intricately affected by each another, in a time of decline we forget about the importance of these cultures and the need to sustain their core values.[2]

Currently government at all levels supports business development, but rarely concerns itself with societal development. National leaders may talk about a decline in values in one realm or another ("family values" has been a popular topic of discussion), but they do not think about how the values in all these orders of society develop together. We are suggesting that we need a creative linking between the values of all these orders. If this were to take place, we would be moving toward a civil republic.

Societal development is very different from business development. It is the extension of the "sensible influence" and creative mix of all the core values listed in Box 5.1. In relation to the kinship order, for example, it is about advancing values such as caring, tenderness, and kindness in the larger society. In relation to the state order, societal development is about advancing values like democracy, justice, and freedom beyond the sphere of political ideology. In relation to the educational order, it is about extending the values of truth, reason, beauty, and human excellence into business, politics, and the professions. In relation to the religious order, societal development is about advancing spiritual values, including love, faith, devotion, and compassion at their deepest levels as part of the life of all people, religious or not. Again, the creative linking and advancement of core values in and across all these orders—and others not categorized above—is the key.

The "civil development of markets" is a special aspect of societal development. It is about how core values in non-business orders are brought into the business order to shape markets. In this outlook, the core values in all orders are then viewed in connection with the economy. In other words, the civil development of markets is about how

Box 5.1. Civil Orders of Society (Examples)

KINSHIP ORDER

The *kinship* order is composed of families and partners that allow for appropriate sexual relations, procreation, and the rearing of children. In this order, we see people developing values that include *love, tenderness, kindness, intimacy,* and *caring.*

STATE ORDER

The *state* order is composed of associations where people create enforceable law. In this order, people determine by assembly what is right and wrong for all citizens in a political territory. They establish and implement values, which include *freedom, democracy, justice, safety,* and *the common welfare.*

BUSINESS ORDER

The business order is composed of for-profit establishments and allied trade associations. In this order, people produce and distribute goods and services to fulfill human needs. They develop core values that include *productivity, efficiency, competition,* and *wealth.*

PROFESSIONAL ORDER

The *professional order* is composed of associations in which experts and specialists organize knowledge according to principles and standards. In this order, we see people developing a discipline (e.g., medicine, law, or engineering) with special expertise and skills. These associations support values like *safety, health, honesty,* and *personal accomplishment.*[3]

EDUCATIONAL ORDER

The *educational* order is composed of associations in which people transmit the culture of society. In this order, people study fields of knowledge like the humanities, sciences, and professions. Here faculties study and advance the major values in society, such as *truth* (e.g., science),*beauty* (e.g., the arts), *physical recreation and well-being* (e.g., sports), and *reason* (e.g., philosophy).

RELIGIOUS ORDER

The religious order is composed of institutions in which people honor a transcendent being or beings beyond all human understanding. In this order, people advance ultimate concerns about life and death. They cultivate values that include commitment, integrity, faith, devotion, compassion, and dedication.

society's core values are integrated into business life, not the other way around. The right synthesis of core values is what produces a healthy economy within society, a situation in which the well-being of people is linked with a healthy economy and a healthy economy adds to their quality of life.[4]

Today economic planners focus upon increasing the material output of society, and they advance the values of business, not the values of other civil orders. Planners of civil development—we will call them civil planners—would work deliberately and consciously to bring the values of these non-commercial orders into business.[5]

As we shall see, this idea is not new. It is already happening to some degree; civil decline is not the only thing going on today. There are churches making ethical investments, not Wall Street investments. There are accountants who insist on honesty and transparency rather than engaging in accounting tricks and budget fixes. There are scientists who insist on a collegial sharing of data and refuse to engage in laboratory secrecy or the quest for private patents for corporate profits. But there are ways to increase the probability that all these civil-minded activities are supported. As we shall see, government can do this by supporting new market structures.

Each civil order in Box 5.1 has a level of integrity that is sustained in the economic activities of its members by its associations. If the core values in any civil order decline, the capacity for its associations to govern decreases and its values are eroded. In our outlook, the core values inherent in all these orders need to be not only sustained but also developed in relation to the economy.

The "state order" (or government), for example, should sustain its autonomy and integrity, its self-rule. When government officials take bribes from business corporations or when lobbyists dictate congressional policy, the state order loses autonomy and self-direction; in effect, rather than governing, it becomes governed by the business order. When accountants and lawyers consort with corporate executives and adapt their high standards to align them with business interests alone, their professions lose integrity; the fields of law and accounting become merely a part of business.

This is why maintaining a level of independence for each order is important as we think about building a new level of *inter*dependence in the development of civil markets. How does this happen?

Sectors of the Economy

In order to understand how the values in these orders of society can not only resist decline but be brought into commerce, we should clarify differences between the business sector and the Third Sector. The business sector is chartered *primarily* for profit and *secondarily* to advance other social-cultural values. Conversely, the Third Sector is chartered primarily to develop social and cultural values in its orders and *secondarily* to advance economic values such as profit or productivity. This idea is outlined in Box 5.2 below.

The juxtaposition of our ideas about civil orders (Box 5.1) and the two non-governmental sectors (Box 5.2) introduces questions for scholars to debate, especially economists and sociologists. Some scholars contend that *society is grounded in the economy.* Others contend that *the economy is grounded in society.* For our purposes both statements are true, relatively, but the latter truth is not recognized in economics or in most mainstream studies of the economy.[6]

Perhaps here we need a quick review of our definition of the economy. The economy, we have argued includes activities in which people produce, distribute, and acquire goods and services; it is also where people utilize scarce resources to meet human needs. The higher ends toward which scarce resources are produced and allocated in the various orders of society are linked with this economy. The economy is where people earn their livelihoods and where organizations produce incomes. It is where material and social needs and wants are met. "The economy" by this definition is not just business and it is connected with the core values of all orders of society. In other words, the civil orders of the family, religion, education, and the professions are not in business, but they are in the economy; their values and goals are advanced in the economy through their (nonprofit) corporations and associations.

Third Sector associations—as we described in Chapter 2—go beyond the common list of bowling leagues, civic organizations, and other voluntary groups. They include nonprofit corporations in science, education, religion, recreation, healthcare, and the professions, and both local and global organizations.

There is no accurate count of these nonprofit corporations. According to the Independent Sector—an organization interested in the social and

---

Box 5.2. The Private (Non-governmental) Economy

Societal Sectors	Business Sector	Third Sector
Charter	Profit	Nonprofit
Primary motive	Economic/Financial	Social/cultural
Secondary motive	Social/cultural	Economic/Financial

charitable dimensions of the economy—in 1998 the nonprofit sector comprised 1.2 million organizations, ranging from hospitals, museums, and schools to houses of worship, orchestras, research centers, youth groups, and similar types of organizations.[7] They serve purposes in the community that are different from those of business and government.

The writer Jeremy Rifkin describes the nonprofit sector as an "outlaw subculture" that could create a new order of life, i.e., fill up the vacuum between the market and the state. Rifkin claims that US nonprofits employ 10 percent of this nation's workforce and involve 90 million Americans as volunteers. He concludes that the US nonprofit sector could be measured as the seventh-largest economy in the world.[8]

But, as we have noted, not all nonprofit corporations reside in the Third Sector. They also exist in the business order as well as other civil orders. "Nonprofits," for instance, include trade associations that advance the purposes of business. We mention this distinction because for our purposes the future of the American economy is linked with inter-sector (profit/nonprofit) development, and strengthening the links between business and other civil orders as a strategy for civil development. In our view, the creation of a civil republic will depend upon nonprofit associations working together at establishing a higher order of values in the economy than those of business alone.

Although it would seem that Third Sector corporations (like churches or colleges) are different and separate from business, they are also in part businesses, as all nonprofits must create net revenue above the cost of production or services; they must compete for scarce resources and must (at least) break even in order to survive. Indeed, the government's internal revenue service (IRS) monitors how nonprofits make money. Many nonprofit corporations have "contingency funds," which represent income acquired annually over and above the costs of operation. This is not called "profit," rather it is considered a capital reserve to be spent in a future year for a social or civic purpose. It is not given to stockholders, as would be the case for a business enterprise.

What is significant about nonprofits is that they carry certain core values of society that become translated into market standards. This changes the character of raw markets, albeit slowly, and provides a basis for building more civil markets. How does this happen?

Public Standards

A public standard is a norm derived from a core value. A value like public safety ("human safety for all") becomes a norm in market organization, a public good so to speak. Market standards for public safety are specified in thousands of arenas, as for circular saws, toys, food, and clothing. Public safety standards are critical for the workplace as well, but their specificity and the degree to which they are followed vary from industry to industry and from factory to factory. The point here is that there is a general understanding about the importance of core values like public safety, which are established for the common good.

When a core value—like safety, health, freedom, or justice—is widely accepted, it must be translated into a market standard. This standard is then calculated, measured, and monitored. For example, a standard like "cleanliness" is a custom, a standard inside business apart from government regulations. It is demanded, measured, and monitored in schools and hospitals, restaurants and theaters, for example, not just by government but also by trade unions, business leaders, and civic groups.

So developing public standards inside markets is not new, but it has not yet been incorporated into a national strategy for societal development. Today nonprofit corporations—like religious, educational, scientific, professional, arts, and recreational associations—do not participate in such strategies like government does. In a civil plan, however, nonprofits would be invited into standard making to become agents of change in the marketplace.

The Role of Nonprofit Corporations: Crossing Sectors

Nonprofit corporations serve a benefit beyond the pursuit of profits. But some nonprofits are serving in the Third Sector, some in the business sector, and some are serving the government; meanwhile, others stand in between sectors.

Nonprofits in the Third Sector include religious organizations, science organizations, homeless shelters, schools, orchestras, youth groups, community service groups, art studios, science associations, dance and music groups, etc. Nonprofits close to business include trade associations like the Chamber of Commerce and special types of nonprofits like the New York Stock Exchange. Nonprofits close to government receive funding from government for performing certain charitable or public services.

Social scientists and government planners fail to see how the economy is regulated through this nonprofit sector. For example, the International Biometric Industry Association (IBIA) is a nonprofit trade association. This means that the IBIA is authorized to take collective action on behalf of the biometric industry in full compliance with antitrust, tax, and lobbying laws. It is granted this status by the IRS under Section 501(c)(6), the provision of federal tax law that is specifically reserved for nonprofit trade associations composed of competitors who wish to advocate common goals and regulate activities in their industry. [9]

Let's look at this point closely because it bears on civil development.

We have said that a decline in civil society happens when corporations in the Third Sector begin to emphasize economic values over societal values or convert their charters to become businesses. Nonprofit corporations that have already converted themselves into businesses include hospitals, community development corporations, schools, universities, museums, day care centers, and environmental groups. (See the "Nonprofit Conversions" column in Box 5.3, "Crossing Sectors," below.)[10]

But "conversions by nonprofits into businesses" is not the total story. Box 5.3 also shows what we call a "public interest domain" developing at the same time. This term refers to the realm of nonprofit corporations whose mission is to cultivate core values and public standards in the market. They link social and cultural goals with business and economic goals in the public interest, and this is not "decline" but development. This is where a synthesis is already being sought between business and the core values of society.

Nonprofit corporations in this public interest domain have members working together in government, business, and the Third Sector. For example, the Social Investment Forum is a nonprofit trade (professional) organization that has public goals for allocating capital in a way that integrates core values with business values.

This shift toward a public domain is catching on. The nonprofit Council of Institutional Investors also has members from government, business, and the Third Sector, that is, council members from all three sectors support its agreed-upon public purpose.

The tendency to cross sectors, then, is a sign of the times. The linking between sectors is happening every day, but of course not all of this activity is civil development.[11] For example, the American Dietetic Association is a nonprofit corporation in the Third Sector that claims to advance professional values, but its connection to markets is close, so close, in fact, that critics say it is colluding (not colliding) with business on diet issues.

Box 5.3. Crossing Sectors

Nonprofit Conversions

Third Sector nonprofits obtaining business charters, e.g., community development corporations, universities, hospitals, schools, museums, environmental groups, etc.

Public Interest Domain

Nonprofits with public goals, e.g., the Social Investment Forum, the Council of Institutional Investors, Joint Commission on Accreditation of Healthcare Organizations, etc.

Fifteen percent of the Dietetic Association's budget comes from food companies. Its website includes "Daily Nutrition Tips" sponsored by the same companies that make the products that it also advertises. Critics ask, Can the integrity of this profession be sustained by such business arrangements?[12]

Nonprofits can become a "front" for business. Nonprofit health care companies in some cases give the appearance of working for the public good but are actually making deals with business on the side. This is civil decline.

To cite another example, an edition of the CBS television program *Sixty Minutes* reported on how people donated tissues from the bodies of their deceased loved ones to a certain nonprofit healthcare organization, thinking that the gift would save lives. They were filled with a strong sense of "giving," but in fact this organization regularly sold donated body parts to a business that is maximizing profits in "skin aesthetics."[13]

In addition, some nonprofit charities have begun to mimic the lifestyle and culture of business. Among some 60,000 charitable foundations, many trustees take no compensation, but this practice is changing. In a climate increasingly saturated by commerce, some trustees of charitable organizations are giving themselves high (CEO) salaries and drawing from nonprofit assets for private gain.[14]

So we would have to say that a civil market develops only when Third Sector corporations link with business *in the right way*. The Third Sector has social (e.g., philanthropic) and cultural (e.g., aesthetic) goals that are beginning to connect with business goals, but this crossing between sectors can be perilous. Each attempt to link such different goals at a higher level may be as dangerous as it is promising.

Standard Making: Two Case Studies

Civil development does occur, however, when core values in contrasting civil orders come together creatively in the market. And it works especially well when nonprofit corporations develop public accountability systems. As we shall now see, nonprofit corporations can create, monitor, and enforce public standards in the market for the public good.

A System of Public Accountability in Healthcare

The nonprofit Joint Commission on Accreditation of Healthcare Organizations (JCAHO) is our first example. Here representatives from the health professions regulate the conduct of business. JCAHO controls and coordinates business activity around health standards and works virtually like a government agency operating in the private sector. Let's look at this case, as it represents one way in which a public domain is currently being advanced.

I would argue that JCAHO is a model for civil development. It does more for the common good than we can summarize in a few paragraphs in Box 5.4. It expedites third-party payments; it fulfills state licensure requirements and strengthens liability insurance premiums. It strengthens bond ratings for members and provides a positive influence on financial markets by its assessments.

Box 5.4. Hospitals and Public Health

A voluntary association called the Joint Commission on Accreditation of Healthcare Organizations (JCAHO) sets public standards for hospitals in the United States. It is an independent, not-for-profit corporation and the main standard-setting and accrediting body in this field of healthcare. It employs roughly 1,000 people and its surveyor cadre numbers more than 400.

The commission evaluates and accredits more than 17,000 healthcare organizations and programs in the United States. Since 1951, it has developed up-to-date professional standards and monitors them in mainline healthcare organizations, evaluating compliance against its professional benchmarks. In other words, JCAHO is a parliamentary body for hospital management.

JCAHO accreditation is voluntary. The organization cannot force all hospitals to comply with its standards. It does not levy fines. It cannot strip licensure, but it can revoke its own accreditation for non-compliance, that is, it has the power to investigate directly whether or not a business seeking to be granted or to maintain accreditation is following its standards. And this is critical for healthcare organizations.

In other words, the commission does not accept what a healthcare organization *says* it does, but examines what it *actually* does. Not only does JCAHO set performance standards for the quality of patient care, it then goes into the field to observe what really happens in a member healthcare center.

The commission develops its standards for conduct in consultation with healthcare experts, providers, measurement experts, purchasers, and consumers. More than 400 physicians, nurses, health care administrators, medical technologists, psychologists, respiratory therapists, pharmacists, durable medical equipment providers, and

Box 5.4 continues

Box 5.4 continued

social workers are employed by the commission to administer ac-creditation surveys.

JCAHO also provides services that "support performance im-provement in health care organizations." It meets Medicare certifi-cation requirements. It formulates public standards for hospitals, healthcare networks, home care, long-term care, behavioral (mental) health care, and clinical laboratories.

JCAHO also accredits ambulatory care organizations, surgical centers, clinics, etc., and has launched a Disease-Specific Care Certification (DSCC) program. The DSCC program certifies that dis-ease management services, such as asthma or diabetes care, are based on public standards. It assumes that when an organization conducts itself properly—does the right things well—there is "a strong probability that patients will experience good outcomes."[15]

The commission is a democratic "stakeholder corporation" gov-erned by a 28-member board of commissioners, made up of nurses, physicians, consumers, medical directors, administrators, providers, employers, labor representatives, health plan leaders, quality ex-perts, ethicists, health insurance administrators, and educators. This board brings together a diverse group of leaders—not only in healthcare, but also in business and public policy.

The Joint Commission on Accreditation of Healthcare Organizations is not governed by business. It is governed by board members representing the American College of Physicians, the American Society of Internal Medicine, the American College of Surgeons, the American Dental Association, the American Hospital Association, and the American Medical Association, all nonprofit or-ganizations in healthcare. Stakeholders in these different healthcare specialties set their own standards and monitor compliance, but the goal of all is to maximize healthcare for the common good.

This commission is inside the healthcare market, but goes beyond the capitalist model. It adds core values and standards to the economy from civil (non-business) orders. It integrates public health values with eco-nomic values. And this method of integration and synthesis not only serves the healthcare field and the public interest, it adds stability to the market as well.[16]

JCAHO is part of the rising public interest domain. Business corpora-tions—like for-profit HMOs and hospitals—are members of JCAHO. They receive accreditation from the nonprofit commission. A business corporation (like a hospital) must adjust to the commission's norms, not the other way around. The commission's standards then prevail over business norms. Thus the commission advances public standards with accountability to stakeholders.

In this healthcare sector, JCAHO standards are drawn from a mix of core values, such as truth, honesty, purity, and cleanliness, which take precedence over economic standards like productivity, efficiency, and profit making. Put another way, for JCAHO member businesses the search for profits must be synchronized with public health values, which are given priority and determine the primary basis for market competition.[17]

In this case we are talking about sustaining "business self-interest" but reconciling it with a higher purpose; the self-interest of a business (e.g., a for-profit hospital or HMO) is reconciled with the common good. And it's not one or two corporations that are trying to do this, it's virtually a whole market sector.[18]

In sum, JCAHO is a nonprofit association that works in a public interest domain. It exists to sustain and improve the safety and the quality of healthcare organizations. It is one example of how civil development takes place as core Third Sector (nonprofit) organizations apply their core values to shape business.

Now let's look at another example, from the field of engineering.

Public Accountability and Professional Standards

We have said that public standards are different from corporate standards like efficiency, productivity, and profitability, that they are grounded in the core values of civil society. In our second case study we look at a Third Sector nonprofit corporation of engineers that creates public standards for business. It is part of a civil (associative) order in the economy.

The American Society of Mechanical Engineers influences market standards through business contracts written with the advice and counsel of engineers. Here we see how markets are not just "natural forces" that impact upon people. Professional associations are part of this "market regulation" inside the private sector. ASME defines public standards for the common good and there are many other nonprofits that perform this public (government-like) function.

Other standard makers include the Underwriters Laboratories, which certifies the safety of electrical appliances and equipment, and Green Seal, which develops standards for environmentally sound products. Standards and ratings are also set in other fields by financial rating services such as Dun & Bradstreet, the Motion Picture Association of America (MPAA), the Comics Code, and the Recreational Software Advisory Council.[20]

Box 5.5. Engineering Standards in Manufacturing

The American Society of Mechanical Engineers (ASME), founded in 1880, is an international educational and technical organization serving a global membership of 125,000. It has a large technical publishing operation, holds some 30 technical conferences and 200 professional development courses each year, and sets manufacturing standards.

A member-elected board of governors presides over five councils, 44 specialist boards, and hundreds of committees in 13 regions around the world. The ASME has developed 400 sections or subgroups to serve its members. Members promote the "art, science, and practice of mechanical engineering" in global markets. The association seeks to strengthen professional values and the competency of its members. This is done by developing programs in mechanical engineering that enable "practitioners to contribute to the well-being of humankind." In civil market terms, the association's councils, groups, and members introduce the core values of their profession into the market economy.

To achieve its objective of continuous training, the AMSE's Council on Codes and Standards has established a goal that all of the applicable training materials be presented to each committee and subordinate group within a three-year span.

The Board on Conformity Assessment, under the direction of the Council on Codes and Standards, supervises the accreditation, registration, and certification activities of the association. It also develops criteria for accreditation and certification for applicable codes and standards; develops recommended policy for accreditation, registration, and certification; and provides an overview for consistency of ASME codes and standards, accreditation, registration, and certification activities. This board serves as a vital link in providing "procedural due process"; develops criteria and selection procedures for survey, review, and audit personnel; and provides internal audits.[19]

Leaders in ASME complain that individual members do not always follow their standards. They see colleagues adjusting standards to suit the special interests of corporations. Nevertheless, they would argue that the market is more "developed" with relation to the values of safety, truth, and accuracy by the presence of ASME than without it. This nonprofit corporation is a check against raw market forces.

Yet ASME is not an accrediting corporation. It is not like JCAHO or the American Zoo and Aquarium Association (AZAA), to cite another example, which has enough power to virtually shut down a member. AZAA counts 212 zoos and aquariums as member organizations that agree to meet higher standards than those set by business or the federal government. They are concerned about core values in animal treatment, safety, and conservation, and with financial stability. (The New England Aquarium lost its accreditation from the AZAA in 2003 due to the association's concern that it lacked the financial resources to pay for much-needed repairs to its waterfront facility.)[21] Accreditors like these are part of the latent (as yet largely invisible and uncultivated) part of markets today.

In sum, if nonprofit corporations outside the business sector do not regulate industries with standards, the government will do it through its regulatory agencies. But many of these corporations *are* performing that public service, and they are part of a developing a public interest domain. The examples cited above show that there is much that can be done to advance civil development through civil associations, and, we propose, government could encourage this development through the mechanism of civil commissions.

Civil Commissions: A New Tool for Creating Accountability

Civil society advocates do not examine the alternatives to capitalism. Our task is to think about that alternative "political economy" in the context of society. How could the government initiate programs that solve social problems in the market system itself? The question is not how the government would solve the problems. It is rather how the government would encourage civil society organizations to work out solutions to the problems.[22]

The president, Congress, state assemblies, and local governments routinely appoint commissions to investigate matters of acute public concern and make inquiry into public issues. So there is nothing new about commissions. What we are suggesting here is that civil commissions should be appointed as a strategy for promoting societal development.[23]

The development of a civil market by such commissions would mean establishing new accountability systems in markets by social contracts (i.e., agreements between government, business, and Third Sector associations), public standards, professional monitors, and authorities that have adjudicative power. Civil commissions would establish these systems with government support.[24]

Government at any level, local to global, would appoint commissions for a variety of development purposes, commissions that would include civic and business leaders and as broad a range of stakeholders as possible. These commissions would then set to work to devise strategies for problem solving and development in the designated realms. Let's start our imagination flowing by considering what civil commissions might look like—and what they might do—in three arenas.[25]

A Civil Commission for Industry Associations

Trade associations have begun to regulate themselves. But without the involvement of Third Sector stakeholders it is difficult to assess their efforts in the public interest. For example, in the last ten years over a dozen industry associations have formed self-regulatory programs focus on environmental protection. The Responsible Care Program of the American Chemistry Council (formerly the Chemical Manufacturers' Association) is one example of an effort to shape standards in chemical manufacturing. It sponsors environmental codes of conduct, but its other goal is to avoid government legislation.[26]

Participants pledge to uphold a set of ten principles and to adopt six codes of management practice. The codes require that member firms embrace specific practices on health, safety, and environmental performance and dedicate staff to advance those practices, as well as employ particular techniques for monitoring. Any firm that wishes to belong to the ACC must abide by its Responsible Care Program's principles and codes. [27]

But Responsible Care does not set specific *performance criteria*. And it does not set up *procedures for judging and penalizing offenders*. In other words, it does not include a system of public accountability and thus it does not work as effectively as JCAHO does in healthcare to bring core social values into its own industry.

What could a government do here?

A civil commission could be appointed to study Responsible Care, and perhaps similar, related programs, and help its members develop a system of public accountability. This would include establishing performance criteria and enforcement procedures, now missing. Members would study how an accountability system could be constructed with Third Sector input (e.g., from science and environmental organizations), one that would emphasize transparency, include "whistleblower" provisions, and suggest how scientific and professional associations could act as monitors.[28]

A Civil Commission for the Beef Industry

Business—and government—cannot regulate all markets by themselves. Let's look at what happened with government's oversight of the beef industry. The crisis provoked by the discovery of a confirmed case of "mad cow disease" in an animal brought a fury of publicity and renewed calls for government regulation. These events are still unfolding but a look at the recent past will serve our purposes here.

In 1998, in creating a system of meat inspection called Hazard Analysis and Critical Control Point Systems (HACCP), the federal government tried something new. Rather than relying on United States Department of Agriculture (USDA) inspectors to enforce government-mandated meat-processing procedures, the new system required plants to develop their own systems for controlling the levels of harmful bacteria in their plants. Then, to assess whether the companies' plans were working, HACCP regulations required microbial testing of salmonella levels in samples of the finished meat and poultry. If a plant's products repeatedly exceeded the salmonella limits imposed by the regulations, the USDA could shut the plant down.

But as the HACCP program swung into operation problems soon arose over the definition of "allowable levels of salmonella bacteria" in meat.[29] Here is where a civil commission would start its inquiry.

Bacteria control is a technical problem for scientists to solve, but individual scientists do not always know the answer to what constitutes public safety, in this case, for instance, with regard to salmonella levels. Furthermore, as individuals, scientists tend favor their employers, whether in business or government, and some may tend to "adjust" empirically debatable standards to favor the interests of the supervisors for whom they work.

To counter these problems, a civil commission could be appointed to investigate how third parties might get involved. One strategy might be to ask scientific and professional associations (not individual scientists) to make these tough "judgment calls"; the government would remain the final authority, but a civil commission focusing on this industry would place more responsibility on scientific and professional associations to answer questions relevant to public health and safety.

The government could bring in its own agencies, like the USDA and the Centers for Disease Control, to work with science associations, which would then be responsible for proposing standards and monitoring processes. They would then advise the USDA and the trade association, in this case the American Meat Institute, and their report would be made public. The commission could also invite neutral parties to enter into the monitoring process, thus making the trade association more directly accountable to the public.[30]

Industry (businesses) and consumers would share the cost of expanding this public interest domain into the private sector, which might be quite minimal if nonprofit associations rather than government are involved in setting standards and monitoring compliance. The government would keep an eye on this self-regulatory process, but the involvement of nonprofit associations would mean that this would cost much less than establishing and running its own regulatory bodies—which means less interference by politicians and savings for taxpayers.

Furthermore, while accountability for sustaining health standards in, for example, the meat-processing industry could increase the price of beef, no single business loses in this strategy. The whole industry is involved. No competitor loses money when each firm follows the same standards and agrees to the same level of monitoring. When such cross-sector or associative arrangements make a commitment to public health, the benefits are great and the costs are reduced and shared more equitably by consumers, businesses, and government.

A Civil Commission on the Pharmaceutical Industry

Georganne Benjamin, assistant vice president of corporate communications of Regence BlueShield of Idaho, says that the results from a Blue Cross and Blue Shield Association survey reveal that prescription drug costs are the "main driver" increasing US healthcare costs. Billions of dollars are being spent to advertise prescription drugs, and state and local governments are beginning to investigate the extent to which those costs are adding to the price of the medications many citizens need. Meanwhile, representatives from consumer groups say promotion and advertising, not research and development, is the pharmaceutical industry's fastest growing expenditure category.[31]

Americans spent about $200 billion on prescription drugs in 2002. This is more money than the federal government paid for education, agriculture, transportation, and the environment combined. It matches what it cost to topple Saddam Hussein with a full-scale attack on Iraq. The price of prescription drugs continues to rise at 15 percent a year, doubling every five years. The government allows drug companies to control the testing of new drugs and it allows them to design and fund trials to suit their own interests, not those of the consumer. This problem extends into the traditional territory of the Third Sector as HMOs and hospitals make deals with pharmaceutical companies to promote new (more expensive) drugs when older (cheaper) ones could often serve the public just as well.

What's the alternative?

A civil commission could be appointed to study drug advertising and the common good. The alternative to this ever-mounting deluge of competitive advertising would begin with the establishment of a civil (public) commission composed of representatives from business, government, and the Third Sector. The commission would then study whether, as many critics contend, competition among drug companies is driving up consumer prices while failing to serve the public good.

Here's a small illustration of the problem as critics see it. Prosilec is a "miracle drug" that helps people overcome heartburn. Its manufacturer, AstraZeneca, earned $4.9 million on Prosilec in 1988; by 1992 it was earning 2.9 billion, and by 2001 it was earning $5.7 billion. Prosilec's success, and the fact that its patent would soon expire, led competitors to come up with comparable drugs. These competitors included Prevacid (TAP/Abbott), Aciphex (Esai/Johnson), and Protonix (Wyeth). But through lawsuits, AstraZeneca managed to keep any competing "generics" at bay while it unleashed a half-billion-dollar advertising program to move people off its own Prosilec and onto a new drug it produced, called Nexium, which the company's own studies showed to be barely more effective than the original but which brought with it the beginning of a new period of patent protection.[32]

In this overheated environment, each company must spend millions of dollars on advertising in a competitive market to convince the public to buy its drugs as opposed to the (usually closely related) products of its competitors. Each competitor would like to bury the other. Now imagine for a moment a different market system.

A civil commission is appointed. Representative organizations from all three sectors of society—let's say a consortium of pharmaceutical industry associations (business), the National Institutes of Health (government), and the American Medical Association (the Third Sector)—are given seats on this commission. Together these and other stakeholders then appoint professionals to study the problem of bias in research, assess test results from various studies, and consider the implications of the escalating advertising wars—all with a mandate to solve business problems while contributing to the public good.

After the commission studies these problems, it could recommend many types of solutions, but let's look at one possibility that focuses on the issue of advertising. The commission could require that financial limits be set on the amount of money spent on by pharmaceutical firms to promote their products. This rule would apply to the whole industry, and business competitors would then be put on an equal footing. (Competition does not stop, but the nature of the competition changes, perhaps raising the quality of the content of advertising, etc.) The commission would set up a neutral monitoring system and estimate the amount of money saved by limiting advertising expenditures. Let's say it stays with the experiment for a few years. On the basis of these savings, it could judge how much money might then be spent to bring broader public health values into the structure of this market—to set standards for research studies, to provide neutral referees to assess test results, to hire professional monitors to ensure product safety, etc.

As part of this effort, the commission would also work to establish a nonprofit public advocacy association (PAA) for the industry, one that could be initially launched with the money saved by reduced advertising. The new public corporation might then build an endowment. It would remain independent, with the primary mission of getting accurate facts and providing transparency for the public. It could coordinate its work with government agencies (e.g., the Food and Drug Administration) to reduce monitoring and other costs.[33]

By then the original commission will have done its work for the common good. As soon as it has created an effective new market mechanism, it is no longer needed and it shuts down and disbands.

Notice the efficiency. If civil commissions were to organize public (nonprofit) corporations to reduce government and business costs, the market sector could become not only a better servant of the public good but also more efficient. Government regulation becomes less expensive and the new market mechanisms save money for the taxpayer.

As we envision these civil commissions and the public accountability associations that they would set up to succeed them, their members would include trade or business association representatives, but non-business parties (e.g., scientific and professional associations) would be in majority control to ensure that the core societal values of public health, transparency, and accuracy would be sustained in the market.

In general, civil commissions would emphasize transparency as one defense against dishonesty in the marketplace. Dishonesty is fostered by secrecy, and secrecy is made legitimate in business by proprietary rights and in government by national security. The "defense industry" is most involved with government and is most especially protected in government contracts. At the time of this writing, a great deal of information on the awarding of business contracts for the "rebuilding of Iraq" is being withheld from the US Congress. So a key issue for civil society planners will be how to balance proprietary and national security interests with transparency, honesty and openness to public scrutiny.

How Civil Commissions Might Support Countervailing Powers

There are many ways to build a public interest domain. What other things could civil commissions do?

To answer that question, let's look, for example, at some science-based Third Sector associations that currently work to sustain public health standards. The National Council Against Health Fraud (NCAHF), for one, is a nonprofit health organization that addresses the problem of "health misinformation, deceit, and quackery." The NCAHF advocates: (a) adequate disclosure in labeling and warranties to enable consumers to make truly informed choices; (b) pre-marketing proof of safety and effectiveness for products and services claimed to prevent, alleviate, or cure any health problem; and (c) accountability for those who violate the law. In our vocabulary, it helps to sustain core values; the NCAHF fits the civil market model, not the capitalist model.[34]

Today agencies like the Federal Trade Commission and the Consumer Product Safety Commission follow the capitalist model, regulating the market from the outside, not.looking for public monitors inside markets. In a civil market model, civil commissions and government agencies would encourage nonprofit groups like the NCAHF to become watchdogs—countervailing associations that keep business honest and accountable.[35]

Nonprofit watchdogs are not to be dismissed lightly. They can have more power than government—especially when they report problems to the mass media. Reporting offenses to newspapers, television, and radio can be more effective in some cases than regulation by a government agency. And we shall see in Chapter 7 how this exercise of power through the media would increase if a civil commission were to be organized there.

Now let us look at broader functions for civil commissions.

A Civil Commission to Monitor the Third Sector

Angels do not organize nonprofit corporations. If Third Sector nonprofits were to acquire more authority in market sectors, they would need their own monitoring. The Joint Commission on Accreditation of Healthcare Organizations (JCAHO) that we described above has ideals and professional goals, but it might also fail to do its job properly. It could grow in size and develop a bureaucracy that fostered red tape. It could become dictatorial. It could become complacent, suffer from mismanagement, make miscalculations, or misrepresent the facts. In short, even nonprofit associations established in good faith are not immune to all sorts of problems that appear in any organization. Civil commissions could serve as public consultants if such problems were to arise, like the General Accounting Office (GAO) but in the private sector. In other words, collectively they would be the audit, evaluation, and investigative arm of the new public interest domain.

Those nonprofit organizations that become accreditors of market sectors or establish public accountability systems would need to be studied periodically. A civil commission would provide follow-up studies on their integrity and effectiveness. For example, an outside monitor could study JCAHO today. Box 5.6 offers examples of questions that might be asked of JCAHO in the course of such a process.

Questions like these would help commissioners and professional consultants evaluate how nonprofit corporations are doing and provide guidelines for planners to improve their work on market reformation.

Box 5.6. Assessment Questions for Systems of Public Accountability

- What is the purpose of this association?
- Who are the stakeholders?
- How is the association accountable to stakeholders?
- How are stakeholders represented in the governing structure?
- How do members define the common good?
- How is this association democratically organized?
- Does the association have electoral procedures and systems to mediate disputes?
- Are there representatives from business and the Third Sector in this association?
- Are the professional monitors of standards competent, impartial and independent, i.e., capable of doing this work with expertise?
- What are the penalties for not meeting the standards?
- Have stakeholders agreed to penalties for breaking the rules?
- How does enforcement take place when standards are not met?
- Does enforcement really work?
- How are economic (financial) values integrated with core values in market transactions?
- To what extent is the association voluntary?
- To what extent are transactions transparent, i.e., made public?
- How is the association financially self-sustaining?
- To what extent is the association decentralized?
- How are principles of justice (e.g., fairness, equal treatment, and impartiality) expressed?
- How do stakeholders cooperate in the context of competition?

A Civil Commission on Science in Business

When scientists hide their data from their competitor colleagues, something is wrong. When they place profit before honesty to protect their employers (as in the tobacco industry), something is wrong. When they fail to allow colleagues to see their procedures for obtaining data, or conceal their methods of verification, something is wrong. And science associations should be concerned.

Here is one example of the problem around secrecy.

John Sulston was part of an international team selected to work on the Human Genome Project. Sulston proclaimed his belief in the free and open exchange of all scientific information that would emerge from the project. Guided by these principles, the Human Genome Project was structured so that all the findings were to be made public. This encouraged international collaboration among scientists.

Then, in May 1998, Sulston's colleague Craig Venter announced that he was quitting the project—with plans to head up a newly launched commercial venture to bring out the complete sequence in three years and market it as a proprietary database. Sulston and a global network of scientists working on the original project opposed Venter's intentions, and this marked the beginning of a major struggle to keep the human genome in the public domain.[36]

Sulston and others argue that when scientists, universities, and business firms privatize intellectual property—a growing trend—this poses a threat to scientific inquiry, which depends upon openness, that the quest for patents and profits interferes with public research goals. They say that in biology, for example, patents stifle research and licensing practices impede access to (and use of) genetic materials and DNA technology for the public good.

The decision about what to do about secrecy in science will require public studies, and here a civil commission that included major stakeholders—science associations, trade associations, and university associations—could be invaluable.[37]

Here are just a few of the major questions that such a commission could ask.

Could accreditors for universities set rules on keeping their scientific research open, i.e., not proprietary? Could science and professional associations assume more responsibility for keeping scientific inquiry open? Could these associations refuse to certify members who hide data that might be relevant to the public interest? Could they penalize members that keep their laboratory work secret while working in a business firm? Could they exclude members who refuse to share data? Under what circumstances should patent rights in science be granted?

The protection of intellectual property rights has helped universities attract research funding and motivated firms to raise investment capital for product development. But it has also generated a growing concern about the concealment of knowledge in the interest of private profit. A civil commission could give us a start on untangling the issues and finding solutions that are fair to all parties.

Socially Responsible Investing

We saw in Box 5.1 how core values are "separated" into different civil orders for analytic purposes, but our discussion also pointed out that connections among them are made in daily life and that higher linkages between them are needed in the economy.

This higher linkage or synthesis of core values is the basis for civil development. It happens when leaders blend different values in the proper way. Again, we are talking about substantive values like truth, freedom, justice, and community. Some pioneers of civil society have begun to do this in financial markets. They do it as leaders of socially responsible investment.

Social investors integrate business values with social-cultural values in financial markets. Civic leaders have been at the forefront of this movement, which began as far back as the nineteenth century, when churches refused to invest in corporations producing tobacco and alcohol, but the practice began to become a significant factor in market activity in the mid-twentieth century, when concerned citizens and religious and educational organizations began to use stockholder resolutions that required companies to address social issues.

In 1970, for instance, public interest lawyers formed a group called Campaign GM and filed shareholder proposals with social policy implications in advance of the annual meeting of General Motors stockholders. The group made sure to get publicity for its proposals, and the SEC ruled that GM would have to bring two of them to a vote. The result was a six-and-a-half-hour meeting attended by three thousand people, during which there was heated discussion of the company's social responsibilities, including questions posed as to why it had no blacks or women on its board.

The publicity surrounding Campaign GM, and an appeals court decision two months later supporting shareholder resolutions related to social and political issues, encouraged more activists-including church groups that hold stock through their pension funds-to submit social policy proposals to other business corporations. By 1972 the number of such proposals to corporations reached more than thirty.

Thus, in the 1970s, Third Sector organizations began to see themselves as "owners" with every right to influence the conduct of businesses in which they had a financial share—and they began to collaborate. One such effort led the National Council of Churches to support the Interfaith Center on Corporate Responsibility (ICCR). The ICCR has been active in the movement for over thirty years, and today its membership includes 275 Protestant, Roman Catholic, and Jewish institutional investors, including those representing national denominations, religious communities, pension funds, endowments, hospital corporations, economic development funds, and publishing companies. Each year these investors sponsor over one hundred shareholder resolutions on major social and environmental issues. The combined portfolio value of ICCR's member organizations is estimated to be $110 billion.[38]

Recently, the realm of socially responsible investment—in which portfolios are screened with an eye to shareholder advocacy, community investing, and the promotion of the public good—has developed rapidly, growing 8 percent from $2.16 trillion in 1999 to $2.34 trillion in 2001. From 1995 to 2003, since the inception of the Forum's publication of biennial Trends Reports, assets involved in social investing, through screening of retail and institutional funds, shareholder advocacy, and community investing, have grown 40 percent faster than all professionally managed investment assets in the US. Investment portfolios involved in SRI grew by more than 240% from 1995 to 2003, compared with the 174% growth of the overall universe of assets under professional management over the same time period.[39]

This social movement exemplifies the creative tension between the two market models we described in Chapter 4. In a capitalist market, money is invested to maximize economic returns. In a civil market, money is invested for a public good by integrating economic values with core (social-cultural) values. This is a big change that is already happening.

Studies reported in journals of finance either find that socially screened investments outperform unscreened investments or show neutral (statistical) relationships between the performance of screened and unscreened companies. But socially responsible investors as a rule seem to make more money than conventional financial investors do. This positive performance is why by 2001 the amount of money invested in socially screened equities had passed the $2 trillion mark. It paid off financially. One of out of every eight professionally managed dollars was part of a socially responsible portfolio.[40]

These positive performance ratings indicate that "social investment" is a logical strategy in the formation of a new republic. It produces public benefits all the way around.[41]

No one knows why this positive correlation happens but financial experts have a good idea. It may be because social (ethical) criteria correlate highly with quality firms, i.e., those that "do well and do good" at the same time. Social investors place their money in "responsible firms" where executives bring their "synthesis" of core values into corporate policy. These firms are responsible and profitable, that is, they are publicly accountable and pay high dividends. They practice good labor relations; they protect the environment and the consumer. As a result, social investment keeps growing in financial markets.[42]

A New Profession

Financial investors build capitalist markets. Social investors build civil markets, that is, post-capitalist markets. And this type of social investment is evolving into a profession, like law and accounting. Social investment is distinguished from political investment. Let's look at this distinction that is clear today.

Political investment happens when an organization like a state, a union, or a bank allocates money for its own strategic reasons. Pension fund managers in the State of New Jersey, for example, wanted to invest their money in companies that would create jobs in their state. This has the tone of an ethical investment, but the goal is to develop jobs and the economic well-being of New Jersey, not the larger good of society. Trade unions have invested in companies that are sympathetic to labor. They have ethical concerns but not all union pensions are designed for the general good. National governments and world financial institutions allocate capital to developing countries that are supportive of their own ideology and foreign policy. While the criteria for investment may be couched in terms of the common good, these are political investments.

Social investment, on the other hand, advances capital by principle for the common good. This means social (non-economic) values are linked with economic values to advance the well-being of society. This type of investment strikes at the heart of capitalism.

Social investment requires expertise to deal with market issues. It is difficult for the average person to identify a corporation's hidden subsidiaries and affiliates, let alone whether they might be engaged in malfeasance, and it can be hard to determine whether certain business practices are legal or not. It is not easy to find out where global firms have tax havens, or whether they are engaged in money laundering. It requires expertise to compare the quality of labor practices among corporations; it is a technical task to assess whether a corporation is polluting the environment or not. This new profession works on the technical problems.

We could foresee a time when, as a public domain advances in this private economy and core values are brought further into markets, this type of social capital allocation could become "civil investment." Civil investment evolves as fiduciaries and scientists are able understand the ground for societal development. Social investors today have important causes—job safety, environmental protection, product safety, etc.—but the answers to "societal development" have yet to be explored. This will be the task of economic sociologists, institutional economists and a Council of Social Advisers.

A National Council of Social Advisers

Implementing any plans for civil development would require a top government agency that can do the research and stay abreast of all the changes. In a civil market plan, we would propose that a Council of Social Advisers should operate in tandem with the Council of Economic Advisers.

The Council of Economic Advisers (CEA) was established by the Employment Act of 1946 to provide the president of the United States with "objective economic analysis and advice" on the "development and implementation of a range of domestic and international economic issues." The CEA today includes three members who are appointed by the president with the advice and consent of the Senate. The summary outline in Box 5.7 below lays out its official duties and functions.[43]

The CEA was developed to research and advance a capitalist economy. But now we propose a Council of Social Advisers (CSA) that will research and advance a civil economy. This CSA would work with the CEA to develop a larger picture of the changes taking place in market institutions. It would assist and advise the president in the preparation of a "Social Report," gathering "timely and authoritative information" concerning civil development

---

Box 5.7. Council of Economic Advisers

Duties and Functions

1. Assist and advise the President in the preparation of the Economic Report.
2. Gather timely and authoritative information concerning economic developments and economic trends, both current and prospective. Analyze and interpret this information for the purpose of determining whether such developments and trends are interfering, or are likely to interfere, with the achievement of public policies on development. Compile and submit to the President studies relating to developments and trends.
3. Appraise the various programs and activities of the Federal Government for the purpose of determining the extent to which such programs and activities are contributing, and the extent to which they are not contributing, to the achievement of policies for economic development and to make recommendations to the President with respect thereto.
4. Develop and recommend to the President national economic policies to foster and promote free competitive enterprise, to avoid economic fluctuations or to diminish the effects thereof, and to maintain employment, production, and purchasing power.
5. Make and furnish such studies, reports, and recommendations with respect to matters of Federal economic policy and legislation as the President may request.

and institutional change. The two councils would study the correlation of their (social-economic) indicators to better forecast changes in the economy.

The Council of Social Advisors would independently gather statistics on demography, health, education, professions, and the sciences, and analyze this information to determine whether economic trends were advancing or retarding the achievement of public goals. It would compile and submit to the president research on civil (social) investment, and assess federal government programs for how they contribute to the development of society.

The CSA would work with different theories of civil development. It would assume that a market could be rooted in a concept of *justice* (fairness, equity, impartiality, and accountability) as well as in *freedom.* It would study the degree to which public standards are being advanced within markets and examine how market sectors become self-governing. It would explore how a "public interest domain" is developed.

It would gather statistics on how types of justice systems (e.g., "due process" and "civil tribunals") develop in the economy. It would study how the values of productivity and efficiency can be synchronized with the values of transparency and accountability; it would examine, for example, how transparency may increase competition in market sectors. It would produce social reports on how corporations can decentralize "command" bureaucracies and increase profits at the same time. It would study innovative ways in which joint Third Sector-business associations could reduce oligarchy by developing multilateral systems of management and democratic practices.

The research this council might engage in would demand a sociological imagination. For example, it could gather facts about how greater *local* responsibility and authority could develop in *global* markets. It could study how *stakeholders* (communities, unions, etc.) could participate in markets and *raise revenue* for responsible business. It could research how *public accountability systems* influence corporate policy and *enhance market efficiency.* It could coordinate with world finance institutions in a joint study of stakeholder involvement.[44]

This Council of Social Advisers would then make recommendations to the president to foster enterprise cooperation (as well as competition) for the common good, and it would furnish public studies on all matters of federal legislation that the president might request.

Conclusion

We started by exploring how society is composed of associations in different civil orders and said that they all link with the economy. All civil orders bring core values to the market, we argued, but more could be done for the economy in the development of society.

We saw how standards develop through nonprofit (Third Sector) associations in healthcare and engineering. Nonprofit associations create standards in ways that could advance throughout the economy with the help of government-sponsored commissions. The purpose of these commissions would be to cultivate connections among leaders in different orders to help solve the market's social problems, a process of building up core values that are missing (or latent) in the market system.

Government leaders are key actors here. As we shall see in later chapters, they would, by a civil market plan, hold conferences with business. They would insist that trade associations be democratic, i.e., true to their charters with proper voting procedures and systems of internal accountability. They would offer tax incentives for civil development and restructure markets with outside monitors. They would impose penalties when firms break the law and in the process encourage contracts with business and Third Sector associations. They would favor socially responsible corporations with tax benefits and persuade financial markets to experiment with social investment.

There is a lot of power in government, potentially, to encourage civil development, but an administration would have to wrest itself free of the old system. It would then encourage societal development, not just business development.

We have also looked at how society's core values are connected in financial markets. Religious, educational, professional, and governmental organizations are linking ethical criteria with economic criteria, making publicly responsible investments-and this is not just finance as usual. These social practices alter the purpose of capital allocation and could begin to change the whole direction of financial markets.

A countrywide reconstruction of markets could take place in the United States, we propose, through the establishment of civil commissions to study market sectors with the help of nonprofit associations and a national Council of Social Advisers. Commissions would encourage civil development while the CSA reports the impact of change on markets and key institutions of the economy as a whole.

Above all, these commissions and the council would assume that people—not just "market forces"—govern the economy. And this would be just the beginning.

Note

1. Decline takes place when core values are lost inside a market price. Senators in Congress have their "price" when they create legislation on behalf of lobbyists as a way to keep their financial support. Universities have their price when donors give funds to establish institutes, as in genetic engineering or certificate

programs simply to advance their technical and job-related needs. Lawyers have their price when they seek profits more than they seek justice. Physicians have their price when they give more priority to high salaries and gifts from pharmaceutical companies than to public health.

2. The German sociologist Max Weber conceived of separate "spheres" or "orders" in modern society. Each "order" has an inner logic, he said, in relation to substantive values. Hans Gerth and C. Wright Mills followed Weber in composing a model of such orders. They included the *military* in their model as institutions in which people "organize legitimate violence and supervise its use." I have not included the military, and have added educational and professional orders. See Hans Gerth and C. Wright Mills, *Character and Social Structure* (New York: Harcourt, Brace, 1953), p. 26. Our own Box 5.1 presents a simplified view. These various "orders" are all exceedingly complex and interrelated. For example, a "religious order" can be theistic or non-theistic, but I am defining it here simply as an institutional phenomenon that offers ultimate meanings for people. A "state order" can also be defined in many ways. Machiavelli took the word "state" as a term for a body politic in the sixteenth century; the state evolved as an autonomous order but closely inter-linked with other orders.

3. There is no agreed-upon definition of the term "profession," either generally or under law. The professional order could be classified under "occupations." I include it here as comprised of disciplines of knowledge. This includes typical professions, such as law and medicine. Then, there are the learned societies (e.g., English and theology) and the sciences (e.g., physics and chemistry). For a discussion of the varying definitions of "profession" see M. Friedman and S. Kuznets, *Income from Independent Professional Practice* (New York: National Bureau for Economic Research, 1945).

4. In other words, the core values of government (e.g., fairness, safety, welfare, and equity), family life (e.g., love and caring), educational life (e.g., knowledge and expertise), spiritual life (e.g., faith, sacrifice and giving), and business (e.g., productivity and wealth making) are an unobserved part of the action of people markets. From an analytical standpoint, a social action happens with these values all the time along with economic action. (A CEO may have sympathy or compassion for employees.) But civil development means notably the kind of social action in which core values shape the way markets are structured.

5. My reference to economic development stands in contrast to civil development. Here is one definition: "Economic development [is] a process of economic transition involving structural transformation of an economy through industrialization and raising gross domestic product and income per capita." Christopher Bass, et al., *The HarperCollins Dictionary of Economics* (New York: Harper Perennial, 1991), p. 150. Here is another: "Economic development contains two key elements. One concerns the total amount of goods and services that are produced and available for consumption, and the other concerns institutions. Economic development occurs when a society is able to increase its total output; it experiences economic growth through the generation and usage of its economic surplus." Tom Riddell, Jean Shackelhouse, and Steve Stamos, *Economics: A Tool for Understanding Society* (New York: Addison-Wesley, 1982), p. 18.

6. Here is a quick look at this problem. Karl Polanyi makes a distinction between the "formal" and "substantive" meanings of the economy. The "formal" meaning for him refers to an economy based on rational action, the abstract way economists use the term. The formal meaning is conventional and used in the field of economics. The term "substantive" refers to the way people make their livelihood. The substantive meaning is in accord with a perspective that indicates how the economy is grounded in society. Karl Polanyi, Conrad Arensberg, and Harry Pearson, *Trade and Market in the Early Empires: Economics in History and Theory* (Chicago: Henry Regnery Company, 1957).

7. See the Independent Sector, under Research, at http://www.independentsector .org/PDFs/inbrief.pdf.

8. Rifkin argues that the nonprofit sector is developing as a new power in society. For example, in Germany the nonprofit sector is growing at a rate faster than either business or government. It had more than 300, 000 voluntary organizations operating during the 1980s. In Japan, the nonprofit sector has grown dramatically, with thousands of nonprofit organizations now attending to the social and cultural needs of millions of people and addressing pressing social issues. Some 23,000 charitable organizations, called *koeki hojin*, operate in Japan. After the war, neighborhood groups resurfaced as self-governing associations without legal ties to the government. Known as *jichikai*, these organizations now exist in more than 270,000 neighborhoods. A local *jichikai* generally consists of between 180 and 400 households. Its leaders are elected and usually serve two-year terms. Jeremy Rifkin, *The End of Work* (New York: G. P. Putnam's Sons, 1995), p. 277.

9. The IBIA is legally permitted to lobby the interests of the industry as a whole but it also serves as a regulator of standards in its market sector. The IBIA focuses on activities that "will promote public understanding of biometric technologies, and encourages lawmakers and regulators to adopt policies that promote industry growth." It has a code of ethics but critics argue that more could be done to emphasize transparency in the work of its members. See IBIA at http://www.ibia.org/press4.htm.

10. A nonprofit corporation is not prohibited from making a profit (collecting more money than it expends in operating expenses and program funding taken together), but there are limitations on what it can do with its "profits." For example, if a nonprofit corporation engages in profit-making activities unrelated to its recognized nonprofit purpose, it must set up a separate corporation to engage in that activity or risk losing its nonprofit, or tax exempt, status. Public benefit corporations serve scientific, literary, education, artistic, or charitable purposes that benefit the public and are listed as "501(c)(3)"s.

11. There is also a blending of Third Sector values into business as professionals and scientists enter the market. Professionals (e.g., lawyers, physicians, accountants, and engineers) and scientists (e.g., microbiologists and chemists) are setting up businesses. This is (too often) a sign of decline, especially when they put profits before their own professional standards. But lawyers who insist on a standard of fairness in the context of profit making and scientists who insist on sharing laboratory data for the common good in the context of corporate privacy are civilizing the market system on a mini-scale. It is part of the creative blending between sectors.

12. Frances Moore Lappé, for one, points out that in a "Nutrition Fact Sheet" used by many, dieticians assure readers that biotech foods are safe for people and the environment; meanwhile, on their professional website (in small print), she sees that Monsanto is helping to bring the reader these "facts." See Frances Moore Lappé and Anna Lappé, *Hope's Edge* (New York: Jeremy P. Tarcher/Putnam, 2002), p. 27. See also Sheldon Rampart and John Stauber, *Trust Us, We're Experts!* (New York: Tarcher/Putnam, 2001), p. 165.

13. See "Skin and Bones," *CBS Recap,* Sunday, 14 April 2002. http://www.cbsnews.com/stories/1998/07/08/60minutes/main13502.shtml.

14. For example, Paul Cabot, son of a legendary Boston investment banker, tapped the assets of the Cabot Charitable Trust from 1998 to 2002 to pay himself $5,185, 216. His annual salary topped out at $1.4 million in 2001. He recently paid $200,000 for a fancy wedding for his daughter by upsizing his salary. See Beth Healy, Francie Latour, Sacha Pfeffer, et al., "Some Officers of Charities Steer Assets to Selves," *Boston Globe,* 9 October 2003, A1.

15. The facts regarding Joint Commission on Accreditation of Healthcare Organizations (JCAHO) were confirmed for me by Mark Forstneger, media relations specialist of JCAHO. For a statement about the organization's mission and accreditation practices, see the Joint Commission on the Accreditation of Health Care Organizations. The quote can be found at http://www.jcaho.org/whatwedo_frm.html.

16. JCAHCO is planning to move into the global economy. It is studying healthcare standards in world markets and assessing "the clarity of its standards, terminology, and the format, and the applicability of the standards to organizations of different types and in different cultures and countries." Ibid. See the Joint Commission on International Standards http://www.jcrinc.com/generic.asp?durki=1235

17. In a capitalist market, economic standards govern transactions, but in a fully developed civil market, public standards govern with them. Core values set the basis for creating public standards in a civil market and these market standards, in turn, set the basis for competition. This is the hallmark of a civil market system. But it is not the end of civil development. Not all public standards may be created for the common good.

18. The meaning of the term "social" and "economic" will vary in the eye of the beholder. For example, cleanliness is a social (health) concern. It is a top priority in JCAHO and it is required for accreditation. When this health standard becomes a requirement for business, it is then viewed as a "business standard." Thus, public standards have become the condition by which profits are made. So, it requires a careful analysis by experts to assess which priorities (social vs. economic) are dominant by definition in a market. Economic sociologists discuss that complexity, but let me illustrate the point. The Commission Standard TX.3.5 of JCAHO says, "Medications must be stored under proper conditions of sanitation, temperature, light, moisture, ventilation, segregation, safety, and security." This standard, based on the value of public health, is more vital to this market than profit, although making an income is essential for all competitors. JCAHO creates the basis for a market to happen in a way is not governed by profit making alone. A healthcare business must make its

income by adjusting to Standard TX. 3.5. Meeting this standard comes *before* profit. It is of course possible to make a profit by raising the price of a product or service, but only by following the standard. So this public standard is governing that market, even though profit making is essential for business. Repeat: only by following the public standard are profits made.

19. For example, there are standards to follow in setting up oil, gas, and coal-fired boilers with heat input greater 10,000,000 Btu/hr. If ASME member engineers adjust such a standard in the interest of profit for a business, they violate their own commitment to standards. See ASME International, http://www.asme.org/about.

20. Underwriters Laboratories tests products for public safety. Its significance is not to be underestimated. In 2002 it evaluated over 18,000 types of products, made over 55,000 follow-up visits to audit compliance, and registered over 55,000 businesses with "standard management systems." See UL, http://www.ul.com/about/index.html. Dun & Bradstreet acquired Moody's in 1962 (along with other companies). Moody's status is reflected in a comment made by Thomas Friedman in 1996: "There are two superpowers in the world today in my opinion. There's the United States and there's Moody's Bond Rating Service. The United States can destroy you by dropping bombs, and Moody's can destroy you by downgrading your bonds. And believe me, it's not clear sometimes who's more powerful." Note. Nonprofits can become too powerful and not function for the common good, but we are talking about balanced development: the principle of advancing countervailing powers in profit and nonprofit sectors. See Ketputa, "Net media profiles D&B," http://www.ketupa.net/dnb.htm and "chronology," http://www.ketupa.net/dnb2.htm.

21. Katherine Lutz, "City's Aquarium Loses Its Accreditation," *Boston Globe,* 14 August 2003, A1, B6. The aquarium's "financial problems" also included bad management. In 2001, Jerry Schubel, head of the aquarium, was paid $313,000 in salary and benefits; he was also paid $138,957 a year as a consultant in a manner that was legally questionable, according to the state attorney general's office. *Boston Globe,* 20 November 2003, C1.

22. The Institute for the Study of Civil Society (*Civitas*), for example, does not propose changing market institutions. It seeks to improve public understanding about "a legal and moral framework for a free and democratic society" and its research is on problems of health, welfare, education and the family. Civil society groups do not seek to resolve the underlying problem of a capitalist system.

23. Civil commissions are forming in the United States. For example, the Local Government Commission (LGC) is a nonprofit, nonpartisan, membership organization in a mixed sector—including civic leaders, local elected officials, city and county staff, planners, architects, and other community leaders—committed to making localities more "livable and resource-efficient." LCG helps communities establish "a healthier human and natural environment, a more sustainable economy, an actively engaged populace, and an equitable society." Stakeholders organize conferences and workshops, and create partnerships, produce guidebooks, videos, slide shows, and "monthly newsletters with new policy ideas." They provide library resources as well as share information on grants. See the Local Government Commission at http://www.lgc.org/index.html.

24. I have discussed public accountability systems in more detail elsewhere. I see them as a market mechanism for development. See Bruyn, *The Civil Economy,* Chapter 8.

25. J. Rees and other scholars suggest that trade associations can help advance self-regulation. See J. Rees, "The Development of Communitarian Regulation in the Chemical Industry," *Law and Policy* 19 (1993), 477; and E. Ostrom, *Governing the Commons: The Evolution of Institutions for Collective Action* (New York: Cambridge University Press, 1990).

26. See Jennifer Nash and John Ehrenfeld, "Code Green," *Environment* 38, no. 1 (1996), 16. In some cases, businesses use these programs to convince consumers of their superiority over non-participating firms. Such actions may forestall government regulation for the industry, but I think that they have not developed far enough for the common good. They require study by a civil commission.

27. Some observers say this effort in business is "the most ambitious and comprehensive environmental, health and safety improvement effort ever attempted by an industry" and "the most significant and far-reaching self-regulatory scheme ever adopted." J. R. Hirl, "Don't Trust Us, Track Us," *Chemical Marketing Reporter* 242, no. 21 (1992). N. Gunningham, "Environment, Self-Regulation, and The Chemical Industry: Assessing Responsible Care," *Law & Policy* 17, no. 1 (1995), 57–108.

28. Mancur Olson argues that some firms willingly provide public goods when their private benefits exceed the private costs. The smaller the industry, the greater the share of the public benefits that accrue to participants. Mancur Olson, *The Logic of Collective Action* (Cambridge: Harvard University Press, 1965). See also A. King and M. Lenox, "Industry Self-Regulation Without Sanctions: The Chemical Industry's Responsible Care Program," *Academy of Management Journal* 43, no. 4 (2000), 698–716. For protocols and codes on safety, environment, health, etc., see the Responsible Care Practitioners website, at http://search.netscape.com/ns/search?query=responsible+care+practitioners&fromPage=nsBrowserRoll.

29. In December 2001, the Fifth Circuit Court of Appeals issued a decision that some believed could be a serious blow to food safety standards. The United States Department of Agriculture (USDA) had developed standards in the wake of the 1993 West Coast E. coli outbreak, but the appeals court ruled that the Agriculture Department does not in fact have the authority to shut down a meat-processing plant that repeatedly fails its tests for salmonella contamination. For more details, see *Frontline,* "Modern Meat," available at http://www.pbs.org/wgbh/pages/frontline/shows/meat.

30. See Centers for Disease Control and Prevention, http://www.cdc.gov/aboutcdc.htm#mission. Notice the logic of a civil commission that would promote cross-sector involvement by industry. It would need the participation of science and professional associations, not just business and government. Appropriate professional, medical, and scientific associations have expertise that can help a trade association assess the facts.

31. See Georganne Benjamin, of Regence BlueShield of Idaho. The Connecticut Committee on Public Health is proposing legislation on this problem. See http://www.pasenategop.com/Issues/Remarks/2000/murphy-prescripdrugs.htm.

32. Sales of prescription medication at retail stores and through mail-order companies totaled $175.2 billion in 2001, an increase of $27 billion over 2000, according to the National Institute for Health Care Management, a private, nonprofit research organization led by physicians, insurance executives, and policymakers from both political parties. For statistics, see National Institute for Health Management, http://www.nihcm.org/DTCbrief.pdf.

33. Outside auditors and medical professionals are needed in this public accountability system to obtain a clear review of what is happening in the industry. Judgments on costs must be made in all fairness regarding all pharmaceuticals. A study from the Tufts University Center for Drug Development found that it costs an average of $802 million to develop and win approval to bring a new drug to market in the United States. AstraZeneca spent $2.7 billion on R&D in 2001 and reported profits of $4.2 billion. Neil Swidey, "The Costly Case of the Purple Pill," *Boston Globe Magazine,* 17 November 2002, 11.

34. The National Council Against Health Fraud, see http://www.ncahf.org.

35. The Federal Trade Commission deals with false advertising, problems in lending money, and many other problems in the capitalist market, but it cannot do the job by itself. See the FTC, http://www.ftc.gov. See also the Consumer Product Safety Commission at http://www.cpsc.gov/about/faq.html#wha.

36. Sulston was the director of the Sanger Centre in Cambridge, England. He is a Fellow of the Royal Society. See John Sulston and Georgina Ferry, *The Common Thread: A Story of Science, Politics, Ethics, and the Human Genome* (New York: Joseph Henry Press, 2002). To read the book free online, see http://books. nap.edu/books/0309084091/html. Also see *Intellectual Property Rights and Research Tools in Molecular Biology: Summary of a Workshop Held at the National Academy of Sciences, February 15–16, 1996* (put out in 1997), Commission on Life Sciences at http://books.nap.edu/books/0309057485/html/R2.html#pagetop.

37. Nonprofit corporations are developing along these lines. See the Center for Science in the Public Interest's website, http://www.cspinet.org/about/index.html.

38. See the Interfaith Center on Corporate Responsibility, http://www.iccr.org/.

39. Many nonprofit corporations have become involved in this movement. The Social Investment Forum, for example, is a national corporation dedicated to socially responsible investing. Its membership includes over five hundred social investment practitioners and institutions, including financial advisors, analysts, portfolio managers, banks, mutual funds, researchers, foundations, community development organizations, and public educators. The First Affirmative Financial Network (FAFN) is another organization composed of financial professionals specializing in socially and environmentally responsible investment. The Social Investment Forum provides research on trends in social investing, offers a comprehensive directory of practitioners in the field, and publishes a monthly "Mutual Fund Performance Chart" on its website. See www.socialinvest.org.

40. The assumption that there is always a loss in financial returns when individuals or investment managers engage in responsible investment is false. The DSI (Domini Social Index) has repeatedly outperformed the S&P 500 on a total return basis and on a risk-adjusted basis since its inception in May 1990.

41. Sandra Waddock, Charles Bodwell, and Samuel Graves, in "Responsibility: The New Business Imperative" (Waddock, Graves, & Gorski, 2000). See the home

page website of Sandra Waddock, http://www2.bc.edu/~waddock/NewBusImp~ Ft~Rev4FNL.doc. Also see John B. Guerard, Jr., "Is There a Cost to Socially Responsible Investing?" *The Journal of Investing* 6, no. 2 (Summer 1997), 11-18; J. J. Angel and P. Rivoli, "Does Ethical Investing Impose a Cost Upon the Firm? A Theoretical Examination," *Journal of Investing* 6, no. 4 (Winter 1997), 57-61; and Sandra Waddock, Samuel B. Graves, and Renee Gorski, "Performance Characteristics of Social and Traditional Investments," *Journal of Investing* 9, no. 2 (Summer 2000), 27–38.

42. There is no evidence that suggests social investment is not as profitable as business investment. See articles noted above and regular reports on SRI mutual fund performance, http://www.socialinvest.org/areas/news/2002-Q1performance.htm.

43. This statement is drawn from the Council of Economic Advisers with a few modifications for readability; see http://www.whitehouse.gov/cea/.

44. The World Bank Group is identifying "stakeholders" for a program in poverty reduction. The purpose of the bank's analysis is for "policy-makers to gain a better understanding of the range and variety of stakeholders." The stakeholder analysis then allows governments "to formulate, implement and monitor new programs." The bank does this through local surveys, studies by researchers, and community-based networks that track "civil society development." See http://www.worldbank.org/participation/tn5.htm

Part 3

The Plan
Civil Development

6

The Process of Development
What are the Guidelines?

Could this civil market model be implemented across the larger society? I think so. In this chapter we examine suggestions to reverse the decline we examined in Chapter 3. Recall for a moment our key assumptions that "the economy" is linked to society, not just commerce, and that those civic leaders in different orders and sectors of a nation are part of societal development. Before we can look at these issues in the larger context of globalization, we need to explore them a bit further in the context of this country.

First, colleges and universities play a prominent role in societal development. They transmit the culture of society. The existing systems of self-regulation for colleges and universities, if strengthened and focused on those market challenges we noted in Chapter 3, might even serve as an exemplar for business. The change agents in this case would be accreditors that are inventive and universities that are daring and imaginative. These educational institutions could be an important force in stopping the decline of civil society.

Second, we shall look at the realm of industry. We said in Chapter 3 that business has too much power over government, and here we will suggest some strategies for solving that problem through measures that would encourage Third Sector groups to engage in monitoring and certification. As we saw in Chapter 5, nonprofit associations can—and do—develop standards, and monitoring and enforcement procedures that can be effective in reducing, for instance, environmental pollution.

Finally, we will add a new perspective to our discussion of the problem of how the power and wealth of big business subvert the policies of government; here our focus will be on local governments, to demonstrate how undue business influence over people's lives might be stopped at a grassroots level. Townspeople and city or county residents become the *change agents*. In this case as they organize community corporations, which then send out statements of their goals, along with requests for bids, to competing firms that might be interested in participating in the development of their neighborhoods. These local corporations, then, "work" business competition to their advantage. By encouraging competition between business firms seeking profit, but insisting at the same time that these firms take the community's values and needs into account, they bring core substantive values into the marketplace. By carefully considering the public benefits of competing proposals, they can choose the one best suited to helping them develop local power and human resources.

This kind of planning is especially critical for communities, and whole countries (in Africa, Latin America, and the Far East), that are struggling against the forces of globalization and want new models for development. Local and national communities want to know how to build a society that goes beyond the current American model. The question is, could the United States point the way?

Higher Education: Cultivating Core Values

Charles Vest, president of the Massachusetts Institute of Technology, is alarmed about one of our principal themes, the state of higher education in this country. In September 2003, he led a discussion at Kresge Auditorium, one of the largest venues for public discussion on campus, in which he sounded like a political activist. He talked about the "fuzziness" of language creeping into federal research contracts and the uneasiness that is spreading on US campuses. His particular concern that day was with new government "barriers against open research and international collaboration." Vest cannot be dismissed as a lightweight fighter. He is a member of President Bush's Committee of Advisors on Science and Technology and has met repeatedly with administration officials "to strike a balance" between the need for university research to be "open" versus "closed" for reasons of national security. Vest says that he is talking about academic integrity at MIT. "History tells us that science and technology advance best in a very open society with lots of communications."[1]

Meanwhile, Henry A. Giroux, a professor of education at Pennsylvania State University, has been arguing that the culture of the market is dominating higher education in general, that the "unbridled commercialization" of academic life is threatening American values. Giroux argues that the corrosive effects of business are evident as universities funnel a disproportionate share of resources into the most profitable areas of study. Universities are downsizing the humanities and reducing funds for research in human services such as public health. Faculties in the more profitable disciplines of the applied sciences are the winners as they are offered opportunities to pursue marketable research.

Any real understanding of the purpose of higher education is threatened by government-imposed secrecy and lost in a market-driven environment. Giroux argues that the problems of education should be addressed in terms of the traditional values of this realm of society, not self-interest and financial gain. If democracy is to remain a defining principle of education and everyday life, the encroachment of business should be stopped.[2]

In Chapter 3 we noted some "leading indicators" of a decline in core values in higher education as a result of the intrusion of business into this realm of society: the increasing number of for-profit universities and the expanding number of for-profit subsidiaries established by nonprofits, the increased outsourcing of campus services to business, the advance of e-commerce, the growth in market-based certificates and types of academic specialization that respond only to market needs, and the emphasis on wealth-seeking and profit-motivated science that is fueled by big research gifts from business. Can universities sustain their own standards against these forces—market-based and governmental—that promote profits and secrecy above inquiry and openness? Let's look at how educational associations monitor standards in their own marketplace.

Accreditors as Change Agents: Upholders of Standards

Colleges and universities sustain core values through accrediting associations that might serve as a model for industry. They struggled to create a higher order of association for accreditation and their common good. What is accreditation?

Accreditation is a process of external quality review. US accreditors scrutinize colleges and universities for quality assurance and quality improvement. They review institutions of higher education in fifty states and a number of other countries. They examine thousands of programs in a range of professions and specialties including, law, medicine, business, nursing, social work and pharmacy, journalism and the arts.

Accreditation is required for access to federal funds such as student aid and other federal programs. Accreditation is also important for a smooth transfer of course credits and the coordination of programs among all colleges, universities, and degree-granting institutions; receiving institutions take note of whether the credit a student wishes to transfer has been earned at an accredited institution. States have adopted minimum standards for degree-granting institutions, but accreditation given for-profits is becoming difficult: Who will decide? What will the standards be and how will they be upheld?

Here is one place where a civil revolution might begin. This accrediting process has been fairly easy and undemanding until recently because a fine tradition had been established. But if accrediting commissions insisted on high standards for online and corporate universities as well as traditional ones, 3,000 institutions (by one count) would have to listen. Accreditors and regional commissions are the overseers, the "polity" of university life. They have the power to act against decline, if they will use it.

The Commission on Institutions of Higher Education of the North Central Association of Colleges and Schools (NCA) accredits the for-profit University of Phoenix.[3] The NCA is committed to advancing excellence, but it faces a challenge in accrediting such global (for-profit) corporations. One question it must consider is, Are such educational businesses causing a decline in core values in this realm or are they making sound innovations? The NCA and the (national) Council for Higher Education Accreditation (CHEA) are working on the problem, slowly. Educators are designing "an alternative accreditation review" to give more attention to the *mission* of member institutions. They want to judge every member institution's "effectiveness" in light of "outside influences." They are evaluating distance learning and the "new providers" of higher education.

Judith Eaton, president of CHEA, defines the new providers as those "corporate universities, virtual institutions and unaffiliated Web-based courses and programs that now dot the higher learning landscape." She says that efforts to evaluate them may be undertaken through existing accreditation standards and policy and/or new guidelines currently under review. Regional accreditors are open to electronically based innovation in higher education, provided that the fundamental values of accreditation are addressed. Online providers need to demonstrate that they provide a community of learning, a degree-granting structure, coherent curricula, careful attention to student needs, and ongoing scrutiny of the quality of their offerings.[4]

Corporate (for-profit) universities are a "growth industry" and going global. In 1999, eight regional commissions reported that they were accrediting 160 institutions and programs that were operating outside the United States. Eaton admits that accreditation of US institutions outside the United States is becoming difficult. To do the job properly, accreditors need more staff and money.

The fight against commercialization has begun. The American Council on Higher Education and CHEA, for example, both declined an invitation to join the World Trade Association (WTO), which guides global markets—that is, they refused to join the "higher (tertiary) education services" sector of the General Agreement on Trade Services (GATS)—because they want to remain an autonomous order. They do not want to be part of global business.[5] But meanwhile, global for-profit universities continue to clamor for US accreditation. There is a market value in a "seal of approval" from the United States, hence more and more foreign-based institutions are approaching US accreditors for review. What should be done? Should an international agency be established for global educational corporations? Should global accreditation move under the auspices of the United Nations?

There are no answers yet, but one thing is clear. If US accreditors get tough on standards for corporate (for-profit) universities, the latter will likely set up their own accreditors. Indeed, the majority of for-profit, degree-granting campuses already get accreditation from their own bodies established for that purpose, like the Commission of Career Schools and Colleges of Technology and the Accrediting Council for Independent Colleges and Schools.

Let me sketch two choices for civil planners. First, traditional accreditors can refuse to certify for-profit universities. They might take a stand that liberal arts and general education institutions should not be chartered for profit. Accreditors would then simply refuse to evaluate big for-profit educational corporations like Phoenix; profit, they would argue, should not be the goal of a public, civic, or liberal-arts–oriented institution.

Second, accreditors could do the opposite. They could accept corporate-oriented institutes, colleges, and universities under their wing, while insisting that they establish strong standards for general as well as career-focused education. In this case the argument would be that while it is a good thing that business is creating special niches in education, it would benefit these new institutions to shape their standards for the common good.

In a civil market model plan, accreditors could accept for-profit universities as members, but they would have tough questions to ask them. Here are a few.

- What are the on-line substitutes for on-campus libraries? How can an e-commerce library be as good as a campus library?
- What are the alternatives for on-campus recreational facilities? Is physical education a part of the online institution's requirements? How could it be monitored?
- What are the substitutes for interpersonal, face-to-face group learning for students? What are the options for personal counseling and for direct talks between professors and students? How are chat rooms on the Internet better than personal conversations between students and professors on campus?

Questions for Nonprofit Educational Institutions in a Business Climate

In Chapter 3 we spoke of the influence of business on academic life in nonprofit universities. Accreditors would have questions even for solid, established institutions like Stanford and Harvard, such as the following:

- When universities receive millions of dollars in royalties on business-linked projects, what are the consequences to academic life?
- Do universities study the consequences of faculty selling their lectures on the Internet? When faculties profit by putting courses on CD ROMs, how does this affect their work? When courses become commodities on the market, does that shape the content of these courses?
- To what extent are scientific experiments—once conducted openly in academic settings—now performed secretly on campus? Do corporate (business) sponsors prohibit the publication of scientific findings in order to protect possible patent rights? How does this practice affect the integrity of the research? How does it affect the integrity of science?
- How does a "research university" study the human and environmental consequences of its programs? For instance, does a university attempt to assess the long-range effects of genetic transfer technology on animals and eco-systems?
- Is there an interdisciplinary conversation among faculties about these science-and-society problems? Are faculties in the physical sciences isolated from faculties in social science and the humanities? How are students involved with faculty in advancing interdisciplinary conversations? Are students encouraged to study the impact of scientific research on people, the environment, culture, and society?

Commercialization on campus and in education in general is a slippery slope. I would argue that accrediting associations must scrutinize the quality of distance learning, explore online modes of "interactive learning," assess the quality of teacher-student relationships, check carefully the student/faculty ratios, evaluate the quality and level of student contact with teachers, and check the credentials of teachers hired by both for-profit universities and the new programs of traditional educational institutions.

Special Accreditation and a Larger View

There are hundreds of accrediting associations that oversee certificate, diploma, and degree programs in professional and technical fields. These programs might very well be legitimate and valuable, but here are some examples of the problems they pose for accreditors. In the health field, there are accreditors for degree programs, like the Commission on Accreditation of Allied Health Education Programs (CAAHEP), the Accrediting Commission for Education in Health Services Administration (ACEHSA). Certain degree programs in public health are accredited by the Council on Education for Public Health (CEPH), and the American Medical Association (AMA) certifies medical schools.

These mainstream associations are devoted to the development of professional skills, but how do these accreditors stop a decline in core values in their fields? Could they become demanding change agents? Some of the questions for change agents in medicine follow below.

- Do AMA accreditors encourage medical schools to study of the impact of business on public health? Do they ask, What are the consequences of HMOs moving into business for profit? To what extent do medical schools study the public health consequence of for-profit hospitals?
- Do medical schools study the consequences to the profession when physicians seek advice so frequently from pharmaceutical companies? What does it mean when psychiatrists ask business sales agents about diagnoses for patients? Do medical schools study the consequences of the current practice in which physicians consult business firms on the best drugs to give a patient or the right devices to use in surgical practice?

I am arguing here that all of the professions—through their accrediting bodies—must pose new questions and hold to their core standards. Let's look at other problems noted in Chapter 3 that bear on systems of certification, such as the impact of business on religious life. Religious denominations too have accreditors for their schools.

- Do theology schools examine how churches today maximize profits and property income?
- Do these schools study the ethical problems of their investment practices? Are they maximizing dividends on Wall Street stock and getting top economic returns from their subsidiaries?
- Do schools that train ministers, priests, and rabbis examine how the practices of hiring business specialists—to get new members or building chapels inside shopping malls—affect their core values?

Each profession has an accreditor. The Council on Social Work Education (CSWE) accredits schools of social work, and they are facing their own challenges.

- Does CSWE ask schools about the "commodification" and "de-familization" of family and healthcare? Do students in these schools study the loss in family values and the growing lack of caring relationships in society? Do they explore alternatives?

The American Bar Association accredits law schools. They too have questions to ask:

- To what extent do law schools question the legal foundation of markets as a system that can be destructive? To what extent do students study how to advance the profession's values fairness, justice, impartiality, and the public interest, as opposed to corporate goals?
- To what extent do law schools examine schemes that will prevent corporate scandals? Do schools study the alternatives to a system in which lawyers support exorbitant salaries for CEOs, special stock options? To what extent do lawyers disregard pension fund problems for employees? How do they study the "alliance" of lawyers with CEOs, politicians, lobbyists, and Wall Street bankers?
- Do these questions, involving systemic issues, deserve more attention than a single course on professional ethics?

Questions, large and small, about the influence of the market on core values exist for accreditors in all fields, from architecture to forestry to the culinary arts.

The New Culture War

In a capitalist market, when business competition becomes unfair and destructive—ruthless, corrupt, or collusive—it leads to government regulation. But in civil market planning, nonprofit associations would step in to control the quality and type of competition, avoiding government regulation. Higher education as a whole already has a plethora of relatively democratic structures to govern its own markets. It is in part a sector that is self-regulating, that is, one with a "civil polity."

At the same time, the problem is this: for the past two decades, universities and other institutions of higher learning have increasingly been copying the culture of business. As far back as 1989, for example, the US Justice Department became concerned about the way certain elite private colleges and universities set both tuition and financial aid awards and whether that process violated antitrust laws. Following up on the Justice Department's investigation, a *Wall Street Journal* article published in May of that year alleged that Ivy League schools were "part of a price-fixing system that OPEC might envy."[6]

How can this tension between value systems be resolved? Can the field of education remain an autonomous (self-regulating) order? If the civil development model we are advocating were to be followed, the government would encourage existing educational associations to address the issues of price fixing and ruinous competition themselves. Federal and state departments of education would work with these associations to help them assess whether markets in their own fields are collusive or cooperative for the common good. They would help them set criteria and appoint monitors or strengthen existing standards and monitoring systems. In the civil market model, competition should be fair, honest, robust, friendly, and lively. For most markets, self-regulation is in its infancy, but, I would argue, the field of education has the potential to lead the way.

Sustaining Excellence by Market Sectors

In my region of the country, the New England Association of Schools and Colleges (NEASC) keeps an eye on what is happening, but it could do more. It is one of six nonprofit regional accrediting bodies in the United States whose purpose is to appraise educational institutions within a given region. It has five commissions to carry out evaluations and provide assurance to the public that the quality of education at a particular institution is high and that the institution's finances are sound. When problems are found, it is customary to give the institution some time to resolve them. "We will be back in twelve months," a regional accreditor might say, "to see whether you have brought the library up to standard," or, "We want a financial report from you in two years that demonstrates your financial stability."

NEASC's Commission on Standards for Accreditation periodically reviews each college program. It expects affiliated institutions to "work toward improvements, increase effectiveness," and "strive toward excellence." The NEASC has eleven "standards," each focusing on one of "the principal areas of institutional activity," that it uses to assess the soundness of an academic institution and the quality of its programs.

Below I have commented on a few of NEASC's standards to illustrate how they relate to the problem of decline we reviewed in Chapter 3, in particular noting how these standards might be made more precise and more supportive of core educational, as opposed to business, values.

Since it is through its interest in science and technology that business today has its greatest influence on higher education, change agent (revolutionary) accreditors would ask each institution whether it has, for instance, an advisory committee on scientific research. They would also ask, To whom does a university report on the size of grants to scientists, the independence of university scientists from business, and the transparency

Box 6.1. NEASC Standards and Market Values

The NEASC's Standard 4.9 asks how much a college or university depends on "resources outside its direct control." The commission's goal is for each institution to have "a clear, fixed understanding of that relationship which ensures the reasonable continued availability of those resources."

The commission should investigate the extent to which a university's business contracts and its gifts increase its dependency on outside capital resources. There should be a balance between outside sources of special funding and its own endowment. In addition, the commission staff should ask members, How do business contracts influence academic research and teaching?

* *

Standard 4.22 assesses how doctoral degree programs will "afford the student substantial mastery of the subject matter, theory, literature, and methodology of a significant field of study."

The commission should ask what it means for a liberal arts university to develop lucrative scientific specialties, like the study of genetic technology. To what extent do these specialties depend on sustaining contracts from business? How do they affect academic values? Do long-term business partnerships affect the mission of a university? How does a university specialize without narrowing or reducing a student's "scope of thought"? How does a research university provide students with a "substantial mastery of theory, literature, and methodology"?

* *

Standard 4.26 asks whether "all faculty pursue scholarship, an activity fundamental to the achievement of institutional purposes."

The commission should ask, How do students and faculties pursue scholarship when a university increasingly offers job-oriented certificate programs?

* *

Box 6.1 continues

Box 6.1 continued

Standard 5.8 is concerned with whether faculty has "adequate time to provide effective instruction, [and] advise and evaluate students" and the degree to which "faculty may participate in scholarship, research, and service" compatible with their mission.

The commission should ask, To what extent do science faculty—especially those who work with large business contracts—have time to advise students in "scholarship, research, and service" in accord with the university's goals?

* *

emphasized in scientific research on campus? And, Are science faculties encouraged to enter into dialogue with students and faculty in the social sciences and the humanities?[7]

In Chapter 3 we presented evidence that business is shaping university norms. Here we are saying that accreditors could—and should—shape business norms in their connection with education. Members of regional associations should set norms for corporate (for-profit) universities and for non-profits deeply affected by business and a market environment.

Creating a Civil Polity in Industry: Accreditation

The field of education has accrediting associations that could be models for private industry. As a change agent for advancing civil society, the government could encourage the development of accreditors for industry markets in this tradition, offering incentives and tax breaks for those trade associations that follow them. Nonprofit trade associations and associations in the Third Sector have the capacity to monitor standards in industry, but they need the assistance of government to enforce them. Here is one illustration of the current state of affairs.

Willamette Industries (WI) is a national forest products manufacturing corporation based in Portland, Oregon, that employs thousands of workers. Well before the 1990s it became clear to local leaders that the company was violating federal pollution regulations, but the government refused to recognize the problem.[8]

Third Sector organizations—the Northwest Environmental Defense Council and the Plumbers and Steamfitters Local 290—reviewed thousands of pages of paperwork that documented that WI was producing excessive discharges of toxins into the air. They brought large volumes of evidence to the state of Oregon's environmental protection agency and asked for corrective action. But the agency did not act on this information. Worse, the state allowed the company to go for many years without requiring, as it should have done, a renewal of its permit to discharge industrial effluents into the air. Could there have been some government collusion here? The leaders of the two voluntary associations stayed in hot pursuit, and eventually a courageous administrator in the federal Environmental Protection Agency looked at the case, took it up, and expanded the original investigation.

Subsequently, violations of the federal Clean Air Act (1970, major amendments 1977 and 1990) were found at about a dozen of WI's plants across the country. According to the EPA, WI's smokestacks illegally spewed invisible clouds of airborne chemicals that could cause cancer, birth defects, and other health problems in nearby communities. (This came as no surprise to people living near the WI plant in Oregon, who had been reporting for years that their lungs ached and their children coughed and wheezed.) Finally, the US Environmental Protection Agency and the Department of Justice filed charges against Willamette Industries, alleging that fifteen WI building materials plants violated air pollution laws and regulations in four states—Oregon, South Carolina, Arkansas and Louisiana. A separate case was then prosecuted against a WI pulp and paper mill in Pennsylvania.

In July of 2000, Willamette Industries agreed to pay a $11.2 million fine to the federal government to settle the claims against it. EPA administrator Carol Browner took note in public, calling this settlement "the largest to date" involving the Clean Air Act and factory emissions. Under the plan, Willamette was required to spend $74 million to install new pollution-control equipment at its thirteen factories in Oregon, Arkansas, Louisiana, and South Carolina. Browner estimated that cleaning up the emissions from the Willamette plants would keep an average of 27,000 tons of pollutants out of the air, the equivalent of taking 287,000 cars off the road.[9]

So this is how modern governments work in this arena today: slowly. All too often no action is taken, even when federal regulations are violated, until Third Sector leaders push hard and/or a conscientious administrator takes notice. In the meantime, citizens pay the costs, both personal and financial. Air pollution causes sickness and death, the "externalities" of business. How could a government act differently?

The Civil Alternative: Government Builds a Civil Polity

Let's imagine a civil market plan of action. First, *some portion of the money from such settlements and/or government fines would be given to those Third*

Sector organizations that bring these matters to the fore. It costs these associations a lot of time and work to monitor and investigate business and industry. A share of the penalty money would reward them as whistleblowers and allow them to continue this work. In the case cited above, part of the money would be given to the Northwest Environmental Defense Council, its parent EDC, and the Plumbers and Steamfitters Local 290. And a smaller share might be given by proportion to other environmental groups working in the same area of concern. These rewards would pay for their labors to uncover problems that affect the welfare of the public and force governments to act to resolve them.

Second, *some penalty money could go toward developing a civil polity within the industrial sector in general.* This would support the work of government, Third Sector associations, and stakeholders to establish wider systems of public accountability. Recall that when we discussed public accountability systems in Chapter 4, we spoke of formal contracts among stakeholders. The government in this case would support (or mandate) a process in which stakeholders (business and Third Sector corporations) agree on *public standards, neutral monitors,* and *juridical authorities.*

One part of such contracts would stipulate that Third Sector stakeholders be given free access to company data related to environmental problems—toxins in chimney emissions, for example. This would permit stakeholders like the EDC and local unions to monitor corporate activities if they suspect that they could be a risk to public health, and it would also provide civil procedures for business compliance with government and trade association standards. Put another way, industry (like higher education) would have accreditors with broad powers of inquiry. Such a public system could be legally mandated and called into action when the law or an industry standard is broken.[10]

In the aftermath of cases like that of Willamette Industries, new accountability systems could also be created that would encourage the development of a civil polity, that is, "self-government," in the industrial sphere. The civil market model of a public accountability system could eventually be applied, with appropriate variance, to every industry that has the potential to endanger public health and/or the environment.

In a civil plan, whenever legal violations occur in big business, new systems of public accountability would be established, systems that would include independent arbiters and professional mediators. The government itself would create professionally staffed arbitration committees to settle disputes between Third Sector associations and industry trade associations, negotiating guidelines for defining transparency and proposing penalties in accord with the seriousness of an alleged offense.[11]

In plain English, this vision calls for governments—state and federal— to become change agents for modifying the structure of industry. They would help associations build a civil polity within this sector of the economy. They would encourage the development of self-regulating markets by involving Third Sector associations as monitors and accreditors, mandating and supporting stakeholder rights to obtain information about all matters that affect the common good.

These mandates for public access, arbitration, transparency, joint monitoring, and civil enforcement would then become stakeholder rights, and such public accountability systems would include the hiring or appointment of appropriate specialists (such as physicians and civil engineers) as representatives of Third Sector and trade associations to assist in the process of adjudication. In following a civil development program, government would remain the ultimate authority, but it would support the establishment of civil associations to set industry standards and monitor them, and the result would be a cost saving—in both financial and social terms—for society. As we shall argue in greater detail below, this is good economics for the whole nation.

Smaller Models of Accreditation: Certification in Agriculture

Accreditation and certification programs have already developed in some business market sectors. Producers in agriculture, for example, organize trade federations (like cooperatives) that monitor standards for everything from organic soybeans and milk to "fair trade" coffee. These trade associations certify that social and/or environmental standards have been met in the production of products they approve. So this is not entirely new.

Certification is done by organizations that can be tested for creditability. In Texas, the state government's department of agriculture certifies producers, processors, distributors, and retailers of organic food and fiber within the state. This program includes the certification of production and processing, from "seed to sewing," of organic fiber products made from organic cotton, wool, and mohair.[12] But governments do not need to do the certification.

In the private sector, the Ohio Ecological Food & Farm Association is a grassroots coalition of food producers and consumers (formed in 1979) to promote "a healthful, ecological, accountable and permanent agriculture." Its bylaws state that its goals are

> to assist producers making the switch to ecological management and production systems; to make consumers aware of the increased value and quality of commodities produced by these systems; to promote research on eco-management systems and techniques; to promote the adoption of alternative technologies where appropriate; to establish and update standards for grower certification; to provide a general sharing of

resources, ideas and information; and to monitor legislation that directly affects ecological agriculture and to provide information on that legislation to the membership.

This is a nonprofit association, democratically organized. One vote is granted for each individual, business, and nonprofit organization. The corporation provides organic certification services at actual cost.[13]

The Sustainability Institute in Vermont has studied these commodity systems as they organize through production, processing, and retailing, and it finds that "collective agreements do not need to depend only on trust and good will. Legally binding enforcement provisions can be built into collective agreements. In designing such measures it is important to provide the resources for enforcement."[14] Why is it important to develop these certification programs?

An Economic Rationale for the Nation: Cost Saving

Capitalist markets "externalize" costs. Civil markets "internalize" costs. Our argument here is that a civil market has an economic advantage over a capitalist market. The purpose of a civil market is to increase wealth, but it includes mechanisms to protect the public and reduce the costs of externality.

How does "externality" happen? When businesses pollute public spaces and resources (air, land, lakes, rivers, and oceans), or cause injuries by selling unsafe products, they do so because their goal is to make profits and this overrides all other concerns. Meanwhile, citizens suffer both directly and indirectly. Aside from personal suffering, they pay the medical costs of an injury. When they get sick from pollution-or their insurance carriers or government health programs do (which drives up premiums and taxes), then, in a "double taxation," they pay for government's efforts to solve safety and environmental problems.

In the end, everybody loses financially. The failure of automobile companies and tire manufacturers to create safer cars is an example of how even the companies themselves eventually lose. People get injured, and they lose when they must pay physicians for treatment and lawyers to seek compensation. But business also loses money. Hundreds of legal actions have been filed against tire manufacturer Bridgestone/Firestone and the Ford Motor Company to recover damages resulting from defective ATX, ATX II, Wilderness AT, and other tires manufactured by Firestone and installed on cars sold by Ford. And lawsuits and settlements are costly.

The same dynamic exists across the economy. In agriculture, pesticides at first lower costs for business, but at some point they increase the ultimate costs, as pests become chemical-resistant and the chemicals poison the soil. Nuclear power at first lowers energy costs, but eventually the high cost of coping with its (non-disposable) waste tips the balance in the other direction. This is bad economics.[15]

Let's look at our alternative model. Civil markets prevent pollution and injuries from happening. The aim of civil planners is to internalize the cost of doing so by creating standards (e.g., good soil, safe tires and chimneys) within the market. Practiced on a wide scale, civil markets would add efficiency to the economy. A civil market, I argue, is a cost saving device for society.

The market sector in this vision includes many stakeholders. As we saw in the case of Willamette Industries, stakeholders (trade association, unions, environmental groups, and communities) should have public access to information and power as whistleblowers. These are necessary elements for "internalizing" costs by changing the market structure and shifting the responsibility for monitoring industry compliance to voluntary business and Third Sector associations. Government still plays a part in this model, but only as the ultimate authority, which decreases the burden on taxpayers.

Note the shift in cost accounting practice. In a civil market, business will pay for this system of accountability, but the increase in cost will go into market prices and have little or no effect on the ability of companies to make reasonable profits. The Third Sector organizations (e.g., the Environmental Defense Council and the Plumbers and Steamfitters Local 290) must be supported financially so that they can serve as monitors though public access and civil procedures, but customers will pay for this monitoring in the market. This new structure saves money directly because it reduces costly government bureaucracy. It reduces the harms (and costs to the public) of environmental pollution and dangerous or defective products.

Recall the two models as we presented them in Chapter 4. The attributes of the capitalist market are modified but retained substantively in the new civil market structure. For example, privacy is altered by an emphasis on transparency but is retained as a basic principle. The market remains "competitive," but public standards help assure product safety, a healthier environment, and that customers will pay the lowest price for goods and services. The "tax" for increased corporate responsibility and accountability—which enhances the well-being of all—goes to consumers as a part of the price for a product, no longer a cost of government.[16]

It is our basic premise that the market system should not determine the values of society, rather society should determine the values of markets. The civil market model we are outlining would include standards hammered out by voluntary Third Sector and trade associations and agreed-upon mechanisms for enforcing them. Furthermore, we would argue that a civil market actually adds a social value (self-responsibility) to the economy. In the lexicon of economics, we might label this a "value added"in the market.

In attempting to regulate a vast array of markets in a capitalist system, governments can become big and inefficient, and weakened before the power of big business. In a civil market plan, government serves instead as a change agent to encourage the more efficient economy. Its purpose: to develop a civil (self-governing) system of industrial production.

Local to Global: Systems of Accountability

Global corporations help develop communities and countries, but they also produce social problems. The dark side is well documented. Global corporations come to cities, towns, and villages and cause social and environmental problems. All too often, they produce harmful toxins, mistreat workers, and do their best to avoid local taxation—and they have the money to pay off elite leaders and any other local authorities that might otherwise restrict their activities.[17]

There are means, however, by which local governments can resist this trend, and the formation of community development corporations (CDCs) is one of them. Community development corporations, as they have begun to evolve in the United States and elsewhere, have the potential to use competitive power in global markets to their own local advantage. Simply put, local people organize a community development corporation—a nonprofit corporation designed to promote local (core) values and avoid outside exploitation—and its leaders create civic partnerships with firms desiring to do business in the community. The goal is to create social contracts that integrate economic development with social development.

A CDC is not a capitalist corporation, it is established, owned, and managed by local people and it focuses on achieving social and economic returns for the whole community. CDCs are democratically organized and run by staff and citizen boards who take responsibility for negotiating with outside businesses. Members of these boards live in the communities they serve, and have a personal interest in improving their lives according to community standards. The board members, who are elected from the local populace, invite big corporations to become partners with them and insist upon written contracts fitting their needs.[18]

How can a CDC have any power in a global market? The answer: by taking advantage of global competition. Any global firm must compete with others (e.g., a US firm vs. a German firm vs. a Japanese firm) to enter a locality. In a civil market in which CDCs are part of the mix, businesses must compete to meet the values and standards of local citizens. The CDC represents a neighborhood "commonwealth," which is not the same as government; rather it is a civic structure in which local people maintain autonomy with regard to the market.[19]

Put another way, CDCs utilize global competition for their local advantage. A foreign company must compete to win a contract with the local CDC for the use of the community's land. In this case, a global firm does not pay a bribe to a top government official so that it can take land or avoid taxes. Rather, residents in the neighborhood control the territory and demand that their values be recognized in any contract to be made.

This is not the same as globalization. It is not an imperial conquest of localities by global firms. Local leaders in this case are in a position to negotiate with corporations that are competing for local resources. They reach a deal on their terms.[20]

This bargaining power makes a big difference. It allows local control to stay even with the advance of global markets. The more public nature of CDCs then becomes a counterweight in local, national, and global economic sectors. It can even help jumpstart a civil market system. We know how community efforts can bring core values into markets from studies of actual cases.

In the United States, for example, churches have worked with CDCs to clean up neighborhood slums. In slum rehabilitation, church members reduce the cost of labor because they serve as volunteers. When volunteers provide business with free labor, there is an incentive for businesses to invest in the projects they sponsor, but churches in turn can insist on premium standards for new housing, refusing to accept big high-rise, walled-in types of apartment buildings. Competition for the construction of housing then takes place within the context of community standards.

In sum, civil development moves forward with Third Sector participation. Clergy insist on rules on safety for housing, streets, and products; educators insist on physical and academic standards for schools; and CDCs become part of this mix, through which intersector collaboration begins to push markets toward a civil structure.

In the civil market model, cooperation goes together with constructive and vigorous competition. The goal is to avoid destructive or cancerous competition. The attributes of the capitalist model remain (e.g., self-interest and wealth seeking), but CDCs turn them toward the common (local) good. When a global firm contracts with a CDC accompanied by Third Sector groups (not just with a government elite), their arrangements become more "people oriented," and more in tune with the substantive values of local communities.[21]

Neighborhoods in the Big Metropolis

This idea of CDCs also applies to neighborhood development in large cities. But here, as elsewhere, there are problems to be solved, as we shall see. In January 2000, New York Mayor Rudolph W. Giuliani proposed that the city spend a record $1.2 billion over the next ten years to renovate and expand the Lincoln Center for the Performing Arts, the Metropolitan Museum of Art, the Soloman R. Guggenheim Museum, and other similar institutions. Such public planning has shown the way for cities from Houston to London as they endeavor to diversify their economic bases from manufacturing industries to banking, law, consulting, and information technology. In this case, New York City "envisioned" cultural institutions as new engines for development.

Museums, nonprofit art galleries, and theaters together have been one of the fastest growing job categories in New York. Studies by the N.Y./N.J. Port Authority describe some $10 billion in annual revenues that such institutions generate when you include the spillover to hotels, restaurants, and transportation services. A flourishing cultural environment has become an advantage for urban centers competing globally. Lifestyle enhancements are a big way to attract and retain skilled people essential to the workforce and an enhancement of the tax base.

But as Jeffrey Garten, dean of the Yale School of Management, says, this "thickening nexus of economic development and culture" raises potential problems. It's important to ensure, he warns, that "public funds not be used to subsidize the relatively well-off, while explosive urban problems go unattended."[22] So what might be done? In New York City and other metropolitan areas, the organization of CDCs is a good option. But they should be organized to include people representing the jobless, the homeless, and the unskilled, along with people who represent the interests of museum and art gallery boards. This bridging of needs and values is what develops a civil market.

Constructing a civil market means solving a puzzle with a hundred unlike pieces. Community development corporations are part of that picture, but without other pieces in place, the old business system could overwhelm a local CDC. To switch metaphors, CDCs represent only one kind of seed in a large garden, all of which need cultivation.

Local Innovation: Studying the Microcosm inside the Macrocosm

CDCs are not for everyone. Other types of community associations (e.g., community land trusts, community finance corporations, housing cooperatives) can be effective in their own ways. No community corporation is faultless, but some work better than others under different conditions. So the options are open.

Let's look at a case study that involves an arrangement concerning local housing. Its core values could be studied as a subset of the larger (non-market) culture. It is like a microcosm inside the macrocosm society. Economists study markets under the axiom of "freedom," now social scientists can study markets under the axiom of "justice." Let's see what this means.

Cambridge Cohousing in Massachusetts is a condominium association whose buildings have a centralized ground-source heat-pump system and a solar site orientation. They were constructed with "low impact building materials" and specifications based on an "EcoDynamic home design." Cambridge Cohousing environmental performance reviews indicate a 60% savings on energy use and a 50% reduction in air pollutants compared to similar developments. All these things are quite advanced for a housing development, but of special interest to us is the way its members promote core values, such as "justice," "freedom," and "democracy." Members are localizing these values in their housing arrangement by interpreting society's great values on their own terms. (See Box 6.2)[23]

Here customers or buyers (the condominium owners) have become the change agents, deliberately bringing core values into the market. As we

---

Box 6.2 Cambridge Cohousing: Justice, Democracy, and Freedom

In the Cambridge Cohousing community, the managing board is composed of elected "apartment community owners." The owners run their community as a democratic association. They define the meaning of "democracy" as decisions based on consensus. They define "justice" in the bylaws of their organization.

The members see justice as important because the organization operates in a capitalist market. The Cohousing bylaws link the "justice idea" with the "freedom idea." They discuss the meaning of freedom in terms of "open space for play and food-growing." They discuss justice in terms of equal "rights" to a parking place and use of "utilities." They specify "fair rights" for all "community owners," and state "equal responsibility" to each other in terms of consensus.

The managing board defines justice in terms of how to collect expenses fairly, distribute profits equitably, manage the property impartially, rent office space on even terms, obtain insurance with probity. They also agree to rely on national standards of justice (i.e., " "fairness" and "equity") set by the American Institute of Certified Public Accountants. They follow the justice-oriented standards defined by the nationwide cohousing organization, of which they are a member, and working with standards of fairness outside their organization as well is required in a public audit of their books.[24]

noted in our discussions about socially responsible investment, they are not the only ones acting in this manner. Today in many cases customers and consumer groups want to know whether markets are fair and just. They want to know under what working conditions the goods they buy are produced; they ask about workplace safety, environmental conditions, child labor, and workers rights in factories. They want information on human rights in order to make the correct choice among competing products. These consumer preference questions combine the idea of justice with the idea of a free market.

Conclusion: Building a Public Domain

Leaders in government, business, and the Third Sector become change agents when they bring society's core values into the market structure. They become civil revolutionaries who change a private domain into a public domain. In a civil revolution, the public domain is composed of government and non-governmental associations.

Recall again the different models in Chapter 4. The private domain becomes "public" when people obtain access to all the information they need to make choices in the market. (Civil markets retain the principle of "rational choice.") A public domain develops progressively with core values and humane standards; it makes its appearance when people debate substantive values against exchange (market) values. It emerges slowly as local, regional, and national associations introduce transparency into systems of exchange. It develops gradually as principles of fairness and democracy enter into the organization of markets.[25]

We saw how the state of Oregon allowed a business corporation to keep its chimney emission data secret until stakeholders (non-governmental organizations) used existing laws to press for access to corporate data. Certain data are relevant to the common good. Now imagine multiplying this argument for transparency to other market sectors. Greater transparency is essential to all market sectors. It is part of this civil revolution.[26]

We have noted how change agents work (and might do more) in different markets. In higher education, a nonprofit association (e.g., the NCA) would evaluate the conduct of a corporate (for-profit) university like Phoenix. In the smokestack industries, nonprofit (Third Sector) accreditors would have access to the production records of a business like Willamette Industries; they would serve as standards monitors and they would check on other competitors in this industry as well. In agriculture, nonprofit accreditors have begun to control pollution. In localities, nonprofit CDCs can protect the environment and judge the worth of global competitors. This sort of development builds a civil polity, step by step.[27]

A civil polity is equivalent to stakeholder self-government. It has developed to some degree in the field of education and it could develop within business and industry. But applying the model for market governance in education to other industries is not simple. It would require policy studies on the relation between production, wholesale, and retail associations in each market. Accreditation is the system used by American higher education to assure quality in its market, but innovations in types of accreditation and certification would be needed for each industry.

What is significant here? The existing system of accreditation in education in the United States was not inherited from Europe. It had to be invented. It is a distinctive American innovation that began to develop some one hundred years ago and relies on a voluntary stakeholder review process. It is based on the belief that those who are affected by institutional decisions must be among those who evaluate the work done in a given market sector.

How is this a new revolution? In previous centuries, violent revolutions have been one way citizens gained a voice in modern government, but today stakeholders can gain a voice in markets through a civil revolution. Existing systems of civil government took a long time to develop, and change was sometimes brutal, but a civil economy can evolve without resort to brutality. A civil economy develops with stakeholder power through social contracts that ensure compliance with public standards in the private sector.

A civil economy—like a civil government—develops in phases. It develops by increasing levels of democratic organization in markets that are now characterized by oligarchies and oligopolies. It develops by augmenting degrees of cooperation for the common good among competitors. It develops by increasing fairness and justice within each market sector. It develops by advancing transparency within a system of proprietary rights. It develops by creating a public (nonprofit) domain inside a private (commercial) domain, a creative mix of new attributes that produce a different economic order.

In the eighteenth century, people fought monarchies because as "subjects" they had no power to hold them accountable. Today people as "stakeholders" struggle to make business corporations accountable to them. Civil development is the frontier as planners build a new type of government. No one can predict the outcome of this effort, but with a little bit of luck and national leadership, it will be what I have termed a civil republic.

Notes

1. Vest began to protest secrecy and the "loss of open science" shortly after the passage of the Patriot Act in October 2001. The issues are critical because MIT has been a key player in national defense for more than a half century. Robert Weisman, "Openness in a Time of Terror," *Boston Globe,* 6 October 2001, F1, 4.

2. Civic discourse, Giroux says, has succumbed to the language of commercialization, privatization, and deregulation. Within the language of corporate culture, citizenship is portrayed as "an utterly privatized affair that produces self-interested individuals." The corporate culture in academic life ignores (or cancels out) injustices in the social order by overriding the democratic impulses and practices of civil society. These trends, Giroux goes on, affect the way we address the meaning and purpose of education, and mark a hazardous turn that threatens our understanding of democracy itself. Henry A. Giroux, "Neoliberalism, Corporate Culture, and the Promise of Higher Education: The University as a Democratic Public Sphere," *Harvard Educational Review,* Winter 2002, 425–464. See article abstracts.

3. The Higher Learning Commission, as a member of the North Central Association (NCA), accredits the University of Phoenix as a whole. Phoenix's Bachelor of Science in Nursing and Master of Science in Nursing programs, however, are accredited by the National League for Nursing Accrediting Commission; the Master of Counseling Program in Community Counseling at the Phoenix and Tucson campuses is accredited by the Council for Accreditation of Counseling and Related Educational Programs. See http://www.chea.org.

4. Judith Eaton, *The CHEA Chronicle,* http://www.chea.org/Chronicle/vol3/no3/focus.html. Testimony of Judith Eaton, "Assuring Quality in Distance Learning, http://edworkforce.house.gov/hearings/107th/21st/accreditation10102/eaton.htm.

5. The letter of refusal—from Stanley Ikenberry, President, American Council on Education, and Judith Eaton, President, Council for Higher Education, to Joseph Papovich, Assistant US Trade Representative for Services, at the Investment and Intellectual Property Office of the US Trade Representative—can be found at http://www.chea.org/international/papovich_wto.html.

6. G.Putka, "Colleges in Collusion," *Wall Street Journal,* 2 May1989, B1.

7. As far back as the 1980s, when new technologies were advanced in business, Nicolas Ashford at MIT said that the first decision in making a business contract is the "general category of research to be pursued." He asked, "Will an engineer, for example, focus on developing new technologies for automation or investigate the effects of automation on labor or work organizations?" Second, Ashford said that engineering faculties should listen to other faculties concerned about the public interest. Those were the old days. See Nicholas Ashford, "A Framework for Examining the Effects of Industrial Funding on Academic Freedom and the Integrity of the University," *Science, Technology, and Human Values* 8 (Spring 1983), 18.

8. WI's violations of government standards at some facilities began in 1980 and continued at least through 1998. See documents that can be obtained from the EPA through the Freedom for Information Act. Also see *Cascadia Times,* http://www.times.org/archives/2000/willamette1.htm.

9. Attorney General Janet Reno applauded the settlement, which required the corporation to spend $8 million on environmental projects. Terry Frieden, "Willamette Industries Settled the Pollution Claims with a $11.2 Million Fine," 21 July 2000, web posted at 12:01 p.m. EDT (16:01 GMT) from CNN Producer Washington (CNN).

10. For example, the Toxic Use Reduction program in Massachusetts creates rules to reduce social costs. This public accountability system requires firms to remain open to inspection, file annual reports, and pay fees to maintain the program, including inspection. The fees go into a public trust that pays the University of Massachusetts to teach professionals how to conduct the inspections and administer the program. See Severyn T. Bruyn, *A Civil Economy* (Ann Arbor: University of Michigan, 2000), 166–67; for another public accountability system, see International Standards Organization in the same book, 213 ff.

11. We do not have space to describe the possible details of such an arrangement. But the authority for outside groups to make investigations—and for the government to set up an arbitration commission—is in accordance with public interest law. The government assumes this power, based on laws related to industry violations. The right of outsiders to make an inquiry and the right to advance disciplinary proceedings by voluntary associations (e.g., trade associations and churches) must by law "satisfy the elementary requirements of any judicial proceeding in government courts." These requirements include "reasonable notice of charges," "notice of a hearing," the right of confrontation and cross-examination, the "opportunity to refute all charges," and a "hearing before an unbiased tribunal." See Severyn T. Bruyn, *A Future for the American Economy* (Stanford, California: Stanford University Press, 1991), Chapter 8.

12. Texas Department of Agriculture, http://www.agr.state.tx.us/license/regulatory/reg_organic.htm.

13. Ohio Ecological Food and Farm Association, http://www.oeffa.org/aboutoeffa/bylaw.html.

14. Beth Sawin, Hal Hamilton, et al., "Commodity System Challenges: A Sustainability Institute Report," April 2003, p. 36; the organization's address is 3 Linden Road, Hartland, Vermont 05048; see also www.sustainer. org.

15. According to sociologist Immanuel Wallerstein, the ecology movement has addressed this last problem by pointing out inexpensive modes of disposal of products that cause damage to the ecosystem. But this "externalizing cost" requires government to solve the problem. Wallerstein says that the only real long-term solution to these problems is the internalization of costs, which, given the limits of the elasticity of demand, means a long-term profit squeeze. Immanuel Wallerstein, "A Left Politics for the Twenty-First Century? Or, Theory and Praxis Once Again," Fernand Braudel Center 1999, http://www.transformaties .org/bibliotheek/wallersteinleftpol.htm.

16. The model policy would be applied nationwide, starting experimentally with corporations that break the law. The cost of regulatory agencies should be reduced by that degree to which a market sector develops stakeholder controls. We would predict that government costs would go down to the extent that public accountability systems go up. *And* society's core values then become active in the market.

17. For more on the story of corporate exploitation, see Charles Derber, *Corporation Nation* (New York: St. Martins Press, 1998).

18. People in a village or a city neighborhood create a special blend of what could be commercial, industrial, residential, and cultural values for local develop-

ment. If local leaders do their job well, using their own skills and the knowledge of outside entrepreneurs, they advance public standards and build a local marketplace. They bring core values drawn from the whole village into development programs. For a list of CDCs and descriptions of some of their offerings, see http://www.ppnd.org/cdcs.htm.

19. Let's go back and see how CDCs fits the model put forth in Box 4.1, Chapter 4. Notice the creative link between the values of capitalist and civil models. Community development corporations emphasize local *cooperation* and civic engagement while they accept *competition* in the market. Local people elect their own boards and emphasize public *standard making* (e.g., health, safety, and environment) while they promote *profit making* (i.e., an increase of wealth) for the community in a context of sharing. A global (capitalist) market emphasizes *competition, efficiency,* and *productivity,* which are fine for the CDC as long as these values can be linked with *cooperation, self-reliance,* and *self-sufficiency.*

20. A host government can supply consultants to CDC leaders who are not always knowledgeable about how to make the best deal. For a specific case on the way this works, see copper mining in Puerto Rico, Severyn T. Bruyn, *The Social Economy* (New York: John Wiley, 1977), Appendix: "The Social Economy of Copper Mining." In this case, after consulting with people in local communities in Puerto Rico who were concerned about the destruction of their environment—when the Kennecott Copper Corporation was exploring to mine their ore—I wrote to commerce agencies in Japan and Sweden to invite their global firms to be competitors in the island's development. They became competitors for the local copper. This competition increased the bargaining power of local residents to protect their environment.

21. There is a strong tradition for community development along these lines. Civic activist Saul Alinsky began the Back of the Yards Neighborhood Council in the late 1930s as an effort to induce citizens to participate more fully in local governance. Carol Gould saw community development as a condition for self-development. Benjamin Barber argued for a "strong democracy" with widespread participation of citizens in community life. Carole Pateman wrote about the need for new "authority structures" in government, business, and non-governmental spheres of social life. Klaus Eder argued that social movements would be critical to developing democratic institutions. See Benjamin Barber, *Strong Democracy: Participatory Politics for a New Age* (Berkeley: University of California Press, 1984); Carole Pateman, *Participation and Democratic Theory* (Cambridge: Cambridge University Press, 1970); Carol Gould, *Rethinking Democracy: Freedom and Social Cooperation in Politics, Economy, and Society* (Cambridge: Cambridge University Press, 1988); and Klaus Eder, "Social Movement Organization and the Democratic Order," in Colin Crouch, Klaus Eder, Damian Tambini, eds., *Citizenship, Markets, and the State* (Oxford: Oxford University Press).

22. Jeffrey Garten, "Cities: Investing in Culture Is Simply Good Business," *Business Week,* 5 March 2001, 26. Other types of community corporations, such as "community land trusts" and "community development finance corporations," are described in detail in Severyn T. Bruyn and James Meehan, *Beyond*

the Market and the State: New Directions in Community Development (Philadelphia, Pennsylvania: Temple University Press, 1987).

23. Cambridge Cohousing is part of a national network of "cooperative neighborhoods" that organize on "social and environmental principles." See the Cohousing Network, at http://www.cohousing.org/

24. See Cambridge Cohousing, http://www.hickoryconsortium.org/cambridge_cohousing.htm.

25. See David Mathews, "What Is Exactly'the Public'?" *Higher Education Exchange* (The Kettering Foundation, 1998), 72, 73. Erik Engstrom believes that the idea of public participation is virtually lost. He says the emphasis on "professional politics" helped destroy the notion that "the public was sovereign." The idea that "widespread participation of the citizenry was mandatory," was surrendered to "professional politicians," and even "progressives" began seeing "the public," like "the masses," as irrational. Slowly, a belief emerged that society could be better managed through government policies based on objective science. These trends "eclipsed the public" as a relevant concept. See Erik Engstrom, "Exhuming the Phantom: Notions of the Public and American Democracy," *Kettering Exchange*, Fall 1994.

26. A public domain should be developed with a social economic rationale. Social economists and economic sociologists should examine the appropriate types of transparency by market sectors. The loss of "privacy" on the Internet has led US senators to propose legislation to restore it; Senate bills on this issue have included the Consumer Privacy Protection Act, the Privacy and Identity Protection Act of 2000, the Notice of Electronic Monitoring Act, the Consumer Internet Privacy Enhancement Acts, the Secure Online Communication Enforcement Act, and the Freedom from Behavioral Profiling Act.

27. How could increased transparency reduce the need for government regulations? See Nancy Fraser, "Rethinking the Public Sphere," *Kettering Review*, Winter 1997, Civil society, Item #R1090 , 23-34. On public philosophy, see Benjamin Barber, *Strong Democracy*, 72; William M. Sullivan, *Reconstructing Public Philosophy* (Berkeley: University of California Press, 1986).

7

The Mass Media
Who Owns It?

Whenever any form of government becomes destructive of these ends [life, liberty, and the pursuit of happiness], it is the right of the people to alter or abolish it, and to institute new government, laying its foundation on such principles, and organizing its powers in such form, as to them shall seem most likely to effect their safety and happiness.
        —Thomas Jefferson, Declaration of Independence, 1776

A popular government without popular information, or the means of acquiring it, is but a prologue to a farce or a tragedy, or perhaps both.
        —James Madison

Such as it is, the press has become the greatest power within the Western World, more powerful than the legislature, the executive and judiciary. One would like to ask; by whom has it been elected and to whom is it responsible?
        —Aleksandr Solzhenitsyn

The mass media system in the United States is a network of private "communication companies" that sends uncountable millions of messages to people every day. Its "hardware" includes television, computers, newspapers, videotapes, magazines, theaters, motion picture films, and musical recordings. It is a vast, complex system that is governed by business and the laws of capitalist markets. Indeed, the mass media in this country are so powerful in shaping public opinion that they serve like a second Congress or parliament. But this is not a system that is democratically organized in any nation.[1]

In dictatorships and the few remaining communist countries, the mass media system (in particular radio, newspapers, and television) is a government monopoly. In capitalist countries, it is a business monopoly. Mass media ownership in the United States is concentrated in the hands of a small number of private firms whose primary aim is to advance profit, not the common good. They are in business to make money, not to work in the public interest. That is, they have established the media as a private domain, not a public one.[2]

We define a *public domain in the media* as a place where people find news and entertainment and debate ideas as a community; where citizens examine their differences and find some common ground; where people across the land converse about who they are and who they could be. It is where people express their opinions fully and honestly, exchange ideas, negotiate and settle problems, and learn from one another. It is where leaders and common folk alike consider *fairness* and *democracy* to be vital, and where they encourage dissent. It is a field of competition but also a field of cooperation.

How could this key realm of society be reclaimed so that the media serve the common good and generate profit for business at the same time? How could the media serve the citizens of the world, not just citizens of one nation? How could they speak to the humanity in people, not just for special interests? These are questions that we address in this chapter.

Today's Media: A Business Domain

Let's look at the current state of the media in this country as a background to subsequent proposals for transforming a private (business) domain into a public domain. We will focus on telecommunications, but similar observations and arguments can be marshaled for other forms of mass media as well.

The Problem of Market Concentration

Media specialist Robert McChesney, at the University of Illinois, sees the mass media in a *hyper-commercialized frenzy.* Fewer than 10 global media conglomerates dominate the worldwide marketplace; fewer than two dozen account for the overwhelming majority of newspapers, magazines, books, films, and television and radio stations. These same media organizations, says McChesney, are responsible for the full-scale commercial exploitation of sports, the arts, and education.

Bill Moyers describes the concentration as increasing over the last decade. In North America there are approximately 1800 daily newspapers,

11,000 magazines, 11,000 radio stations, 2,000 television stations, 3,000 book publishers. The increasing concentration of control over the media listed above is clear. In 1987 the number controlling all these media above was 50; in 1996, the number was 10; in 2002, the number was six.[3]

Let's look at this case in a little more detail, focusing on the United States. With regard to radio, in October of 2003 the nonprofit Center for Public Integrity released a report showing that in each of 43 different cities a single company owns a third of the radio stations. No corporation should own more than eight in any market, but the rules are ignored. In 34 of those 43, one corporation owns more than eight stations. Cumulus Media owns eight of the 15 radio stations in Albany, Georgia. Clear Channel Communications has 1,200 stations altogether. In Mansfield, Ohio, Clear Channel owns 11 of the 17 radio stations, and in Corvallis, Oregon, it owns seven of 13.[4]

AOL Time Warner is one of the top five US/global leaders in film production, TV show production, cable TV channels and networks, movie-theater ownership, book publishing, music, and magazine publishing. It also owns amusement parks, retail stores, professional sport teams, and Internet services. It is a huge cross-sector media conglomerate.

The Walt Disney Company has also mastered the art of conglomeration. Its animated films *Pocahontas* and *The Hunchback of Notre Dame* were only "marginal successes" at the box office—roughly $100 million in gross US revenues—but both films will generate close to $500 million in profit once Disney has exploited tie-ins to all other venues, such as TV shows on its ABC network and cable channels, amusement park rides, comic books, CD-ROMs, CDs, and merchandising through six hundred Disney retail stores.[5]

General Electric owns NBC television. NBC's $5 billion sales revenues are less than 6.5% of GE's massive $80 billion revenues from electric machines manufacturing, but, with GE's approval, NBC intends to move beyond its current ownership of radio and TV broadcast networks and 11 TV stations into cable and satellite television as well. NBC has purchased or created several cable channels and acquired shares in another twenty, including the Arts and Entertainment network. All this "growth," of course, makes good business sense.

The largest media firms began "equity joint ventures" in the 1990s, and while the increased concentration of ownership in the mass media remains invisible to the public, under these arrangements media giants now share "silent ownership" of important media markets and projects. Fox Sports Net, for example, is jointly owned by Rupert Murdoch's News Corp, the Comedy Central cable channel is co-owned by Time Warner and Viacom, and these media firms have joint ventures with each other. Meanwhile, Murdoch's News Corp has at least one joint venture with every one of them. In such intertwined and therefore noncompetitive markets, McChesney claims, media firms have enough market power to dictate content on the basis of pure self-interest and joint profitability.

Today the big media moguls see the Internet too as a telecommunications frontier. Barry Diller's company, InterActiveCorp (IAC), is becoming the world's largest consumer e-commerce business. It has acquired a group of businesses that range from the online travel powerhouse Expedia to the Internet dating service Match.com. This makes it bigger than e-commerce giants Yahoo!, eBay, and Amazon. IAC's Expedia and Hotels.com are the two most profitable online travel agencies in the world; Ticketmaster gives Diller a 90% share of ticket sales for its concerts and sporting events; LendingTree Inc., an online mortgage-referral service, provides a major entree into real estate; and Diller's cable-TV retailer, HSN (the Home Shopping Network), makes profits that he can use to spin an even wider net of companies on the Web.[6]

Meanwhile, the trend toward conglomeration across media sectors is going global. General Electric, for example, signed a deal on October 8, 2003, with a French media group called Vivendi Universal to join with its US film studios and cable TV channels. This will bring the film studio behind *ET, Jaws,* and *Jurassic Park* together with the producers of NBC's TV hits, like *ER* and *West Wing,* in an arrangement that will also encompass its Universal Studios film operation and cable channels, including the USA network and the Sci-Fi Channel, and Vivendi Universal's five US theme parks. The new company is called NBC Universal and will compete with Walt Disney, MTV owner Viacom, and Rupert Murdoch's News Corp, owner of Fox and DirecTV.[7]

Viacom is one of the largest of the global media empires with a financial interest in broadcast and cable television, radio, Internet, book publishing, and film production and distribution. Its conglomerate's properties include the CBS network, MTV, Infinity broadcasting, Simon & Schuster, Blockbuster and Paramount Pictures.[8]

Critics like Robert McChesney argue that because owning properties in different media markets gives each competitor more opportunities for profit and power, these huge firms have become oligopolies with strong barriers to new entrants. Small businesses simply cannot compete in this market environment, which is why media giants increasingly dominate this domain. And as competition decreases, whether people are seeking news, information, entertainment, or cultural and educational programming, they have fewer and fewer real choices.

The Question of Values

Critics also contend that in today's climate the media communicate a commercial culture, not America's core values. Television is at the heart of the communications industry. In the US, 98% of all homes have a TV set and the average person watches more than four hours per day. In the past decade, the number of commercials on network TV has increased by 50%. In the 1990s, commercially saturated programming for children was the fastest-growing and most profitable branch of the TV industry.

In the United States, the average person-no matter what his or her age—sees 25,000 commercials a year on television alone. Commercials are more than a pitch for a particular product; they represent the attitudes, values, and "lifestyles" that advertisers foster in order to promote their products. Mass entertainment captures a mass audience and mass advertising promotes, above all, mass consumption.[9]

Furthermore, for many people, television has become the primary window onto the world. Indeed, most people get most of their news from television. Television has become the principal source of the information that forms public opinion. This has grave implications for democracy itself. In our vision, the media would provide people with a wide range of views and analysis on political issues, reflecting a diversity of citizen opinion. But neither television nor the rest of the mass media are organized to do this. They do not represent the public or the core values of civil society.

Public Service, Power, and Profit

Three-quarters of a century ago, lawmakers foresaw the dangers inherent in new, more far-reaching forms of media communication and attempted to guard against them. Based on legislation dating back to 1927, radio and television broadcasters in the United States have had an "overriding" obligation to "serve the public interest, convenience, and necessity." Media corporations are obligated by law to inform the public on local, national, and global issues that affect the lives of all citizens. Their duty is "to serve the public, first and foremost," not business and corporate profit.

The Federal Radio Commission—predecessor of the Federal Communications Commission (FCC)—set down the principle that the "airwaves" belong to the public and the basic requirement that broadcasters must give *first priority* to the public interest: "[B]roadcast stations are not given these great privileges by the United States Government for the primary benefit of advertisers. Such benefit as is derived by advertisers must be incidental and entirely secondary to the interest of the public."This "public obligation" has remained in effect since the inception of broadcasting. It is expressed in the Federal Communications Act of 1935 (which regulated telephone and television as well as radio) and the 1969 Supreme Court decision that clarified the responsibilities of broadcasters, in which the Court said, "It is the right of the viewers and listeners, not the right of the broadcasters, which is paramount." In addition, the Court continued, "It is the purpose of the First Amendment to preserve an uninhibited marketplace of ideas in which truth will ultimately prevail, rather than to countenance monopolization of that market, whether it be by the Government itself or a private licensee." This legal position has been affirmed by more than a half-century of law in the US Supreme Court, Congress, and the FCC.[10]

In the meantime, however, the communications media have grown ever more powerful as new technologies have emerged, and they have become ever more closely linked to commercial interests. The Telecommunications Act of 1996, which relaxed media ownership regulations and thus encouraged mergers and joint ventures, is grounded in the theory of laissez-faire capitalism: its premise is that the free market, with business at the helm, should rule. This 1996 act is now the basis for shaping the course of virtually all aspects of communication in the United States as it shifts into digital technologies. And in the end, the 1996 act assumes that business will control all mass communication. But should business be in control?

Newspapers and television did not alert the public to the details of the congressional debates about the telecommunications industry that took place in the 1990s. The business and trade press covered the political debate as a story for investors and managers, but not as an issue for the general public. Business ownership and control of the media has become an accepted phenomenon in the United States.[11]

The broadcast industry—the private media domain—protects its profits through the power of its lobby in Congress. This power was documented in a study by the Center for Public Integrity entitled "Off the Record: What Media Corporations Don't Tell You about Their Legislative Agenda," published in September of 2000. According to this report, from 1993 through the first six months of 2000, media corporations and their employees gave $75 million in campaign contributions to candidates for federal office and the two major political parties. In addition, from 1996 through the first half of 2000, the fifty largest media companies and four of their trade associations spent $111.3 million to lobby Congress and the executive branch of government. The study found that from 1996 through 1998, the National Association of Broadcasters and five media firms— ABC, CBS, the A.H. Belo Corporation, the Meredith Corporation, and Cox Enterprises—cumulatively spent nearly $11 million to defeat a dozen campaign finance bills mandating free airtime for political candidates.[12]

Interestingly, television broadcasters—both network and local stations—accumulated a record $606 million from political advertising in 2000, a 34% increase over 1996 and the previous presidential election year.[13] And, as of early 2004, the National Association of Broadcasters remains in a powerful position in Congress and continues to lobby the FCC for further loosening of any government regulations that might curtail the trend toward media conglomeration. The media corporations would never allow a debate to take place about their own aims and lobbying power, of course. Not in their publications or over what they see as *their* airwaves.

Some lawsuits have already been filed to challenge the near total dominance of business interests over the media. Civic groups leading the way in this effort include the Rocky Mountain Media Watch and a national consortium of civic associations of lawyers and academics with support from Unitarian Universalist groups.[14] As we shall see, there are plenty of legal arguments that can be mustered to support a different media system. And a growing number of organizations are calling for change.

Could the mass media be organized to represent society? Could they help reverse the decline in core values in religion, education, the professions, and the arts and sciences? Could the media be made more democratic and more accountable to the public? These are the questions that grassroots leaders are asking.

Challenging the Status Quo

Over the past decade, grassroots organizations have developed across the United States to oppose the concentration of media ownership and to push for a reclamation of at least some significant part of "the media" as a public domain. Our Media Voice, for example, is a nonprofit organization that wants to hold television broadcasters accountable to *all* stakeholders. It wants a "socially responsible media." Its members envision a healthy media environment in which programming "inspires, enlightens and empowers people to create a healthy, sustainable, democratic society."

Today more than forty nonprofit groups cooperate in ongoing efforts to challenge the media oligarchy/oligopoly. Box 7.1 entitled "Grassroots Public Media Organizations" lists and briefly describes a few of them.

These organizations argue that the mass media—with its deluge of marketing and programming that serves corporate interests—are biased. The media ignore and dismiss too much of what should be conveyed to the public for the common good.

Bias and Self-Interest: What You Won't See or Hear

CIPB points out, for example, that US public broadcasters produce nightly programs that feature Wall Street and business news but no similar programming that focuses on the concerns of workers, consumers, and environmentalists. Nor is there a program comparable to PBS's *Nightly Business Report* that is devoted to issues of the Third Sector—religion, education, medicine, science, and the arts. Even on PBS, which most people see as more socially responsible than the commercial networks, there aren't even any weekly programs that address these issues in an ongoing way.

Box 7.1. Grassroots Public Media Organizations[15]

Fairness & Accuracy in Reporting (FAIR) is a national media watch group offering documented criticism of media bias and censorship since 1986. It exposes neglected news stories and defends working journalists who are muzzled.[16]

The Institute for Public Accuracy is a consortium of policy researchers who seek to broaden public discourse by gaining media access for those whose perspectives are commonly drowned out by corporate-backed think tanks and other influential institutions. The institute promotes outlooks that usually get little media attention.[17]

The Media Education Foundation (MEF) is a nonprofit educational organization devoted to media research and production of resources to aid educators and others in fostering analytical media literacy. They believe that a media-literate citizenry is essential to a vibrant democracy in a diverse and complex society.[18]

MediaChannel is a media issues website that features criticism, breaking news, and investigative reporting from hundreds of organizations worldwide. It is a media watchdog that keeps an eye on current events.[19]

Citizens for Independent Public Broadcasting (CIPB) is a national membership organization dedicated to putting the "public" back into public broadcasting. At the national level, CIPB has developed a detailed proposal for a Public Broadcasting Trust (PBT) that would be independently funded, publicly accountable, and true to the service's founding mission. At the community level, CIPB builds chapters and is working with national partner organizations to democratize community public broadcasting service. CIPB offers a training manual, a video, and a national clearinghouse for organizing.[20]

Citizen Works is a nonprofit, tax-exempt organization founded by Ralph Nader to strengthen citizen participation in power. The aim is to give people the tools and opportunities to build a wider base for democracy. The strategy is to enhance the work of existing organizations by helping to share information, build coalitions, and institute improved mechanisms for banding activists together; and to recruit and train citizens to act as watchdogs in their own communities and nationally.[21]

People for Better TV is a coalition of national organizations that are pushing to improve public broadcasting and to tighten regulation of commer-

Box 7.1 continues

Box 7.1 continued

cial broadcasting. The members see themselves as "parents and teachers and doctors and viewers and voters." The Steering Committee is composed of representatives from organizations such as Children NOW, Civil Rights Forum on Communications Policy, Communications Workers of America, Consumer Federation of America, League of United Latin American Citizens, National Association of the Deaf, National Organization for Women, National Urban League, Project on Media Ownership, and the US Catholic Conference.[22]

Commercial Alert organizes campaigns against the commercialization of culture, from sports and museums to literature and media. Commercial Alert's mission is to keep the commercial culture within its proper sphere, and to prevent it from exploiting children and subverting the higher values of family, community, environmental integrity and democracy.[23]

The Center for Digital Democracy (CDD) is a nonprofit organization "working to ensure that the digital media systems serve the public interest." It sees itself committed "to preserving the openness and diversity of the Internet in the broadband era, and to realizing the full potential of digital communications through the development and encouragement of noncommercial, public interest programming."[24]

The Independent Press Association (IPA) was founded on the fringes of the 1996 Media & Democracy Congress in San Francisco. It promotes and supports independent publications committed to social justice and a free press.[25]

The Media Access Project (MAP) is a twenty-seven-year-old nonprofit tax-exempt public-interest telecommunications law firm that promotes the public's First Amendment right to hear and be heard on the electronic media. MAP is a Washington-based organization devoted to representing listeners' and speakers' interests in electronic media and telecommunications issues before the Federal Communications Commission, other policy-making bodies, and in the courts.[26]

The same, of course, is true of the commercial networks. As Susan Thompson, the editor of MoveOn.org, puts it, "At networks owned by multibillion-dollar conglomerates like General Electric, Viacom and Disney, the news divisions solemnly report every uptick or downturn of the markets," but "when was the last time you heard Tom Brokaw, Dan Rather or Peter Jennings report the latest rates of on-the-job injuries or the average wait times at hospital emergency rooms?"[27]

In considering why this is so, political analyst Edward Herman says bluntly that it is because the media carry out "propaganda" on behalf of the corporate and political establishment. This is reflected in their choice of topics, such as the cost of welfare rather than Pentagon costs, the terrorism of America's enemies rather than that of governments supported by the United States (e.g., Guatemala). It is also revealed in the way they frame the issues—GDP growth rather than the distribution of wealth, federal policy effects on inflation rather than on unemployment—and choose their sources of information, depending on almost exclusively on officials and "think tank" representatives. Their reliance on these particular sources further limits both the content and the vocabulary of any discussion of issues (e.g., "terrorist" is applied only to America's enemies-Iraq or Hamas and the PLO).[28]

Meanwhile, Citizen Works complains that PBS's one nightly news program, *The Newshour with Jim Lehrer,* "duplicates" the same official voices heard commercial network news: you hear from the secretary of defense or the secretary of state but not from articulate critics like Noam Chomsky, Howard Zinn, or Ralph Nader.[29] When John Stant, a Virginia-based writer on national security affairs, and Wayne Madsen, a Washington, D.C.-based investigative journalist, criticize the "selective reporting" of the business-owned media, they focus on corporate self-interest. As one example, they cite an instance when ABC, owned by the Walt Disney Company, featured an "investigative report" on *World News Tonight* about whether time travel is possible, a story (or rather a thinly veiled movie advertisement) timed to coincide with Disney's release of its remake of *The Time Machine.*

Other examples are not so amusing. Disney also owns interests in petroleum and natural gas production facilities; Stanton and Madsen believe that it is not hard to figure why oil as a factor in foreign policy was not part of ABC's news coverage of Iraq. When "the corporate megaliths took over the news networks, the first casualties were the foreign bureaus," the authors write. "No longer would network journalists be able to build up a base of sources and contacts within major cities and financial centers." The result is that the networks now depend more than ever on government spokespeople for "news." But Stanton and Madsen agree with Edward Herman that this is mainly propaganda.[30]

Paul Taylor, founder of the Alliance for Better Campaigns, focuses on the media's role in political campaigning:

> The United States is one of just a few countries that does not require television stations—as a condition of receiving their government licenses—to set aside free airtime during the height of the political campaign season for candidates and parties to communicate to voters. It's almost certainly the *only* country in the world to permit its television industry to

profiteer on political campaigns, and to do so by using billions of dollars' worth of airwaves they have been given, free of charge, in return for a commitment to serve the public interest.[31]

Looking at the issue of news coverage from yet another angle, Neil Hickey, editor-at-large at the *Columbia Journalism Review,* writes that broadcast news people seldom cover media mergers and their public consequences because they are directly implicated in the problem. Media executives claim that these stories are too complex and boring to tell in TV terms, but, Hickey argues, that claim is disingenuous. The companies that reap the economic rewards of the media oligopoly, he goes on to point out, own TV news and they do not want to tell citizens about issues that might affect them adversely. At best, newspapers bury the story of mergers and deregulation in the business pages.

Don't forget many big newspaper companies own television stations and stand to benefit from deregulation. The News Corporation owns 33 stations, for example; the Tribune Company has 23; Gannett owns 22; the New York Times Company, eight; the Washington Post Company, six. Some newspaper companies may decide to buy up many more television stations. Or newspaper companies themselves might be seen as attractive takeover targets by AOL Time Warner, GE, or Disney, for example.[32]

Meanwhile, small media enterprises say they cannot grow. This is because government subsidies and policies encourage big conglomerates. The government, in effect, "grants monopoly rights" to the TV broadcast spectrum. It is not setting the terms of fair competition; rather, it is picking the winner. In effect, government provides "corporate welfare" to the aforementioned media giants to the tune of tens of billions of dollars. These decisions are made in the public's name, but without the public's informed consent.

James Carey—a scholar, media critic, and teacher of journalists—says that he has one major concern: How do we reverse current trends—to make democracy work in the mass media? One of Carey's worries is that he sees monopolies developing at the local level; there are monopoly systems in the print media (newspapers), cable television, and, increasingly, in radio, with a consequent narrowing of offerings. The press is being systematically sold off (with government approval) to the entertainment industry. We would not have tolerated this, he points out, when the major industries in question were steel, or automobile or chemical production. The fact that the public views Disney as a communications company— rather than a basic industry like oil—allows monopolistic sales and mergers to go forward with government approval.[33]

Carey argues that when the mass media is driven solely by the stock market and opportunity costs, news has no justification in the eyes of managers other than its contribution to overall corporate profits. How much sacrifice of the journalism component of AOL Time Warner was driven by the collapse of the AOL part of the company? CNN was sacrificed to the decline of AOL stock prices-prices that were over inflated at the time of the merger.

Reversing the Decline: The Critics Speak

What should be done? Let's look at some of the possibilities offered by the critics; then we will offer proposals of our own. Robert McChesney would apply anti-monopoly laws to the corporate media, and expand "the reach of those laws" to restrict ownership of radio stations to one or two per owner. He would break the hold that newspaper chains have on entire regions and initiate a federally funded study to identify a more "rational set of media-ownership regulations." He wants a broadcasting system without "commercial pressures" that would serve communities "without significant disposable incomes."[34]

Ben H. Bagdikian, a Pulitzer Prize winner and dean emeritus of the Graduate School of Journalism at Berkeley, would convene a nonpartisan, nongovernmental, noncorporate commission of citizens to study the present and future status of the country's news media. And he has put forth a host of other proposals based on years of study of "the media monopoly."[35] Bagdikian argues for inexpensive licensing of low-power, city- and neighborhood-range radio and TV stations. A majority of local townships are served by only one cable TV company, which means there is no competitive pressure to increase quality of programming and community service or to maintain reasonable cable rates; as a counterweight he recommends a "community-wide voter approval of monopoly franchise renewal."

Bagdikian would revive the National News Council, which existed from 1973 to 1984. The council, supported by foundations, used to hear serious complaints about specific cases of national news media performance. Its public recommendations were not mandatory, but the council provided the public with "a voice" and alerted the news media about weakness and abuse. It would be required that all of the council's recommendations be announced in the broadcast news media or printed in the newspapers and magazines in question.[36]

Bagdikian believes that public broadcasting should be financed through a "nonpolitical system." Today, even "noncommercial broadcasting," he says, depends on appropriations by federal and state legislatures that are heavily beholden to government and corporate interests. The new system could be funded by a small surtax on all consumer electronic equipment—computers, VCRs, TV sets, radios, and the like. It would be "miniscule" at the individual retail level but could provide enough revenue to fund a full-fledged multi-channel radio and TV noncommercial system, and a substantial national broadcast news and documentary operation as well.

To reverse the increasing commercialization of the Public Broadcasting Service, designed as a bastion against business interests, Citizens for Public Broadcasting (CIPB) believes that PBS should be restructured as an independently funded public trust. CIPB argues that this would remove corporate advertising, stop the desperate search for money, and free public broadcasting to pursue its original mission with editorial integrity.[37]

The new (proposed) Public Board of Trustees (PBT) would be insulated from direct political pressure. It would have nine members: three representatives from the public broadcasting community, three from the educational community, and two from the President's Commission on the Arts and Humanities. The PBT managing director would be the ninth board member, selected by the original eight. All members would serve staggered six-year terms. Participants in the nominating process would include representatives of public television and radio stations, independent producers, and associations for school administrators, teachers, academics, librarians, and school boards.

Finally, critics agree that "media literacy" should be taught in public schools. The average American child spends more time in front of a TV set than in front of a teacher. The young are targets for commercials and business-oriented programming. They need to know how the media influence their lives and how to analyze its advertising, commercial programming, and news presentations.

A Modest Proposal and a Vision for the Future

How could concerned citizens create a public domain inside the private media? Again, for the purposes of this discussion we'll focus on telecommunications, the ideas here are relevant to other media as well.

The Establishment of a Civil Commission

Let's imagine that the US government appoints a civil commission to examine the future of telecommunications. This Civil Commission on Telecommunications (CCT, for short) would be different. It would include representatives from business, government, and the Third Sector and be mandated to investigate how all sectors (i.e., civil society) could be involved in the ownership and management of the airspace that ultimately belongs to all of them.

Our proposed commission would look first into American history to see how mass media have functioned in all sectors—nonprofit, government, and business. During the early twentieth century, they would discover, nonprofit groups in the United States controlled almost one-third of the broadcast stations, and for decades, the Third Sector and business were complementary. Nonprofit broadcasting developed as a "public service" and business developed commercial broadcasting with "popular programs." Then gradually, and with government support, the business sector began to gain more control over radio and television stations and networks as they emerged, developed, consolidated.

Now let's say that the commissioners remember their history and their mandate to work for the common good; as they consider the possibilities of the new technologies just now being developed, they decide that broadband communication might be a basis for rebuilding a public domain. The commissioners read the literature on the innovations that many predict this particular technology will make possible, and come to believe it could allow them to change this market sector radically.[38]

The CCT anticipates that this telecommunications technology will transform the Internet and the World Wide Web to include a network of "stations" providing programming of all kinds. People will then be able to navigate through television "airspace" like they use search engines on their computers. Furthermore, the cost of becoming part of the mass media, rather than just a consumer, could become the same as the cost of building a web page—very little. Every organization would have an opportunity to compete on fairly equal grounds; each could decide how it wanted to provide up-to-date news reports, commentaries, films, dramas, documentaries, and panel debates.

Members of our civil commission are now free to think about how all sectors of society could have public (equal) access to "the airwaves" in a new context, one that looks at existing structures as well as new technologies. Assuming that they want to give people a greater diversity of views and provide for more competition from all three sectors they represent—business, government, and Third Sector—their next task would then be to decide how these sectors could be organized together to offer, in particular, a diverse and balanced outlook at the news at all levels from local to global.[39]

Mandating Public Standards

Markets tend to move from one extreme to another, from mutually destructive competition to monopoly. Every market needs some regulation to be reliable and it needs public standards to be trusted. The CCT would proceed to examine how the federal government could help develop a public (self-governing) system to regulate the new media realm. The government in the past has demanded fairness, democracy, and transparency in markets. If our commissioners were to place this outlook in their first public report, its basics might look something like those set forth in Box 7.2.

The commission's legal arguments would be debated in law schools and schools of management; in the meantime, they extend their inquiry.

Box 7.2 The Commission's Report on Market Standards

The Government Requires Public Standards for Media Markets

The federal government has always required public standards for markets. We find that fairness, democracy, and transparency should be translated into standards for the mass media. We note below how the Justice Department and US courts apply this reasoning.[40]

Standards of Fairness

In separate one-count felony charges filed on October 5, 2000, in the US District Court in Manhattan, Sotheby's auction house and its former CEO were charged with participating in a conspiracy lasting more than six years.[41] The government issues penalties against corporations that do not engage in fair competition. This standard should be applied to the mass media.[42]

Standards of Democracy

A trade association is deemed a monopoly or oligopoly if its members are "vertically or horizontally integrated." Vertical integration is created when members control an entire buying and selling process, say, from production to retail. Horizontal integration is created when firms collude in one trade area.[43] The courts and government agencies require trade associations to practice democracy. Trade associations must be organized with equal voting rights, equal membership rights, and proper due process for settling differences. In effect they charter themselves to be democratic with self-enforcement procedures. If "due process" procedures are not followed, the government takes action.

Federal agencies judge the extent to which a trade association represents its members in an "evenhanded and impartial manner."

Box 7.2 continues

Box 7.2 continued

The US government requires trade associations to integrate the values of democracy (e.g., equity) and justice (e.g., fairness) with market freedom. The court demands that a trade association reduce "the possibility that it can be controlled by a small group of members." The court can forbid any group of member corporations to use a trade association to violate antitrust laws. Any dominance by a small group of corporate members is illegal. Indeed, corporate lawyers advise business firms on how they can avoid any sign of monopoly by following these two principles: appoint an executive director who is not an employee of any member, and provide equal opportunity for all members to have one vote per member, instead of weighted votes based on assets or sales; and provide election of the board of directors by members that involves, selection by the board of an elected to the board of directors and to serve on nominating committees.[44]

Standards of Equity

The federal government requires that members of trade associations make their decisions on a "fair and equal" basis to "prevent commercially interested voters from having a disproportionate voice" in decision-making.[45] The law also requires trade associations to follow procedures to prevent "packing a meeting" with inappropriate voters. Voters should be held to a "realistic level of relevant expertise." Associations must make sufficient knowledge available to members on the issues they decide upon as a body. Trade groups must be democratic associations. [46]

In case of doubt, the government can require trade associations to show evidence of "equal voting rights for members." It can demand that associations have "proper judicial proceedings." Private judicial proceedings involve "reasonable notice of charges by complainants, proper notice of a hearing, the right to confrontation and cross-examination, and the opportunity to refute charges, by means of an unbiased tribunal."[47]

When a federal court determines that corporations have violated the law, it is empowered to "fashion appropriate restraints on the defendants' future activities both to avoid a recurrence of the violation and to eliminate its consequences." A court may enter such orders and decrees "as are necessary and appropriate to assure compliance with the antitrust laws." In addition, the court can give "adequate relief" to stakeholders. The court will "remove impediments to the restoration of competitive conditions in the affected

Box 7.2 continues

Box 7.2 continued

market and prohibit conduct that might cause a recurrence of defendants' unlawful behavior." In effect, courts can use discretion to promote fair competition, honest conduct, and democracy. Judges are advised to model their decisions " to fit the exigencies of the particular case." These high principles should now be applied to trade associations in the media industry.[48]

Standards of Transparency

The US government requires transparency and openness in all market transactions. But questions of "how much?" and "where?" remain. The financial scandals of the 1980s with inside traders are well known, and the issue of transparency in business has become more significant since the revelations about accounting problems at Enron, WorldCom, and other corporations. The government must establish new rules on transparency.[49]

Global corporations in the mass media are subject to the Foreign Corrupt Practices Act of 1977, which imposes a standard of transparency on American business overseas. The act requires business to establish a "paper trail" to make it possible to detect secret and illicit payments to foreign government officials. But transparency should go further in building a public domain for the media because mass media organizations do business around the world.[50]

Intergovernmental agencies should set these global standards. The issues of transparency concern the relationship between markets and the development of democratic institutions in all nations. A civil system of global markets will require transparency for corporations that link with authoritarian regimes. Transparency in the media is not separate from politics. The Commission concludes that a system of global media cannot co-exist with governments that control public discourse. Intergovernmental agencies must set those standards for global media markets.[51]

A Public Discussion: Peril and Promise

Our CCT commissioners would call for nationwide debate on how a public (self-governing) media domain could be created. Seeking broad citizen involvement, they would conduct public hearings on key questions they would set forth in their second public report, noted in Box 7.3.

Citizens ask many different questions at public hearings. Should "popularity" be the main basis for selecting programs? That is, should all media

---

Box 7.3. The American Public Media: Questions for Debate

(1) *Public Purpose:* What is the purpose of telecommunications? Could it become self-regulating? Could it be organized in the public interest and for the common good?

(2) *A Public Media:* Could a nonprofit public corporation be organized? If so, how would the governing board be selected?

(3) *Major Organizations:* What organizations in society should be represented on this public corporation? Should representatives come from the field of business, government, and labor, and include youth, elder citizens, women, and members of public interest groups, the professions, and religious life?[52]

(4) *Legal Status:* Could the media in America be a combination of profit, nonprofit corporations, and government? Or should all media corporations be chartered under Section 501 (c)(3) of the Internal Revenue Service (IRS) Code? Should media corporations retain business holdings? Should media corporations not be allowed to lobby and influence legislation? Should corporations and their trade associations not be allowed give money in political campaigns? Should the media be chartered so that no part of net earnings accumulates to the benefit of private individuals?

---

stations be judged by a popular "rating" system? To what extent should the government control the media on issues of obscenity and national security?

The commissioners will have models in other countries to examine. In Germany, for example, an independent Broadcasting Council (*Rundfunkrat*) governs all broadcasting corporations. Its representatives are intended to reflect the "socially relevant groups of society, according to a Federal Constitutional Court's ruling." These delegates are elected from major organizations in society, including *political parties, business associations, labor organizations, religious organizations, farmer associations, sports federations, women's organizations, youth organizations, cultural organizations,* and more. In effect, the whole of society (not business alone) is represented. Any complaints against the public service broadcasting are heard judiciously before local "broadcast councils."[53]

To adapt such a model to this country, the CCT could ask the presidents of major American associations in civil orders (education, religion, science, professions, etc.) if they would appoint representatives to a new public corporation. This would be the core of a proposal to Congress on how a public domain could be organized in the media sector—a proposal that offers a portrait of what could be done, leaving details for Congress to work out, but just enough "particulars" to start political leaders thinking about how to develop it.[54]

A Civil Market Model for the Media

What follows is a vision of how a new structure for the media might evolve, one that involves the establishment of a new public corporation to represent "society" and the supervision of the public media domain by voluntary associations as well as government. To avoid verbal gymnastics in describing how this model might be translated into reality, we'll speak about it here in the present tense.

The Creation of a Public Domain Board for the Media

To begin with, the commission suggests that Congress approve a Public Domain Board (PDB), whose members will be stakeholder representatives chosen from three sectors of the economy—business, government, and the Third Sector.

The PDB is a voluntary (nonprofit) federation, not a government. It does not regulate the media, which, in the final analysis, is the job of government. The constitution of the PDB states that it should operate for the common good and by legal terms "in the public interest." The PDB board staff coordinates the efforts of leaders in this new media organization.[55] The commission summarizes its proposal to Congress (see Box 7.4) and spends time explaining to the public how it would work.

In this proposal, all three sectors of society (government, business, and Third Sector) have representatives on the Public Domain Board, which coordinates their work. Each sector has its own board of trustees that serve in both a management and an advisory capacity. Media associations like the National Association of Broadcasters (NAB) and major media corporations appoint their own members to the Business Sector Board. Agencies in the US government (like the Environmental Protection Agency and Department of Justice) have their own board of directors; the president appoints the government sector's board chair. And the Third Sector has its representatives appointed by presidents of major associations who together elect their own chair.

Each "sector board" manages the media activities of its own broadcasters and stations. These boards have no powers of law over individual

---

Box 7.4. Civil Governance in Broadcasting

The Public Domain Board
(Representatives Chosen from the Three Sectors)

Third Sector

Civic Board: NGO representatives, e.g., major associations in religion, education, family, professions, science, art, and special interest groups (e.g., ethnic/gender/racial groups) and corporations for public broadcasting.[56]

Business Sector

Trade Board: trade association representatives,e.g., the National association of Broadcasters (NAB).

Government Sector

Government Board: e.g., government agency representatives with the chair appointed by the president, approved by Congress

---

members in this voluntary media system. They have only the power given to them by the legal contracts of their nonprofit corporations. Each sector elects its own board and its bylaws outline the delegation of authority. As mentioned, in the case of the federal government, the president appoints representatives of major agencies and the chair. The Civic Board has the authority to admit or reject members based on the status of their media stations; to be included in this Third Sector set of media stations, an organization must be judged by the board to be part the "independent sector,"(i.e., not funded by government or business).

The commission points out to Congress that this PDB governing system is a confederation, organized like the US Chamber of Commerce and the National Council of Churches—that is, its main powers derive from the bottom levels of organization. It follows the principle of subsidiarity. In other words, the Public Domain Board outlined in Box 7.4 has no legal ground to demand that any media station alter its schedule, modify its style, or eliminate content from its programming. It serves only as a public advisor, coordinator, and manager of administrative details. It has influence but no legal power to stop any broadcasting or alter the policies of any station.

The PDB is strong by virtue of the collective power of its constituencies, and it is legitimate by its democratic authority and especially by the electoral process in the voluntary sector. The board recognizes that part of the media's role in society is to entertain as well as to inform, but it is also designed to represent the core values of society, organized for the common good.[57] Now the commission must explain how such a system can be funded.

Sources of Income

In our theoretical scenario, Third Sector non-governmental organizations or NGOs have said in earlier public hearings that they do not have the cash to produce high quality news broadcasts, and they do not have the "liquid assets" to invest in "high quality programs to command a national audience" or to negotiate with Hollywood firms and directors to provide great drama. They could not match the technical quality of programs offered on business stations. So how can they participate in this scheme?

Our commissioners have studied the Public Broadcasting System and observed how it developed in the private sector as a nonprofit corporation. Whatever justifiable complaints its critics may lodge, today PBS provides TV programming to 349 noncommercial stations serving all fifty states, Puerto Rico, the US Virgin Islands, Guam, and American Samoa. It manages program acquisition, distribution, and promotion; education services; new media ventures; fundraising support; engineering and technology development; and video marketing. Its members include 171 noncommercial, educational licensees that operate 349 PBS member stations. Of the 171 licensees, 88 are community organizations, 56 are colleges/universities, 20 are state authorities, and seven are local educational or municipal authorities. It has developed important and innovative (and expensive) programs like *Frontline, Nova,* and *NOW with Bill Moyers.*

PBS has also developed close ties with the field of education. It has a Ready to Learn Service that provides educational and entertaining children's programming. It has an "outreach" to local communities with workshops and learning resources to aid parents and childcare providers to prepare young children to enter school. It has an Adult Learning Service that involves a partnership with colleges. It provides college-credit TV courses to "nearly 500,000 students each academic year," and has become a top television resource for classroom programming. It features topics on art, education, history, nature, news, public affairs, and science. It moves on the frontier of online programming. PBS Online (PBS.org) produces web programming and pioneers the convergence of television and the Internet.[58] Again, while PBS may be increasingly vulnerable to the influence of the corporate (private) sector (in news coverage and program choices), it has shown that a nonprofit corporation can do good programming.

The commissioners have also studied PBS's funding sources. Its revenue (national, regional and local) in 1999 was $1.6 billion. Its leading sources of revenue: members (23.5%), state governments (17.1%), the Corporation for Public Broadcasting and federal grants/contracts (14.8%), businesses (14.3%), state colleges and universities (6.1%), and foundations (6.1%). In addition, 4.7 million individuals and families contributed $373 million to public TV in 1999.

Our Civil Commission on Telecommunications now suggests that Congress consider options for funding the new PDB system. The "public domain" should have multiple revenue-making capacities. Third Sector organizations had told the commission in public hearings that they would invite businesses to advertise on their sites, according to their values. They would use social screens to influence advertisers to follow their goals and value orientation. All the ideas given to the commission from the Third Sector are placed in a third public report for congressional review, a portion of which is summarized in Box 7.5.

Box 7.5. Sources of Income for the PDB

Income for Third Sector Media Corporations

> (1) *Gifts:* The constituencies of Third Sector organizations (bandwidth listeners/viewers/readers) make voluntary contributions to finance their nonprofit media corporations.
>
> (2) *Endowment:* Special constituencies in Third Sector organizations (e.g., faculties, parishioners, lawyers, dentists, accountants, scientists, etc.) help build an endowment for their media corporation.
>
> (3) *Advertisers:* Advertisers are selected according the principles of the respective Third Sector organization, as in science, medicine, history, therapy, law, religious, and recreational organizations. NGOs would compete for the best-screened advertisers.
>
>   For example, in the field of education, state and local boards select only advertisements that meet their standards as "healthy" and "safe" for children. Teacher associations and unions assess "screening" for nutritious foods and reliable toys. Nonprofit organizations contract with professional social investors to make the selection based on their expert knowledge.[59]
>
> (4) *Taxes, benefits, and subsidies:* The government gives additional support to this part of the "public domain" through tax arrangements deemed appropriate.

On Point 4—taxes, benefits, and subsidies—the commission reminds Congress about previous recommendations for funding a public broadcasting system. In 1967, the Carnegie Commission advocated a federal trust fund based on a manufacturer's *excise tax* on the sale of television sets. The Communications Act of 1978 proposed that commercial television *spectrum fees* should support public broadcasting. The Communications Transfer Fee Act of 1987 called for the creation of a Public Broadcasting Trust Fund, to be financed by a 2% tax on the *sale price* (to be paid by the seller) *of the transfer of radio and television licenses.* The following year, the Working Group for Public Broadcasting advocated a *factory tax* of 2% on sales of consumer electronic products and broadcast equipment. In 1993, the Twentieth Century Fund called again for independent funding for public broadcasting based on a share of spectrum auctions or spectrum usage fees.[60]

The Civil Commission on Telecommunications recommends that Congress should revive these proposals for fees and taxes, and choose those among them that favor self-regulation. The government should plan for the Third Sector wing (Civic Board) of the PDB to be independently financed and locally organized with ties to the national network. It should favor financial disclosure for all media corporations. It should encourage civic engagement in local-to-regional and national programming.[61]

Civil Media

Today business controls the mass media, but in this PDB model, representatives of both the Third Sector and the government would have equal influence. Each of these three sectors would have a voice in shaping the media according to its own interests, but the Public Domain Board would debate and attempt to balance those special interests for the common good.

For example, Third Sector representatives would "socially screen" advertising in their own realm. If advertisers want to reach an audience of children by sponsoring a TV program to be used in public schools, they could be required to first prove that the goods they are marketing are wholesome and safe. The Civic Board could insist that they follow the standards set by school boards, families, teachers, and professionals, thus putting the core values of education—not profit alone—in the driver's seat.

If the American Medical Association (AMA) opened a public media station, for instance, it could choose to screen advertisers on the basis of public health values. If the AMA station drew a large audience because of its attractive programming—panel discussions, news stories, and dramas focusing on issues of personal and public health—outside advertisers would compete to meet AMA standards and the core values of the AMA on health would have an influence on business decisions.

In this scheme, Third Sector organizations would have a stronger influence over business even as the private sector retained its own for-profit stations. Of course, not everything that a given Third Sector organization supports is good for the nation. But all organizations that conflict with the AMA, for instance (e.g., chiropractic associations, alternative medicine organizations, public interest groups, and insurance associations), would be free to establish their own stations in the new media marketplace, to tell their own stories. Notice how this becomes a competition for core values more than for profits. Money is still a big factor, but the structure has changed those priorities.

Will Third Sector organizations participate? There are precedents in the media business. *The Christian Science Monitor,* for example, is a daily newspaper published by the First Church of Christ, Scientist, in Boston. It reaches a wide audience nationally and internationally with its print and electronic editions. When she established the Monitor in 1908, the church's founder, Mary Baker Eddy, said she wanted to have an influence on the way the media present the news. The paper's motto is "to injure no man, but to bless all mankind," and while religious principles influence its editors, its supporters—including many outside the church—argue that the *Monitor* holds to high journalistic standards and has had a positive, leavening effect in "an age of corporate conglomerates dominating news media."[62]

In our market model, national religious organizations (churches, temples, mosques and synagogues) would be free to set forth their priorities and values. The same would be true for other Third Sector organizations. A media station established by the American Bar Association, for example, might focus on the values of law, justice, impartiality, and fair play in its station programming. Stations might be established by scientific and learned societies of chemists, biologists, and historians to inform the public about their fields and promote the values of scientific validity, objectivity, and historical accuracy. Associations of artists would focus on aesthetic values.

The development of Third Sector media, under the umbrella of the PDB and its Civic Board, could lead to competition between core religious, social, and cultural values. What is deemed good (aesthetically valid) on an arts channel might be quite different from what would be deemed good (objective or provable) on a science channel. What is seen as good by religious organizations may conflict with what's "good for business." And so on. But this is a civil market model, and I would argue that public debate about values and priorities is a good thing for civil society.

In this model, as Third Sector stations and media networks evolve, standards would be set at the discretion of the organizations that found and maintain them. These stations would screen advertisers (if they wish) according to their principal values (e.g., honesty, integrity, decency, health, and safety).

Finally, Third Sector associations would provide a counterweight to the influence of business interests alone defining the media. They would do so as competitors with their own media outlets, as partners in the standard-setting process, and as providers of potential venues for advertising.

Conclusion

For geologists, fault lines are studied as places where portions of the earth's crust rub against each other and earthquakes happen. For social scientists, fault lines are more abstract—places where values collide and social disasters can happen. Today the major fault line in society runs between the paramount values held by citizens and the political economy of markets and states. This is where high ideals like democracy and justice might fail if overwhelmed by business values such as the pursuit of profit.

In the eighteenth century, Thomas Jefferson wrote that if a "government" loses its core values, the people should overthrow it; if democracy fails to sustain itself, a revolution is legitimate. In the nineteenth century, Karl Marx saw that a fault line existed between the culture of modern society (i.e., democracy, freedom, equality, justice, and truth) and the culture of capitalist markets. And in the twentieth century, Aleksandr Solzhenitsyn argued that the press, having become the greatest power in the Western World, was more powerful than government.[63]

We have suggested that this need not be so, and proposed that the federal government should appoint a civil commission to study the problem of media governance and make recommendations to Congress. The commission would examine how a new public domain could be organized to bring civil society values into a self-regulating media. In this realm the government should be a "preventive state," acting directly only when a problem becomes too big to handle.

Leaders in all three sectors—nonprofit, for-profit, and government—have views on what is "significant" in the news and what is "entertainment." The media market should be a space where problems in the nation are debated and dissent is safe. It should be a place where citizens can argue and have a "public conversation," just as citizens did, according to history, in the agoras, the market squares of ancient Greece. The creation of a public media system will entail a struggle between leaders in government, business, and the Third Sector. And the struggle would be worth it, if it led to a media system that represents society, not business or government alone.

Notes

1. Critics say that big corporations govern the airspace without proper representation from the people who are indoctrinated and "programmed."For this outlook, see the Center for Cognitive Liberty and Ethics, http://www.alchemind.org/issues/mass_media_index.htm.

2. The assertion that the media do not represent the core values of society is argued by many writers and past studies. Here are some examples of research: W. E. Adam and F. Schreibman, *Television Network News: Issues in Content Research* (Washington, D.C.: George Washington University Press, 1978); D. L. Altheide, *Media Power* (Beverly Hills, California: Sage, 1985); A. N. Crigler, ed., *The Psychology of Political Communication* (Ann Arbor, Michigan: University of Michigan Press, 1996); Elfriede Fürsich and Eli P. Lester Roushanzamir, "Corporate Expansion, Textual Expansion: Commodification Model of Communication, *Journal of Communications Inquiry* 25, no. 4 (October 2001), 375–395.

3. *NOW* with Bill Moyers, Facts and Figures, http://www.pbs.org/now/politics/media.html, 1/31/04

4. Bill Moyers reported this information on *NOW, October 10, 2003.* http://www.pbs.org/now/politics/localmedia.html.

5. Robert W. McChesney, *Rich Media, Poor Democracy* (New York: The New Press, 1999); see the author's "Conclusion."

6. Timothy J. Mullany and Ronald Gover, "The Web Mogul," *BusinessWeek,* 13 October 2003, 62.

7. The deal means that GE will own 80% and Vivendi will retain 20% of the newly merged entity, with the option to sell its stake at fair market prices beginning in 2006. Owen Gibson, "Vivendi Finalises NBC Universal Deal," *The Guardian,* 8 October 2003, http://media.guardian.co.uk/vivendi/story/0,11919,1058493,00.html. For an update on the ownership structure of all media companies, see *Columbia Journalism Review,* http://www.cjr.org/ tools/owners.

8. With such a diverse portfolio of properties, Viacom is one of the most profitable media giants. CBS is a top draw for older viewers while MTV remains the most popular "teen oriented" media outlet. *Columbia Journalism Review,* http://www.cjr.org/tools/owners/viacom.asp. 1/31/04.

9. For more on this standpoint, see Robert McChesney, "Making Media Democratic," *Boston Review,* Summer, 1998, http://www.bostonreview.net/BR23.3/mcchesney.html. TV journalist Bill Moyers says that the big media companies keep getting bigger, and gain more and more power over American culture, politics, and news reporting. The deal between General Electric and Vivendi means in effect that GE's NBC picked up not only Universal Studios but also the nationwide newspaper *USA,* to go with its news networks CNBC and MSNBC, plus the Trio and Sci-Fi cable channels.

10. For more, see Our Media Voice, http://www.ourmediavoice.org.

11. McChesney, *Rich Media, Poor Democracy.*

12. See Center for Public Integrity, John Dunbar, "Broadcast Industry Defeats Shays-Meehan Bill," 18 July 2002, available at http://www.publicintegrity.org/dtaweb/report.asp?ReportID=7&L1=10&L2=10&L3=0&L4=0&L5=0.

13. These figures were prepared by Competitive Media Research and the Television Bureau of Advertising, a not-for-profit trade association of the broadcast television industry.

14. See Our Media Voice, http://www.ourmediavoice.org/article_movement.html.

15. For a longer list of alternative news websites, see the list I posted on www. alternative-views.org. under the green button "Alternative News Sites."

16. FAIR believes that "structural reform" is needed to break up the dominant media conglomerates, establish independent public broadcasting, and promote strong nonprofit sources of information. See FAIR, http://www.fair.org/whats-fair.html#mission.

17. News releases from the Institute for Public Accuracy provide documentation and analysis of fast-breaking events that involve major public issues. See the institute's website, http://www.accuracy.org/index.htm

18. The MEF argues that global mergers involving media giants and multinational corporations have threatened the public sphere. These giants hold a monopoly on airwaves, television, the movie industry, print journalism, and the Internet. The voice of the citizen is driven out of the public domain by the "colonization of public space, from schools to ball fields, by an all-pervasive commercialism that bombards us with thousands of advertising images daily." See http://mediaed.sitepassport.net/about.

19. See http://www.mediachannel.org/about. Or contact MediaChannel, 1600 Broadway, Suite 700, New York, NY 10019.

20. See CPIB, http://www.cipbonline.org/video/cipbcut_dsl_300.ram.

21. Citizen Works; see http://www.citizenworks.org.

22. See People for Better TV, http://www.bettertv.org/about.html. Protestors ask, "Why is the press the only business granted explicit constitutional protection?" (There is no clause in the constitution saying that Congress shall make no law abridging the freedom of shoe manufacturers.) The press is accorded a special place because it is a domain that partakes of a public interest. This view is implicit in the US Constitution and affirmed in Supreme Court decisions. In 1971, for instance, in the famous Pentagon Papers case, Justice Hugo Black wrote the majority opinion for the Court, which defended a newspaper's First Amendment (free speech) right to publish material that the government would rather had been kept secret. Today many grassroots organizers say that this First Amendment right has been converted from a political right to an economic one, that the first duty of the press is no longer to form and sustain a political community but to guarantee a protected economic environment in which media corporations can pursue their goals of maximizing profit. And the latter does not lead automatically to the former.

23. See Commercial Alert, https://www.egrants.org/donate/index.cfm?ID=2404-0| 1236-0.

24. CDD has broad goals: (1) to enhance public understanding of the changing dimensions of the US digital media system by "explaining the communications options and the public-interest resources that citizens should have at their disposal"; (2) "to foster the development of a new generation of activists to work on digital media policy issues"; and (3) "to make the media industry more accountable to the public." See CDD's website at http://www.democraticmedia.org.

25. Today IPA's membership includes large-circulation magazines, desktop-published "'zines,"and alternative newsweeklies, monthlies, quarterlies, annuals, and publications serving African-American, Asian, Latino, and working-class communities. See IPA at http://www.indypress.org/programs/index.html.

26. On MAP, see http://www.mediaaccess.org. The study of the "free press" has a long history. To look at the problem of government control and censorship in English-speaking countries, see Ralph E. McCoy, *Freedom of the Press* (Carbondale, Illinois: Southern Illinois University, 1993).

27. MoveOn.org argues that noncommercial TV and radio outlets are supposed to be insulated from the "inordinate power of money." But across the country, each year "public broadcasting"relies on hundreds of millions of dollars from corporations that provide underwriting to burnish their images to upscale listeners. Corporate donors exert hefty influence on programs by "underwriting"—and, in some cases, literally "making possible"—specific shows. "Private money is a big determinant of what's on'public' broadcasting."Susan Thompson, susan.thompson@moveon.org Media Concentration 7 Nov 2002 Moveon.org, http://www.moveon.org.

28. Edward S. Herman, "Word Tricks & Propaganda," *Z Magazine,* June 1997, http://zena.secureforum.com/Znet/zmag/zarticle.cfm?Url=articles/june97herman.htm. Note the findings of a two-week study done by FAIR (1/30/03-2/12/03) of on-camera network news sources quoted on Iraq. FAIR, "In Iraq Crisis, Networks Are Megaphones for Official Views," 18 March 2003, http://www.fair.org/reports/iraq-sources.html.

29. Citizen Works organizes monthly meetings of leaders among citizen organizations—from PIRG to Transafrica to the Democracy Action Project. These meetings provide a space for citizen leaders to share ideas, campaigns, and strategies. Grassroots organizations want business advertisers out of public schools and classrooms. They would prohibit fast-food promotions. MediaSpace, http://www.mediaspace.org/index.html.

30. John Stant and Wayne Madsen, "Champions of Profit, Propaganda, and Puffery,"in Counterpunch, http://www.counterpunch.org/madsen0425.html.

31. Paul Taylor, "Cornering the Airwaves," *The American Prospect,* 9 April 2001, 16.

32. "Neil Hickey Interviews Neil," *Columbia Journalism Review,* May/June 2002, and "Media Monopoly Behind the Mergers: Q&A," see http://www.cjr.org/year/02/3/hickey.asp.

33. Carey argues that in fact the charge of monopoly at the national level is not so sustainable as it is at the local level. For example, around 1980 there were three television networks (excluding the public one), one telephone company, national and local, one major computer firm (IBM), and one mobile phone company, Motorola. There are now many more such companies. Therefore, the argument has to be less about economic oligopoly than about political oligarchy: the concentration of political power given the size of the dominant firms and the role of trade associations. In his view, the existing antitrust laws should be used to break up entertainment conglomerates; otherwise, the government could insist that if a company (e.g., GE, Disney) owns news operations, the corporation as a whole would fall under a strict regime of government regulation. This policy, he suggests, would "end the mergers soon

enough." It is not so much that such conglomerates determine public opinion as that business (as a whole) in cooperation with the party in power "silences public opinion or renders such opinion ineffective." These notes are drawn from my correspondence with James Carey in March 2003. Carey has been a board member of the Public Broadcasting System and published numerous books, among them, *Television and the Press* (1988) and *Communication as Culture* (1989).)

34. McChesney would allow a $200 tax credit for any nonprofit media company and lower mailing costs for nonprofit and noncommercial publications. He would eliminate political-candidate advertising as a condition of a broadcast license and cut back TV advertising directed at children under twelve. He would grant journalists on local TV stations an hour daily of commercial-free news time, thus "decommercializing" local news.

35. Ben Bagdikian, *The Media Monopoly*, fifth edition (Boston: Beacon Press, 1997). When this book was first published in 1983, 50 corporations owned most of American media; in this update of his book, Bagdikian says that by 1997, 10 corporations controlled virtually everything we see, hear, and read. This has led to loss of depth and quality in the news and limitation of subjects addressed on the national agenda. See http://www.ourmediavoice.org/article_reform.html. Bagdikian argues that paid political advertising should be banned from American broadcasting. In the two months before elections, every station should be required to provide prime-time hours for local and national candidates, with fifteen-minute minimums to avoid slick sound bites without content.

36. Bagdikian believes that the Telecommunications Act of 1996 should be replaced with a new law that could be used break up the most "egregious conglomerates" and reinstate mandatory local community access. The government should put teeth into the requirement that stations demonstrate their record of public interest programming when they apply for renewals of their licenses. He feels that "license challenge procedures" must be made more accessible to civic groups that are dissatisfied with their local radio and TV broadcast stations. Ibid.

37. PBS was created in 1967 not to sell products but to "enhance citizenship and public service." The Carnegie Commission on Educational Television proposed a system "free of commercial constraints" that would serve as "a forum for debate and controversy." It should provide a "voice for groups in the community that may otherwise go unheard" so that we could "see America whole, in all its diversity." But the Federal Communications Commission has given PBS permission for public broadcasters to commercialize new digital channels. For more on this issue, see Citizens for Independent Public Broadcasting, http://www.cipbonline.org/trustMain.htm.

38. George Gilder predicts that the frontier is wave division multiplexing (WDM), a technique for sending many different colors of light down a hair-thin fiber optic thread that will radically change this sector. Gilder argues that this thread will increase the capacity of world communications systems by "a million-fold." George Gilder, *Telecosm* (New York: The Free Press, 2000), 4.

39. The task of a US civil commission would be to assess how both business and Third Sector organizations could compete and learn from one another. "A Report of the Committee on the Future Funding of the BBC" (known as the Davies report) argues that digital technology creates strong pressures for government participation in the mass media, like the BBC. See "A Communications White Paper at the BBC," at http://www.communicationswhitepaper. gov.uk/by_chapter/ch5/5_3.htm.

40. The Clayton and Sherman Acts are the basis for the government to "restructure" an industry. See McChesney, *Rich Media, Poor Democracy.*

41. For an example of fair competition, see "Former Chief of Sotheby's Gets No Jail Time for Price Fixing," *New York Times,* 29 April 2002; Ralph Blumenthal and Carol Vogel, "Ex-Chief of Sotheby's Gets 3-Year Probation and Fine," ibid., 30 April 2002.

42. Government agencies, such as the Federal Trade Commission, set specific rules for fairness in market sectors. For example, see Public Notice, 1919 M Street, N.W., Washington, D.C. 20554, News Media Information.

43. For details on vertical/ horizontal integration, see Severyn T. Bruyn, *A Future for the American Economy* (Stanford, California: Stanford University Press, 1991).

44. The study of democratic and "juried" decision making in a trade association is relevant to studies of "market concentration." For example, the US Supreme Court held that a steel firm "unreasonably restrained trade" when it recruited new members to a "standards organization" on the eve of an important vote. See law partners Carter, Ledyard & Milburn, "Partners for Your Business", http://www.clm.com/partners.html.

45. For more legal details, see Bruyn, ibid.

46. See ibid., Chapter 8.

47. The Federal District Court system is invested with jurisdictional power to prevent and restrain violations of the Sherman Act, which was established to maintain the "public trust." The law says that a market cannot work without democratic trade associations. For more, see ibid., Part 3, 171ff.

48. My assessment here is based on court decisions, such as *Nat'l Society of Professional Engineers v. United States, Northern Securities Co. v. United States,* 193 US 197-, 344 (1904); *International Salt Co. v. United States,* 332 US 392, 400-01 (1947); 435 US 679, 697 (1978).

49. The need for transparency became notable during the Great Depression. The US Congress passed the Securities Exchange Act (1934) to require open transactions on the stock market. Today accounting regulators around the world are encouraging companies to identify their "transparency risks"—currency, political, and operational. This includes publishing cash-flow statements, the latest disclosure requirements enclosed in Statement of Accounting Standard (SAS) 23 Segmental Reporting, quarterly reporting, publishing uncertainty in profits of crucial importance in making investment decisions.

50. Even in market sectors where standards have become a custom, competitors still keep an eye on each other in their self-interest. Customers also watch market standards, and businesses in associated fields will monitor them. PriceWaterhouseCoopers has been a monitor for whole industries. See

"Global Oil Industry Overview 2000," by Michael Cooke and Don Kinnersley, The Petroleum Group, ABAS TICE Energy, London, PriceWaterhouseCoopers. But we are suggesting that monitors in the business sector alone are not wise: this is a task for the nonprofit sector as well. So "monitoring" should be done competitively in business and Third Sector markets. In the stock market and the mutual fund industry, independent firms monitor "performance." All expense and performance numbers are obtained from security and exchange filings. This includes Valueline, Morningstar, Wiesenberger, and Standard and Poor's, a field of competition that generates fair reliability. There are also separate reports by magazines, including *Money, BusinessWeek, Fortune, Barron's,* and *Smart Money.*

51. The World Bank has linked transparency and press freedom to a wider endorsement of freedom in civil society. Ann M. Florini, "Does the Invisible Hand Need a Transparent Glove? The Politics of Transparency," Annual World Bank Conference on Development Economics, Washington, D.C., 28-30 April 1999.

52. For an example on how a "society-wide" TV corporation was created in Germany, see Severyn T. Bruyn, *A Civil Economy* (Ann Arbor, Michigan: University of Michigan Press, 2000, 111.

53. In the commercial broadcasting media some of the large television programmers employ a commissioner for youth protection (*Jugendschutzbeauftragter*) that reports only to the company. The new Staatsvertrag proposes to establish informal councils of advisors to the licensed programmers. See the European Media Landscape, http://www.ejc.nl/jr/emland/germany.html#4. Also see The German Embassy http://www.germany-info.org/relaunch/index.html. My thanks on these references go to Elfriede F̈rsich, professor of communications at Boston College.

54. Media representation by members of "society" (not just business or government)) is critical here. James Carey of Columbia University, asks students, How is society possible? John Pauly speaks about Carey's teachings in his "Introduction/On the Origins of Media Studies and Media Scholars," in Eve Stryker Munson and Catherine A. Warren, eds., *James Carey: A Critical Reader* (Minneapolis, Minnesota: University of Minnesota Press, 1997), 3-4.

55. Media analysts believe that George Gilder's vision is far off in time. Other trends in the telecom industry have more immediate significance. Wireless networking, for example, is becoming a successful market. But in the technology of electromagnetic fields (George Gilder's "telecosm"), anyone will be able transmit any amount of information, any picture, any experience, at any moment. There will be an opportunity for anyone, at any time, instantaneously, to transmit information without significant barriers of convenience or cost.

56. The Corporation for Public Broadcasting (CPB) is a private, nonprofit corporation created by Congress in 1967. The CPB is not a business or a government agency. CPB invests in more than 1,000 local radio and television stations. The Public Broadcasting System (PBS), on the other hand, is a private nonprofit media enterprise owned and operated by member stations. It produces and distributes programs, funded by CPB and member stations. The Corporation for Public Broadcasting (CPB) is a private corporation created by the federal

government that does not produce or distribute programs. The federal government funds it.

57. The field of telecommunications is moving rapidly beyond the control of national governments. On the organization of media corporations in world markets, see http://www.mediaspace.org/MMI/mmi_frame.html.

58. PBS.org has more than 135,000 pages of content, including companion websites for more than 450 PBS programs. See Inside PBS, at http://www.pbs.org/insidepbs/facts/faq1.html, January 2002.

59. Members of the civic board that choose this option of selecting advertisers based on their ethical standards could hire professional investors for this purpose. Social investment is a technical process and is a profession. Peter D. Kinder, Steven Lydenberg, and Amy Domini, *The Social Investment Almanac* (New York: Henry Holt, 1992).

60. See the Carnegie Commission on Educational Television, *Public Television: A Program for Action* (New York: Bantam, 1967); the Working Group on Public Broadcasting, "Public Broadcasting: A National Asset to be Preserved, Promoted and Protected," John Wicklein, ed., December 1988; and The Twentieth Century Fund Task Force on Public Television, *Quality Time?* (New York: The Twentieth Century Fund Press, 1993). In 1998, Rep. Billy Tauzin (R-LA), the chair of the House Subcommittee on Telecommunications, proposed a spectrum fee on commercial broadcasters to fund public broadcasting. My thanks go to David Croteau and John Hoynes for these sources. See David Croteau and John Hoynes, *The Business of Media* (Thousand Oaks, California: Pine Forge Press, 2001), 228.

61. The government in this proposed model is a "competitor," an "intercessor," and a final arbiter in legal cases. Government agencies compete in this airspace along with business and the Third Sector.

62. See the *Christian Science Monitor,* http://www.csmonitor.com/aboutus/about_the_monitor.html.

63. The question is whether the mass media will gain as much power as government in the twenty-first century. Today's Jeffersonians have this concern as they refer to the mass media as a "private government." On these Jeffersonians, see the Institute for Free Speech and Media Law, Ellen K. Solendar, http://library.law.smu.edu/Free_Speech/, and the Thomas Jefferson Center for the Protection of Free Expression, http://www.tjcenter.org/about.html.

8

The Market Struggle
Who Are the Agents of Change?

Bringing civil society values back into the mass media is an enormous undertaking—one that will require the establishment of a whole new structure for the setting of public standards. It will require the entry of new players into the market, and the encouragement of real competition. But civil action can take place in other market realms as well.

In this chapter we will look at the efforts of grassroots groups and educational associations to create a system of public accountability in apparel manufacturing. We want to know how these efforts might be a change-agent model that could be extended to the industry as whole—and to other industrial sectors.

When associations in the Third Sector buy and sell in a market they influence the production of goods on the basis of their values, not just the values of business. Economists call this "consumer preference" and interpret it as a matter of individual choice. But when this choice is collective and applies to nonprofit associations in the Third Sector, the picture changes. To get a picture of how systems of public accountability can be developed by Third Sector associations, we need case studies.

Here is one story that is ongoing. In this chapter we will see firsthand how nongovernmental organizations demand that their core values be translated into enforceable standards in the market.

Higher Education and the Wearing Apparel Industry

Institutions of higher learning are in business when they buy and sell land. They are in business when they erect buildings, purchase vehicles, buy

191

furniture, advertise their programs, or set up cafeterias and restaurants. At each of these points, they are buyers with preferences that have the power to shape markets.

All Third Sector corporations have such an influence on the market. This includes nonprofit corporations in religion, the professions, sciences, the arts, and recreation, indeed, in every major field of civic activity in America. And Third Sector federations are intricately linked with business and trade interests at local, regional, and national levels. These federations are growing in the private sector like a silent republic.

What do we mean by federations? As an example, let's take a brief look at one federation in higher education. The Association of American Colleges and Universities (AAC&U) was started in 1915 by a group of presidents of liberal arts colleges. Today it is the leading national association devoted to advancing undergraduate liberal education. The members of the AAC&U represent a wide spectrum of American colleges and universities: large and small, public and private, two-year and four-year. There are more than seven hundred accredited member institutions, drawn in approximately equal percentages from research universities, master's degree institutions, and liberal arts colleges. The AAC&U supports "excellence" in the standard making process of higher education.[1] There are many federations in higher education and all of them have dealings with the business sector. As we shall see, some of them have gotten involved in the wearing apparel industry.

Issues and Actions

Our story opens when American clothing manufacturers began moving the production of their goods overseas to lower costs, writing business contracts stipulating that "hosts" in foreign countries where wages and labor standards were low would own and manage the factories.[2] An industry-wide crisis ensued when college and university students heard that "deplorable conditions" existed in these facilities and went overseas to see with their own eyes. The results of their firsthand investigations led to the formation of protest and activist groups that addressed the issue on campuses across the country.

As part of their campaign, the students and their allies complained publicly about the practices of companies such as the GAP in El Salvador, the producers of Kathie Lee Gifford apparel in Honduras, and Nike in Indonesia. And these campaigns had an effect. Members of Congress and the executive branch, including Robert Reich, then the secretary of labor, became involved. In this case the government functioned as a mediator, enabling civil development to happen. These government officials, by their actions, became legitimizers of this student movement, giving them credibility and public acceptability. In August of 1996, fearing the impact of this controversy on free trade, the Clinton administration established the White House Apparel Industry Partnership (AIP) to examine and resolve the problems the protestors had brought to light.

Meanwhile, the student campaign became more focused with the establishment in 1998 of United Students Against Sweatshops (USAS), an organization designed to coordinate the ongoing campaign nationwide. The USAS took an activist role with textile unions to work for better labor conditions. They put pressure on educational institutions to join the cause.

The college-licensed sector of the apparel market is a $2.5-billion industry annually. It makes up only about 2% of the American clothing business, but it is a high-profile sector involving global firms, and the publicity given to this campus campaign had implications for other corporations in the market as a whole.

In November 1998, the AIP created the Fair Labor Association (FLA), a task force designed to develop minimum standards to assure consumers (buyers) that henceforth the apparel they purchased would not be made in sweatshops. Among its tasks were to establish standards and a monitoring system. The original members of the AIP included business representatives from Liz Claiborne, Reebok, L.L. Bean, Nike, Patagonia, Phillips-Van Heusen, Wal-Mart, and also from Third Sector organizations. These Third Sector (non-business) groups included the National Consumers League, the Interfaith Council on Corporate Responsibility (ICCR), the RFK Memorial Center for Human Rights, Lawyers Committee for Human Rights (LCHR), and labor groups, including the Union of Needletrades, Industrial, and Textile Employees (UNITE), and the AFL-CIO. Seeking to function as a "public official" on standard making in their markets, the FLA then solicited the approval of universities, and more than a hundred schools signed up.

The profit versus nonprofit struggle began immediately. Soon after the FLA was established, nonprofit representatives decided that the new organization did not have adequate powers for clear standard making and monitoring. The differences were so strong that the AFL-CIO, UNITE, and ICCR pulled out, saying, among other things, that the FLA did not represent the "collective buyers" of apparel in higher education.

As these events unfolded, it was disclosed publicly that businesses accused of organizing sweatshops had funded three of the four Third Sector nonprofits on the board of the FLA, which implied a conflict of interest. Nike, Gap, and Reebok, for example, had donated to the Lawyers Committee for Human Rights (LCHR) and the RFK Memorial (RFK). In the case of LCHR, there was a specific increase in donations from the apparel industry companies after the formation of the Apparel Industry Partnership. Furthermore, the board of directors of the RFK Memorial and

LCHR included directors that allegedly had ties to sweatshop and other special interests. The National Consumers League, also on the board of the FLA, had received funding from garment manufacturer Liz Claiborne. Moreover, the coalition had been organized with the support of the textile unions but without the support of larger federated unions and religious organizations. This left the International Labor Rights Fund (ILRF) as the only nonprofit that appeared properly independent of the (sweatshop) companies.

In April of 1999, the United Students Against Sweatshops, now represented on a hundred campuses, urged the universities to quit the FLA and create a more rigorous standards and monitoring system. The FLA was neither "public" nor "official," they argued, and they pointed to inadequacies in FLA's monitoring standards. For example, the companies involved had refused to make public the location of their factories.

How then could human rights and labor groups independently monitor their labor practices to ensure that these global firms would pay a "living wage?" Students immediately mobilized support for a new association, one that would give more power to a wider range of stakeholders, including the universities that license the use of their logos on clothing. Furthermore, it had become apparent to many observers that no monitoring effort could work effectively unless it was embraced by a critical mass of the whole US apparel industry.[3]

Students organized sit-ins on campuses, held public debates and demonstrations. They brought sweatshop workers from Latin America to speak on campuses and waged campaigns to demand that the location of factories be made public. They wanted stronger codes of conduct than the FLA had developed. They wanted solid licensing agreements. As a result, business corporations like Nike and Champion began to disclose the locations of some of their factories. This created some legitimacy for the FLA, but some student leaders still did not believe that the FLA would establish strong standards and monitor them.

Working together, students and administrators in some colleges and universities began to develop codes of conduct that they felt could ensure that the goods they bought were produced under fair and safe conditions. But how could they be monitored professionally and truly enforced?

As the battle for legitimacy in monitoring standards for production intensified, the United Students Against Sweatshops, in consultation with university administrators and workers' and human rights groups, developed the Worker Rights Consortium (WRC). The WRC began as an activist task force that would follow the federal Occupational Safety and Health Administration (OSHA) model. It included Duke, Cornell, and twelve other colleges and universities. The goal was to write one code of labor standards for use by a broad range of educational institutions, one that could substitute for a multitude of codes being developed on individual campuses. The WRC would verify and inspect conditions in factories producing apparel for colleges and universities. Members of USAS also wanted the WRC to make information on industry malpractice public and to pressure firms to improve conditions in their factories.

The WRC would verify licensee compliance with production codes of conduct in a way that was stricter than the FLA industry code. It believed that a school's code should have provisions for *"a living wage, the right to organize unions, the protection of women's rights, public disclosure of factory locations, and independent monitoring."* It was a core principle of their effort that the business sector should not control the monitoring process.

Major accounting and consulting companies—including KPMG and Ernst & Young, and PricewaterhouseCoopers—had been asked to serve as monitors for the FLA, but activist observers complained that these were business monitors and therefore not "neutral." They argued that as a business itself, PricewaterhouseCoopers, for instance (upon which the FLA most heavily relied), would be biased in favor of the apparel firms, hence independent professional monitors should be assigned from outside the business sector.

Now the issues of transparency and monitoring became the battlegrounds in the struggle between the WRC and the FLA. The WRC's concerns about "legitimacy" and "enforcement" were not the same as those of the FLA. The FLA did not require all its companies to release the names and locations of its factories to the public. The WRC argued that full public disclosure would not only give the manufacturers an incentive to correct violations, it would also help prevent them from quietly "cutting and running" to other nations, as many global firms had done when threatened with higher standards.

Furthermore, the WRC contended, the FLA's existing monitoring system required that only 10% of a company's factories be monitored in a given year, and the companies were allowed to choose their own monitors. Since they were also given a list of the factories to be inspected, it seemed logical that they would notify the factory owners ahead of time, who would then have the opportunity to "stack the deck" in any number of ways. (In this country, OSHA requires independent monitors and unannounced visits.)

The struggle intensified. A draft for an industry-wide labor standards code was circulated in December 1998 for feedback from campus constituencies, including faculty, students and administrators, as well as manufacturers, government and non-governmental organizations, labor and human rights groups, and consumers. The WRC also began negotiations with the Collegiate Licensing Company (CLC), which licenses athletic products for over two hundred universities and about two thousand retailers and also participated in this process.[4]

The WRC called for annual independent monitoring in "at least 30% of factories, as well as independent monitoring in all factories in countries where basic workers' rights are denied." The list of factories to be monitored was to be determined by local human rights, labor, or religious groups, people who had the trust of the workers and knowledge of local conditions, not by representatives of the companies, either local or multinational. The WRC argued that monitoring information on all sites would provide better information for buyers on the status of workers in overseas factories.

The companies countered that information about the location of factories and what they do in them is proprietary, whereupon the WRC responded that this argument was specious since competing shoe and apparel companies often produce their goods in the same factories as their competitors and most of the information about who is producing "what and where" is already well known inside the industry itself.

Nike Retaliates

Business contracts with colleges and universities are extensive across the country. Not only do these educational institutions earn a significant amount of money by licensing their names and logos and selling the resulting T-shirts, sweatshirts, caps, hats, jackets, on campus, but in exchange for cash and athletic uniforms, shoes, and equipment, they agree to having all these latter items—worn and used by their athletes and coaches—feature a display of the contracting company's symbol, in Nike's case the famous "swoosh." For the companies it's an effective advertising technique; for the schools it's a way of defraying the cost of athletic programs.

In April of 2000, Nike announced that it would terminate its three-year contract to provide hockey equipment to Brown University. (The contract had one year to go.) Brown had decided to join the Worker Rights Consortium, and Nike defended its action with the argument that by doing so the university had changed the terms of its initial FLA-based arrangements on inspections at Nike's overseas factories.

Grassroots advocacy organizations (e.g., the Campaign for Labor Rights, Press for Change, and Global Exchange) and student activists denounced Nike's action as "blatant economic coercion," an attempt to "intimidate" other campuses and dissuade them from following the Brown example, and a move to take unfair advantage of its position of power in the apparel industry. But there was more to come.

The University of Michigan and the University of Oregon were also among the prestigious schools that had joined the WRC, and they too suffered Nike's retaliation.[5] Michigan's teams have been among the nation's most successful in many sports. It was one of the first schools to reach a comprehensive agreement with Nike, in 1994. Among the things Michigan initially received from Nike were $620,000 in endowments for shoes, uniforms, and practice gear for players and coaches on its twenty-three teams, plus summer internships for a number of Michigan students at Nike headquarters. Michigan's contract extension would have been worth between $22 million and $26 million over six years. Now it was announced that this longstanding arrangement was in jeopardy.

Finally, Nike's chairman, Philip Knight, is a graduate of the University of Oregon. He had generously given his alma mater $50 million over the years, and he had promised to donate another $30 million toward an $80 million renovation of the university's football stadium. Now, along with Nike's outfitting and merchandising contact with Oregon's athletic department, due to expire in 2003, that proposed donation was in serious doubt. The power of business in university athletics had been trumpeted loud and clear.

Toward a New Social Contract

The Washington, D.C.-based American Council on Education (ACE) is a federation of the nation's colleges and universities. Sheldon Steinbach, its vice president and general counsel, showed alarm at Nike's decisions against universities. "Clearly, the CEO of Nike and the corporate entity [is], in this triple shot across the bow of the institutions involved, seeming to say,'Our financial support is not unconditional,'" Steinbach said. "[This] sends a message to institutions who are beneficiaries of Nike largess." This was counter–fire at Nike, and it came from the general counsel of a major player in the field of education.[6] What additional Third Sector organizations might enter this battle?

Notice that there are voluntary federations with natural affiliations for the various "societal orders" involved in this conflict. The AFL/CIO would be ready to defend UNITE in the labor movement. The National Association of Manufacturers (NAM) would be ready to defend US apparel manufacturers in the business order. The ACE would be ready to defend universities in the educational order. These three non-governmental federations (ACE, NAM, and AFL/CIO) have not yet become actively engaged; so far, they stand in the background. If the stakes were to become high, however, they could go into action. The statement by the lawyer for ACE was a wake-up call to Nike.

A Tri-Sector Map of Stakeholders

In Box 8.1 we sketch the tri-sector stakeholders who are already involved or might take part in seeking a system of public accountability in the marketplace where the values and interests of the apparel industry conflict with those of higher education. Here the term "civic" indicates a partnership between business and the Third Sector. The FLA, for instance, is a partnership that has representatives from both business and Third Sector organizations. It contracts with Verité as a principal monitor. Verité, founded in 1995, is now the largest nonprofit organization devoted to monitoring, operating in fifty countries. It would conduct employee interviews as "the best gauge of factory conditions."

Box 8.1 is a map of the possible "public functions" for the organizations that have a stake in this dispute. Those we have called "principals," such as FLA and the WRC, are rivals. (The WRC has less funding, but it has symbolic power. It is capable of arousing public attention.)

Box 8.1. Wearing Apparel Industry: Standard Making and Monitoring Structure
Stakeholder Organizations (Roles)

Business Sector	*Third Sector*	*Government Sector*
Principal Civic Overseer (Task Force, Legitimizer): Fair Labor Association (FLA) *Business Monitors:* Pricewaterhouse-Coopers and KPMG	*Principal Civic Monitor:* Verité *Activist/Monitor:* Worker Rights Consortium	*Principal Mediators and Legitimizers:* U.S. Labor Department's Occupational, Health, and Safety Administration (OSHA)
U.S. Background Players: National Association of Manufacturers (NAM), the American Apparel Manufacturers Association (AAMA)	*Global Background Player:* International Labor Organization (ILO) *U.S. Background Players:* The American Council on Education (ACE), American Federation of Labor -Congress of Industrial Organizations (AFL-CIO)	*Global Background Player:* The United Nations

---

"Background players" are organizations like the NAM and AAMA in the business sector and the ILO, AFL/CIO, and ACE in the Third Sector. To date they are mostly "observers" of this standard-making battle, but they have a potential stake in the outcome. Any one of these associations or federations could step forward take a more active role if their values were threatened. The United Nations is listed in the background as an intergovernmental organization; this is because it could ultimately play a role in setting worldwide standards in many industries in the future.[7]

In Box 8.2 we note nongovernmental organizations that have played a part in the action or might do so in the future. These are Third Sector activists offering leadership and support. They could increase their engagement and take a more active role at any time.

Box 8.2. Grassroots and Third Sector Activist Organizations

Global Exchange www.globalexchange.org
    Global Exchange is a nonprofit research, education, and action center dedicated to promoting people-to-people ties around the world. Since its founding in 1988, its members have been striving to increase global awareness among the U.S. public while building international partnerships around the world.

UNITE www.uniteunion.org
    Representing 250,000 members in North America, the Union of Needletrades, Industrial, and Textile Employees (UNITE) is known for aggressive organizing and fighting for workers' rights. Members work in the apparel, garment, and textile industries.

Clean Clothes Campaign www.cleanclothes.org
    The Clean Clothes Campaign sponsors efforts aimed at improving working conditions in the garment industry worldwide. Its campaigns are mounted by coalitions of consumer organizations, trade unions, researchers, solidarity groups, and other activists.

Campaign for Labor Rights www.summersault.com/~agj/clr/
    The Campaign for Labor Rights mobilizes local support in the United States and Canada for the campaigns of their partner organizations. They build bridges between local activists and other labor rights organizations around the world.

Box 8.2 continues

Box 8.2 continued
Sweatshop Watch www.sweatshopwatch.org
Sweatshop Watch is a coalition of labor, community, civil rights, immigrant rights, and women's organizations, including attorneys and advocates committed to eliminating the exploitation that occurs in sweatshops. They believe that workers should be earning a living wage in a safe and healthy working environment, and that those who benefit the most from the exploitation of sweatshop workers must be held accountable.

United Students Against Sweatshops
United Students Against Sweatshops (USAS) is an international coalition devoted to stopping sweatshop labor. USAS is an organization of 200 campuses working on a national campaign to stop sweatshops. Their members focus on using their power as students to support issues of economic and social justice on their campuses, in their cities, and globally. They formed in 1998 as a loose coalition of students from campus groups working on the Sweat-Free campus campaign, to facilitate communication and coordination among the campus groups working on the campaign, to give students a unified voice in taking on national targets, and to provide a national network and base.

Public Citizen's Global Trade Watch www.citizen.org
Global Trade Watch is the division of the larger organization Public Citizen that fights for international trade and investment policies promoting government and corporate accountability, consumer health and safety, and environmental protection through research, lobbying, public education, and the media. Global Trade Watch conducts research and advocates in the field of international trade and investment. Public Citizen is a national consumer and environmental organization founded by Ralph Nader in 1971.

International Forum on Globalization www.ifg.org
The International Forum on Globalization (IFG) is an alliance of sixty leading activists, scholars, economists, researchers, and writers formed to stimulate new thinking, joint activity, and public education in response to the rapidly emerging economic and political arrangement called the global economy.

Alliance for Democracy www.afd-online.org/index.htm
The Alliance is a "populist movement" "not designed to be a political party" that seeks to end the domination by large corporations

Box 8.2 continues

Box 8.2 continued

of the economy, the government, the media, and the environment. Its members aim to promote democracy in this country and to help achieve a just society with a sustainable, equitable economy. They work together with other organizations that share these goals.

Democracy 180 www.corporations.org/democracy/home.html
The 180 Movement for Democracy and Education is dedicated to helping students and youth build a movement for political empowerment and participatory democracy. Through education and organizing they hope to encourage a radical political presence in the schools in order to transform communities into democratic spaces.

National Labor Committee (NLC) www.nlcnet.org
The NLC's mission is to educate and actively engage the U.S. public on human and labor rights abuses by corporations. Working with a strong network of local, national, and international groups, the NLC builds coalitions that mount campaigns to pressure companies to adhere to labor and human rights standards.

Other Support Organizations
Campus Action Network, In Fact, United for a Fair Economy, Mobilization for Survival, As You Sow, Campaign for Labor Rights, the Council on Economic Priorities, the Farm Labor Organizing Committee, Global Survival Network, Human Rights Watch, Interfaith Center on Corporate Responsibility, Investor Responsibility Research Center, Child Labor Coalition, Resource Center of the Americas, International Youth Foundation, Social Accountability International (SAI).

Intersections: From Producer to Consumer

Our case study, involving an effort to establish a "social contract" among so many players in so many roles, challenges simple economic models and vocabulary. In a traditional scheme, Third Sector universities would be seen as *buyers*, the businesses as *sellers*, and the students as *consumers*. But this does not capture the complexity of the situation.

Universities are also *retailers* because they sell products on their campuses. Businesses are also *producers* insofar as they write the critical contracts with overseas host affiliates, and they are *distributors* in supplying products to universities. Together this profit/nonprofit field of exchange represents the complications of the whole cycle of modern market organization, from producer to consumer. In this case, the FLA and WRC are in the middle as civic-oriented organizations that are competing to set standards and settle conflicts of interest.

Notice the rationales in this set of buyer/seller/consumer conflicts. Some are economic and some involve the values of civil society. Businesses want low production costs and high profits. Universities want high-quality products and low prices. The ultimate consumers (mostly students) want both low prices and humane standards in factories.

I would argue that this case represents natural conflicts that have become ever more common in the context of globalization—and that they can be resolved by negotiators and arbitrators, that public (civil society) standards can be established for this industry and others through government, retailer, and consumer pressure.

New labor standards—including more transparency on the part of business and professional (neutral) monitoring—could, of course, raise production costs and thus the market price of the goods in question. This is a problem in "conflict resolution" between buyers and sellers. If markets are to become more public and accountable, consumers must agree to higher production costs and higher prices, but increasingly they seem willing to do so. Meanwhile, standards can be set that allow businesses to continue to make reasonable profits.[8]

The Recent Situation

To return to our case study, the Fair Labor Association and the Worker Rights Consortium are working on improvements in their monitoring. The former has become the principal civic monitor in this realm, and at a board meeting in January 2001, it certified its first group of monitors. The first applications from companies seeking a declaration from the FLA that their products are produced "sweat-free" have been submitted.

According to civic leaders, establishing the public legitimacy of this organization will take at least two years. Sam W. Brown Jr., its executive director, says he expects that "nearly every" factory that is inspected will not meet FLA standards at first. Members of the association will not want to do business with companies that fail to comply with its standards, but the practical side is another matter. Some compromises will have to be made. The FLA will concentrate on getting monitors in place in the twenty countries that produce about 80% of the world's apparel, but, Brown says, it will be years before a thorough, reliable, and ongoing monitoring process is established.

The FLA has 144 members that are American colleges and universities. The Worker Rights Consortium has 66 members and far less money.

(The consortium has been struggling with just one full-time staff member, with an annual budget of about $400,000, while the FLA budget is $2 million.) But there is an overlap between these two nonprofit "competitors" on standards: thirteen institutions belong to both the FLA and the consortium at the same time.

Leaders of United Students Against Sweatshops remain closely aligned with the consortium and insist "staying alive is a deliberate strategy." They do not rule out going back to protests and civil disobedience if their goals are not met, and the organization is strengthening ties to labor organizations domestically and abroad. They are looking for students who are personally committed to the labor struggle.

Most observers agree that the complex organization of apparel production hinders the enforcement of labor standards. One barrier to enforcement is the fact that local laws often operate against provisions included in the FLA's code of conduct. For example, in Thailand and South Korea, the maximum allowed work week is longer than the sixty hours that is stipulated by FLA provisions. And in China, independent labor unions are illegal.[9]

And there is more complexity. No one knows exactly how many factories are producing collegiate-licensed apparel. One factory produces the textiles, another factory sews the clothing, and the apparel is then silk-screened or monogrammed in another factory. And another factory makes the zippers. Sometimes licensed items are not produced in a factory at all, but by families in individual homes, or by local residents working in a common area as a cooperative. How many of those workplaces should be, or can be, monitored? Under these circumstances, how do you define "a factory"?[10]

The University of Michigan at Ann Arbor and Nike, Inc., have reached an agreement for uniforms and equipment for all the institution's athletics teams for the next seven years. The contract was signed on January 8, 2000, and doubles the amount of cash payments (to $1.2 million) that Michigan will receive annually from Nike, compared with their former contract.

Civil Alternatives for the Future

College sports are heavily tied to business contracts. In light of these close ties, critics like Andrew Zimbalist, who has written extensively on the subject, would cut football scholarships, shorten seasons, shorten practice hours, and eliminate shoe contract windfalls for coaches. He is one of many—including mainstream media commentators—who argue commercialization has corrupted collegiate sports and eroded academic standards.[11]

Some of these problems are beyond the scope of this chapter, but to return to the question of how academic institutions could influence business practices in the apparel industry, there are other possibilities. In the simplest economic model, universities are the buyers from business and businesses are the sellers. Together they can set rules, monitor production, and raise prices if necessary. They can do this legally as long as competition is sustained and their agreements work in the public interest. In other words, business competitors on the board of the FLA can improve labor standards and raise market prices as long as they stay in competition. This is civil development.

When this is done properly in the public interest, this market sector takes a small step toward becoming a civil market. If core values were to be brought in by educators and public advocates to shape this market, we would see it characterized by cooperation, transparency, and public standards as well as competition, proprietary rights, and profit making. It would become based on fair trade as well as free trade.

If this development process were to continue properly, the market would move toward "intersector regulation," not government regulation. As standards that serve the common good as well as business interests are put into place, it would become self-governing to a great degree.

But this market is also part of a global economy, and we could expect that the United Nations, through UN High Commissioner for Human Rights, and global NGOs like the International Labour Organization could play a stronger part in supporting labor rights worldwide.[12] Verité, today the principal global monitor, could also play a role.

What else could happen? A variation on this plan for the United States could be for universities to support a backup activist monitor, a spot checker, and a whistleblower. But universities could also bring the problem under academic study. Many colleges and universities offer students in various disciplines the opportunity to study with fieldwork projects overseas. There are natural links here with many disciplines: anthropology, sociology, political science, and, of course, business management and economics. The question of how business affects communities is germane to them all.

In a future plan, universities could make arrangements for students to visit and live in host communities where factories are located and where monitoring agencies like Verité make their visits. Whatever the focus of their specific studies, students could also record their observations about the impact of those factories on the community, taking care to keep a clear separation between this activity and their fieldwork for their academic projects.[13]

Academic standards for conducting fieldwork overseas are important. The methodological standards for doing participant observation require students to be respectful, factual, discrete, and objective in their reporting.

Safety is an issue, and discretion is especially important in places where political repression exists. Good fieldworkers learn as much of the local language as they can, and they keep journals as they observe the life of the people around them.[14]

In some cases, special fieldwork programs that focus on labor and economic issues could be designed in collaboration with global corporations, host governments, and local factory owners. The very presence of students working into this field could have a positive effect on local development "on the ground," and their research and reports would likely be very useful to scholars, policymakers, and business leaders as well.

Universities can also help NGO/business partnerships "develop" overseas. They can work with international agencies and encourage community development programs where US factories are located. Their purpose would be to promote community development along with business development.[15]

Conclusion: What's Ahead?

Universities are linked financially and socially with business. This social-financial link is the basis for Third Sector associations to help set standards and take a monitoring role. In the wearing apparel industry, universities could became the accreditors of products, setting standards and monitoring compliance just as they do for their own academic associations.

In Chapter 3 we saw how for-profit universities and for-profit hospitals have been moving into global markets and how nonprofit accreditors have followed them. Now we are seeing how, as the wearing apparel industry has moved into a global market, universities are following them to insist on fair labor standards. The Third Sector, in this case a coalition of educational associations and activist groups, has the collective power to do this by virtue of their purchasing power and the legitimacy that their certification can provide.

Independent nonprofit accreditors are needed in world markets. When domestic corporations go global, nonprofit accreditors can go global as well. The Third Sector could be swept into globalization and virtually disappear, becoming part of the business sector. Or it could do something very different. It could help establish and monitor standards in the development of civil markets.

In the next chapter we will examine how associations in all three sectors—government, business, and the Third Sector—become involved in world markets. International associations have the power to develop a just, fair, and accountable economy. This does not fit the character of capitalist markets, but it does fit the character of civil markets.

Notes

1. Trade associations are a *manifest* (developed) power in the economy while non-profit associations in the Third Sector like AAC&C are a *latent* (undeveloped) power. The AAC&U forges links among presidents, academic administrators, faculty members, and national leaders committed to educational excellence. It does not think of itself as part of capitalist markets. The institution's president, chief academic officer, and three other faculty leaders represent each campus member. See the Association of American Colleges and Universities website at http://www.aacu-edu.org/About/about.html.
2. Nike has gone further. Everything in Nike that was not "core management" was disassociated from its business. Production, distribution, advertising, and even design were outsourced and managed at a distance through electronic communications.
3. Aaron Bernstein, "Sweatshop Reform: How to Solve the Standoff," *BusinessWeek*, 3 May 1999, 186. The development of "civil markets" in this case was about fair wages, safety, health, transparency, social auditing, and a system of neutral monitoring and enforcement.
4. The University of Michigan participated with thirteen other universities on a task force facilitated by the Collegiate Licensing Company in drafting licensee code of conduct, beginning in 1997 and continuing to April 2002. See Actions taken by the University of Michigan, http://www.umich.edu/~newsinfo/BG/actswshp.html.
5. WRC membership had surged to at least 29 colleges and universities, but the Fair Labor Association (FLA) appeared to have the upper hand after persuading administrators on more than 100 US campuses to join its monitoring system.
6. On Steinbach, see Mark Asher and Josh Barr, "Nike Cuts Off Funds for 3 Universities: Schools Thursday, May 4, 2000; Page A01. ACE was founded in 1918 and is the nation's largest association that coordinates the work of universities and higher education. If it were to enter this "market battle" as a full participant, the situation could change dramatically. ACE is dedicated to "the essential cornerstones of a democratic society." It has about 1,800 members, which include accredited degree-granting colleges and universities from all sectors of higher education.
7. In this connection, on July 26, 2000, fifty companies signed a voluntary "Global Compact," promising to end child labor, protect human rights, and allow unions to organize. They also pledged to operate with ecological principles in mind in all countries where they do business, even when national laws do not require it. Among the fifty multinational corporations that made these promises were Nike, Royal Dutch Shell, BP Amoco, BASF, and Rio Tinto, the British-Australian mining company. Among the watchdog groups that also signed the compact were Amnesty International, Human Rights Watch, the International Confederation of Free Trade Unions, the World Wildlife Fund, and the Lawyers Committee for Human Rights. Philip Knight of Nike told the *New York Times*, "This Global Compact has the potential to become a historic partnership," but because the agreement does not include an enforcement policy, some labor unions have called it the "infamous Global Compact." On the term

"infamous,"see the progressive magazine *Third World Traveler,* at http://www. thirdworldtraveler.com/United_Nations/UN_Sells_Out.html.

8. Some trade association agreements have anti-competitive effects, which lead courts to consider them in violation of Section 1 of the Sherman Act. See R. L. Miller and F. B. Cross, The Legal and Regulatory Environment Today (St. Paul, Minnesota: West Publishing Co., 1993), 585; and G. D. Webster, "Avoiding Antitrust Liability,"Association Management, January 1995, 167.

9. The Independent University Initiative (including Harvard and Ohio State universities, and the universities of California at Berkeley, Michigan at Ann Arbor, and Notre Dame) studied the problem. Other studies, conducted by Verité, brought officials into factories where goods are produced for the brand names, such as College Concepts, Gear for Sports, M. J. Soffe, JanSport, and Zephyr Graf-X. Each company selected one factory to be visited. They were located in Costa Rica, El Salvador, Mexico, South Korea, and Taiwan. The report was done on behalf of Boston College, Duke and Georgetown universities, and the universities of North Carolina at Chapel Hill, Southern California, and Wisconsin at Madison.

10. Martin Van Der, " Idealism Into Real Change,"*Chronicle of Higher Education,* 5 January 2001.

11. Zimbalist considers antitrust laws applicable to college sports and asks whether student athletes are exploited by the system. He suggests eliminating freshman eligibility for sports, restricting coaches' access to " sneaker money "from corporations, and more. See Andrew Zimbalist, *Unpaid Professionals* (Princeton, New Jersey: Princeton University Press, 1999). See also Allen Sack and Ellen Sturowsky, *College Athletes for Hire* (New York: Praeger, 1998).

12. The International Labor Organization (http://www.ilo.org) is affiliated with the United Nations System and monitors labor conditions worldwide. The ILO contributes information regarding labor rights and the fight against sweatshops and child labor. The UN High Commissioner for Human Rights seeks to bring together " social and economic values,"a key to civil development. The United Nations Commissioner for Human Rights, http://www.unhchr.ch/ html/menu2/10/e/rtd_main.htm.

13. Faculty members in sociology, for instance, could engage in this fieldwork, preparing data for monographs on social, economic, and cultural life. Management schools have programs in which students serve as interns in business enterprises. Students assist business managers in record keeping, budgeting, and marketing, with no charge to the enterprise; these interns learn the practical side of business under faculty supervision. Students gain perspective on the difficult details of business management, and would in this case face the human problems incurred with overseas contracts.

14. Fieldwork in anthropology could take steps in this direction with safety precautions. Students then provide a local presence in host settings. See Severyn T. Bruyn, *The Human Perspective: The Methodology of Participant Observation* (New Jersey: Prentice Hall, 1966).

15. International grassroots nongovernmental organizations (INGOs) help to foster expertise in community development. For example, Social Accountability International (SAI) is a nonprofit organization whose mission is to improve workplaces and communities. It helps companies develop codes of conduct. Another support organization is the International Youth Foundation (IYF).

Part 4

Conclusion
The Global Picture

9

A Global Political Order
How Does a Civil Society Develop?

World trade opens a path for free markets and democracy, but it is also a struggle for power, and global markets are linked to issues of war and peace. For many, like citizens of the United States and its allies, the World Trade Center was a symbol of freedom, but for others around the world it was a symbol of dominance. Its destruction and the war in Iraq have brought the problems of globalization into sharp focus for the American public.[1]

It seems clear now that countering terrorism and reducing the scourge of war will depend upon organizing a new global system of governance. This includes organizing a new political economy, and we argue in this book that this means developing civil society at the same time. Organizing new systems of governance to stop terrorism and promote economic justice concern political economists and sociologists together, and combining the outlooks of such different fields should give us a new global vision and a fresh foreign policy. This is what we will discuss in this chapter in a brief way.

First, we will look at the globalization problem. Nations create political alliances that sustain capitalist markets and world cartels but this practice does not solve the issues that we discussed in Part 1. It is not the way to build a global civil society.

Second, we will look at a different type of political order that fits with the idea of a civil society, one in which, just to begin with, national leaders stop the production of weapons of mass destruction and the sale of dangerous arms in world markets. We will look at strategies for developing a political (democratic) global system of governance designed to stop terrorism and prevent war.

Third, we will describe strategies for developing a civil market. The ideal is a global market that develops its own accountability systems and reduces the necessity for world government. Ideally, global commerce should develop through civil regimes in "theaters of action" to be described. We argue that a system of civil governance is essential for sustainable development on the planet.

Finally, we will examine the steps that world leaders have already taken to create a new civil order in markets. There are no simple answers to the problems of globalization, but we must start with the reality before we can envision the ideal and describe a set of methods for reaching it.

The Political Reality: **The Problem with Current Regimes**

A global political economy does not develop simply under the auspices of the United Nations. It develops equally through regional (political/economic) regimes. We argue that current regimes are inadequate to solve the problems of global capitalism.

What are examples of these regional regimes? We can start with the European Community (EC), which is developing a body of "Community law" and "member state law," and a system of judicial remedies to be used by litigants to interpret these laws in European markets. Another example is the Organization of Petroleum Exporting Countries (OPEC), composed of 11 countries that are reliant on oil revenues as their income source; membership is "open to any country" that is a substantial net exporter of oil and which agrees to abide by strong controls on production in the interest of keeping prices high. These regimes would also include the North American Free Trade Agreement (NAFTA), which was negotiated in 1994 to foster trade and investment in Canada, the United States, and Mexico and has a schedule for tariff elimination and reduction of non-tariff barriers, as well as comprehensive provisions on the conduct of business in the free trade area.

These are political agreements instituted to support capitalist markets, not "civil markets." As hundreds of giant corporations transmit a commercial culture around the world, the problem is that this type of globalization does not represent the higher values of society. These political/economic regimes demolish forests, produce chemicals with dangerous levels of toxicity, increase the gap between the rich and poor, destroy animal species, and change DNA without studies of its public impact. They are the offspring of capitalist states.

Global corporations are linked with political regimes in market sectors, as in mining, oil, banking, media, and chemical production; they rely on nation states to support them. A few hundred corporate giants lead this global economy, many of them richer and more powerful than sovereign nations.[2]

Global cartels do not intend to advance the core values of civil society. The political/economic regimes in which they are embedded are *not* grounded in global rules that sustain physical safety and health. They are *not* founded on principles of justice like equity and fairness. Rather they are based on alliances designed by nations to advance world commerce as usual.

In other words, multinational corporations have developed under the auspices of nation-state alliances that promote economic development, not civil development. We will propose remodeling these "political/economic regimes" into "civil regimes" that can bring the core values of the rest of society into the marketplace.

Envisioning a New Order

Nations can regulate markets within their own territories, but they cannot regulate global markets. Even the efforts of the United States to try to control world commerce, for all its military and economic power can only go so far. There is no global Environmental Protection Agency to keep markets from destroying the environment. There is no global Securities and Exchange Commission to regulate the sale of stocks. There is no global financial system for banks to provide nations with a safer, more flexible, and more stable monetary system. There is no international agency to regulate international arms sales, curtail the spread of dangerous chemicals, or halt the destruction of the environment upon which all human life depends. In sum, there is no system for governing world commerce with enforcement powers to advance the common good.

Values and Costs

Here is the basis for our vision of a civil republic. *The common good is not based on political and economic values alone.* Why? Consider some of those values we have talked about in our discussions of civil society—truth, love, faith, justice, and beauty. They become politicized in every nation, but they cannot be reduced to one government or explained in a political category. These core values cannot be defined by single nations or by political parties alone. They are part of a larger culture, rooted in the larger lives of people in civil society associations.

Capitalist markets too often generate cartels and lose these values. They produce patterns of domination through globalization and become part of the causes of war and terrorism. Civil markets develop when stakeholders—not just stockholders and heads of state—influence and organize markets. Stakeholders may include international non-governmental organizations (INGOs) in tension with commerce and government. INGOs can bring those core values into markets and establish a civil regime. Every regime depends upon political order but the question is—what kind of order cultivates core values? Developing an order that cultivates those values is a task for world leaders, but here we suggest a few directions.

The Immediate Task

Let's be clear. The current world order is rooted in beliefs based on capitalism and nationalism. These beliefs do not lead to world peace. The current world order is not organized to promote justice, fairness, or even-handedness. It is a world order that generates injustice and terrorism. A new world order would begin with policies that stop terrorism. This means that the United States would reverse its foreign policies and support international law. Such a radical shift in policy goes beyond simple nationalism to link with the core values of all nations.

The US government rejected the Anti-Ballistic Missile Treaty. It rejected an international agreement to track the global trade in small arms and a protocol to the Biological Weapons Treaty to make compliance more verifiable. It rejected the Comprehensive Nuclear Test Ban Treaty. It rejected the Kyoto treaty on reducing carbon emissions. It rejected an international convention to ban child soldiers. It rejected the START III treaty with Russia to codify and verify planned deep cuts in nuclear arms. It refuses to accept the jurisdiction of the International Criminal Court (ICC). It must now reverse those policies.

The US Senate has done no better. It did not ratify the Convention on the Rights of the Child. It did not ratify the Convention on the Elimination of All Forms of Discrimination against Women (CEDAW). It did not ratify the Mine Ban Treaty, banning anitpersonnel landmines, also known as the Ottawa Treaty. It did not ratify the Law of the Sea. It must now reverse those policies.

When the United States acts in this way, it is no model for building world peace, a civil world order. At great cost to the nation, the United States has troops deployed in more than a 100 countries and full-scale military bases in more than 60 of them. Since 9/11 it has added military bases in seven new countries. It has over a 100,000 troops in Iraq and other parts of the Middle East. The consequences of the United States maintaining its troops in other nations and serving as the world's policeman have become a disaster.

The domestic consequences of this global posture are equally a disaster. In fiscal year 2000, the national debt increased an average of $1.25 billion per day, rising to a total for that year of $6.2 trillion. That's an increase of $420 billion over FY2001. Since September 30, 2002, the debt has continued to increase an average of $1.65 billion per day. The federal government debt today is $7.4 trillion and climbing. The bulk of funds that could go toward building the US economy are flowing overseas.[3]

Here's the irony: *The US spends a billion dollars per day just paying the interest on this debt—more on that interest than it pays for military defense.* How might new US policies help stop terrorism, cultivate civil markets, and reduce the debt? What kind of policymaking would promotes the values of a civil society?

Civil Governance on a Global Scale

Sharing the cost of global peacekeeping through a system of civil (mutual) governance with other nations would reduce the terrorism and save money on military defense. We argue that the United States should use diplomacy and work with other nations to build a multilateral world (military) peace force. It should honor the UN Charter and the enforcement of world law, including an appeals process. US support for world law would quicken the pace of true peacemaking in all regions of the world.

That is just the beginning, of course. Political economists should join with civil society advocates to plan the development of a world order based on peace and justice. Political economists should think about how core values link with markets. This means looking for new monetary structures, fiscal policies, and economic development based on international law. It will mean developing a new theory of international interactions, innovative approaches to world trade and financial analysis, and new global models for industrial organization.[4]

Without an effort to "civilize" the global economy, we can expect destructive competition among nations and the regional alliances we mentioned above. Without world law, we can expect regional wars and even WW III. We may see a twenty-first century version of the British Empire, which American colonists fought against in 1776. Historians know that all empires became self-destructive and eventually turn to dust.

One nation cannot act alone for the common good. Without a system of world law and a multilateral peace force, there is no way to stop terrorism or prevent war. World peace and stable economies come through finding a new system of governance in tandem with justice-oriented markets.

First Steps to Address Imminent Dangers

The United States and other nations can begin now to work toward these goals through the UN. To begin with, they would ask for a new order of mutual security among nations. A different political order is needed to build a global society, but its first task will be to protect people from terrorism and the use of weapons of mass destruction.

The United States, I believe, should ask all nations to join it in taking these first steps:

(1) Renounce the first use of nuclear weapons,
(2) End the development, testing, and production of nuclear warheads,
(3) Seek agreements on the mutual and verified destruction of nuclear weapons,
(4) Strengthen nonproliferation efforts by ratifying the Comprehensive Test Ban Treaty,
(5) Support international efforts to locate and reduce fissile material worldwide and negotiate a ban on its production.

The United States should then take its nuclear weapons off hair-trigger alert and work with all other nuclear powers—the United Kingdom, France, Russia, China, India, Pakistan, and Israel—to reduce the risk of accidental or unauthorized use of those nuclear weapons they do not destroy.

Central to our concept of a new global order is the principle that all nations must share the load for policing against terrorism and reducing the threat of weapons of mass destruction. This is done through an expanded system of international inspections. All nations could reduce military costs by sharing this responsibility, gradually. This is an urgent matter and these issues require exploration now under UN auspices. As this is being done, existing institutions of international law should be strengthened. The UN should pursue the issue of arms sales in private markets.

In July of 1998, in Rome, 120 member states of the United Nations adopted a treaty to establish—for the first time in the history of the world—a permanent international criminal court. This treaty came into force on July 1, 2002, 60 days after 74 nations became parties to the Rome Statute through ratification. This international court—the ICC, headquartered at The Hague, in the Netherlands—is a step toward what could develop as a system of world courts.[5]

The advancement of world law and the establishment of associated courts begin in world conferences. While the United States has yet to ratify the Rome Statute, nonprofit associations that have been studying world law have advanced good models to advance a new governing system. A world conference should be held that includes these organizations, such as the Inter-parliamentary Union (IPU), which is an international organization of "Parliaments of sovereign States" founded in 1889 and headquartered in Geneva, Switzerland, Citizens for Global Solutions, and the Coalition for a Strong United Nations. These organizations know how important it will be, as systems of world governance develop, to protect and maintain civil liberties everywhere.[6]

In sum, international arms control, peacekeeping efforts and a system of international law are essential ingredients for a political order that could promote justice and human rights. Not only would US support for international law and a multilateral peace force save lives and reduce the human misery caused by war and terrorism, it would foster cooperation and free up resources for the development of civil society.

Toward a Civil Regime in a Global Society

In July 2000, UN Secretary-General Kofi Annan joined with the heads of key UN agencies to inaugurate the Global Compact, which set forth civic and environmental principles for multinational businesses and recommended civic partnerships with the Third Sector. Although, as we saw in Chapter 8, it has its critics, this was an important attempt to suggest how a global capitalist economy could develop into a civil one.

We will come back to that compact later in this chapter, but we will look first at how world (nonprofit) associations are developing through business and the Third Sector in education, religion, science, and the professions. As we shall see in the last chapter of this book, many of these associations are federations that already have enough power to make a difference. Civil development depends upon the active engagement of civil federations that develop and acquire influence through common law. This is the ground for a civil republic.

Common Law and Civil Regimes

Common law is a system of jurisprudence administered by secular tribunals. It is distinguished from both statutory law and ecclesiastical law. In *Black's Law Dictionary*, "common law" refers to "juristic theory and social norms" that are of general application in keeping civil order. This is interesting because it points to the fact that "social norms"—not just "legal norms"—play a huge part in governing society.[7]

Indeed, studies show that the conduct of people is governed *more* extensively by social norms than by legal norms. Social mores, etiquette and decorum, fashions and fads, folkways and customs—all embody social norms, as do conventions, covenants, compacts, codes, protocols, and agreements. Delinquents and criminals will break the law but not their own rules of etiquette or codes of conduct. Most people will follow the "mores" of the groups to which they belong with greater scrupulousness than they follow government laws.[8]

The question in civil development is how common law and the social norms that underpin democracy and justice can become the basis for "doing business." As we argued in Chapter 4, the norms of democracy (e.g., fairness in conducting electoral procedures) and justice (e.g., equity in applying due process) are not in the model of capitalist markets, which are ruled by the principles of efficiency, productivity, and profit making. Democracy and justice, however, can be seen across society, as in the charter law of US trade associations and citizens' advocacy groups. We believe that the common law based on these social norms is vital to the development of civil regimes.[9]

Every regime depends upon common law, which begins in social conventions, customs, and compacts. A global civil regime is beginning to develop today inside capitalist markets through a body of rules and principles and agreements advanced by international bodies of authority like the Forest Stewardship Council, which we will describe below. This process—which governments should encourage—links Third Sector values (social/cultural) with state and capitalist values (political/economic) worldwide. It begins to develop a public commons with the help of international business organizations (IBOs), international governmental associations (IGOs), and international non-governmental organizational (INGOs).

Put another way, a body of common law developed through IBOs and INGOs, with the support of the United Nations, could be the foundation of a global civil regime. This regime will be strengthened as people everywhere see public norms—and their enforcement—to be in their self-interest. It develops through the ratification of existing international agreements, like the Law of the Sea and the Kyoto Protocol, by more and more nations, and by the construction and implementation of new ones.

The Emergence of a Civil Regime

In political science, the theory of "regimes" has traditionally referred to alliances between nations, but scholars now conceive of regimes that transcend political boundaries. This new outlook encompasses what happens when IBOs (e.g., global trade associations) and INGOs (e.g., the

International Committee of the Red Cross) develop principles, standards, norms, and procedures that have worldwide influence through international agreements between non-governmental "actors" as well as governments.[10]

Such a global regime is a system of authority with rules that are not all derived from government but also from those compacts that form among non-governmental organizations that have identified a common ground of interest.[11] A common ground can develop any sphere of activity—art, accounting, mining, law, medicine, science, religion, education, or business.

For our purposes, a "global civil regime" is a system of authority made up of norms to which actors give consent for their common good. It is a space where IBOs, IGOs, and INGOs operate as stakeholders independent of a single government, one in which for-profit and nonprofit organizations agree to abide by principles and standards based on social conventions and agreed-upon rules of conduct, not just national or even international law.[12]

Non-governmental occupational health and safety, environmental protection, and labor relations regulations are called "standards regimes." They cut across market sectors and are supported by world organizations. NGOs today create standards regimes when they set rules to apply, for instance, to Internet fields of commerce. They are acting together in a field of trust to establish "the rules of the game."[13]

Compliance with Civil Regimes

Ian Hurd, a global analyst, says that all civil regimes confront the problem of "social control," that is, finding ways to get organizations with their own agendas to comply with the rules. When and why, he asks, do actors obey a non-legal rule or standard? His answer is threefold:

(1) The actor fears the punishment of rule enforcers,
(2) The actor sees the rule in its own self-interest, and
(3) The actor feels the rule is legitimate and ought to be obeyed.

Hurd begins his analysis by offering an explanation of why people obey rules in any social system. The three mechanisms he cites (presented above) are based respectively on "coercion, self-interest, and legitimacy." They operate at all levels of any social organization—a classroom, a crime syndicate, the state, or any "regularized field" of global markets. It seems clear how the first two mechanisms (coercion and self-interest) apply to capitalist markets, but Hurd's concept of "legitimacy"—which involves actors defining their "shared perception of the milieu within which they work"—has to be studied carefully. It has a special role in civil development.

As we shall see, when actors feel that a rule is right for them, compliance is strong and not governed by fear. An actor following the rules feels their legitimacy and is not concerned about retaliation or retribution. When many members of a regime share a common definition of what is right, they share that group's identity and think themselves as a community. They establish allegiance as citizens do in a nation.[14]

A strong regime develops with all these social mechanisms: compliance based on fear, compliance based on self-interest, and compliance based on legitimacy ("the right thing to do"). An international civil regime develops when all three sectors—IBOs in business, IGOs in government, and INGOs in the Third Sector—provide the ground for that legitimacy. It is based on a set of norms for conduct that fit the common good in all three sectors of society worldwide.

How does this happen? World markets have rules set by the WTO and by regional governments like NAFTA, but so far this has not solved the problems of dominance and exploitation. Hence we need more effective means for core values and common law (standards) to enter global business. We need to see how civil regimes can work for the common good by connecting with INGOs, (i.e., global non-government organizations).

In appendix L we examine how three theaters of action create a global civil regime. We look at the potential for intersector governance in global markets. In the first theater, for example, there are the world's economic actors (IBOs), building world markets in a thousand fields of economic exchange, as in aluminum, automobiles, coal, foods, computers, oil, machine tools, military arms, petroleum. Some IBOs develop some core values but they need other theaters of society to support and monitor them. In the second theater there are political actors (IGOs) like the UN Environmental Programme (UNEP) working with IBOs on such problems as "persistent organic pollutants" (POPs), and industrial chemical products such as PCBs. In the third theater there are social actors (INGOs) in a hundred different fields like the sciences, the professions, charities, recreation, art, education, and the world's religions. We show how industries endangering the environment can link with INGOs (e.g. science associations) and IGOs (e.g. UNEP) to anticipate the dangerous consequences of their regime policies and take corrective action.

Creating Civil Regimes: Linking the Core Values of IBOs, NGOs, and IGOs

A capitalist regime develops when IBOs (e.g., trade associations) follow a common set of market rules. A civil regime is different. It develops when business and Third Sector associations follow a common set of public standards drawn from core values. Common ground is established as commerce adopts Third Sector norms found in the fields of science, law, or religion. Let's see how it works.

Inter-Sector Cooperation: Learning Together

Every business market has IBOs. The aluminum industry, for example, has trade associations that build a capitalist global regime. These associations will exploit the earth's resources in their own interest, which is natural to capitalist markets. But how could this pattern be changed so that IBOs work for the common good?

The UN plays a role here. The first step for this industry to work toward the good of all nations is by linking with Third Sector associations, like the International Union of Geodesy and Geophysics (IUGG). The IUGG is an INGO dedicated to the promotion of scientific studies of the Earth (physical, chemical, and mathematical) and its environment in space. It's operations are based on the core values of science and upon its public standards. There are hundreds of scientific federations like IUGG with connections to the global economy.

How could IUGG make a difference here? The IUGG is a federation that is devoted to sharing scientific knowledge in a global society. It is not based on proprietary knowledge like the aluminum industry or any other capitalist regime. It shares its knowledge about mineral resources, the mitigation of natural hazards, and environmental preservation. It is comprised of "seven semi-autonomous Associations," each responsible for a specific range of themes. It establishes "inter-Association Commissions," organizes "topical symposia," and connects with other scientific bodies with similar interests. It is governed by general assemblies and each of its member associations organizes its own scientific assemblies. It is organized by membership principles of equity, fairness, democracy, and sustained by core values in science not business. It is committed to "the principle of free exchange of data"—for instance, it provides public data on global warming—and shares scientific information among nations. It has a potential connection to all businesses pulling out the earth's resources—oil, coal, copper, zinc, tin, uranium, lead.[15]

The UN has a role to play by advancing civil order here. It can encourage global regimes like the aluminum industry to find connections with scientific associations. The bylaws of the Aluminum Association Inc. (AAI), for example, say that it wants to know more about "mineral resources, the mitigation of natural hazards and environmental preservation." Hence, AAI could learn much from IUGG scientists about "best practice" mining and recycling techniques, resource development and conservation, and research on their industry's contribution, if any, to global warming. The aluminum trade association could write a social contract with IUGG and develop techniques for environmental protection. This is a common cause between business and INGOs, and for business it also represents an opportunity to gain potentially useful information and (especially if publicized) a good marketing strategy.

A civil regime develops when a significant number of trade associations and Third Sector associations link their work for the common good. Together they support competition in business, but also resolve the conflict between sectors. And there is and should be plenty of conflict. In our hypothetical contract between the AAI and the IUGG, for example, business will want to keep its information private while a Third Sector association like IUGG will want scientific information made public. One of the tasks in civil regimes is to find solutions to the "private vs. public" problem.

The aluminum industry has begun to bring core values into its market (see Appendix L), but building civil regimes requires another step: public accountability systems established through IBO/INGO alliances. Public accountability systems involve agreements (i.e., enforceable formal contracts), standards (e.g., corporate codes and trade rules), monitors (e.g., official observers and advisors), and authorities (e.g., judges and tribunals).

As global civil regimes develop, they promote standards in commerce for the common good. With support from the UN, accountability systems are institutionalized; these systems become a way of doing business in markets. A civil regime is based on legitimacy and authority, by solid agreement between all parties, and civil regimes within market sectors are the building blocks of a new system of global commerce.

In sum, civil regimes begin with codes of conduct—like the Global Charter of the Keidanren, the CAUX Principles, the UN Draft Code of Corporate Conduct, the International Code of Marketing of Breast Milk Substitutes, and the International Code of Conduct on Distribution and Use of Pesticides—and work slowly toward enforceable systems of accountability.

Let's look briefly at some current examples accountability systems: the Law of the Sea (LOS), the International Standards Organization (ISO), the Coalition for Environmentally Responsible Economies (CERES), and the Forest Stewardship Council (FSC). These are relatively civil regimes that uphold core values in the marketplace.[16]

Civil Regimes in Development: LOS, ISO, CERES, and FSC

In the following cases we see how political, economic, and social actors together develop civil regimes based on consent and common law through the efforts of stakeholders working for the common good.

Law of the Sea: A Civil Regime Developing with IGO Support

The Law of the Sea began in capitalist markets with voluntary agreements based on a body of common law. The Comité Maritime International (CMI) was the first international organization to work on programs of self-regulation (soft law) in this arena. Originally established in 1897 as a private organization of maritime lawyers and insurers seeking to promote international law. Today CMI is a nonprofit corporation that deals with commercial issues on the high seas: marine collisions, ship-owner liability, salvage, freight, navigation safety, maritime mortgages, liens, bills of lading, ship arrest, stowaways, registry of ships, and maritime arbitration. The national government of Belgium supports its conferences on global rules and regulations for maritime commerce.

The CMI is a lobbyist for uniform maritime laws among nations. It has spent a century building a public commons that served as a model for the UN-sponsored Law of the Sea. It has constantly sought government support in cases where customs, etiquette, and agreements on the use of the seas need the strength of uniform enforcement.[17]

The United Nations Convention on the Law of the Sea (LOS) was opened for signature on December 10, 1982, in Montego Bay, Jamaica. This marked the culmination of more than 14 years of work involving participation by more than 150 countries representing all regions of the world, all legal and political systems, and the full spectrum of socio-economic development. The convention entered into force on November 16, 1994, and enshrines the notion that all problems of ocean space are closely interrelated and need to be addressed as a whole.

The LOS Convention authorizes a "territorial sea" of up to 12 nautical miles from a nation's shores, and a coastal state's sovereign rights over fisheries and other natural resources in an exclusive economic zone that may extend to 200 nautical miles from the baseline. It also accords coastal states sovereign rights over the nonliving resources, including oil and gas, found in the seabed and subsoil of the continental shelf, which is also defined as extending to 200 nautical miles from the baseline.

The LOS has become the basis for advancing "effective global, regional, sub-regional, and national measures for sustainable ocean use." Global leaders say it is a "living constitution" for the oceans. To date, over 120 countries have ratified or acceded to the convention as modified in 1982.[18]

An international tribunal has been established for settling disputes arising from different interpretations of the convention. The tribunal comprises 21 judges whose appointments reflect "equitable geographical representation," and who serve under a system of rotation that ensures that seven seats are vacated for election every three years. On May, 24, 1999, the "States Parties" reelected six members to the court for nine-year terms; a seventh, from the "African Group of States" was newly elected.[19]

Under the LOS Convention, the secretary-general of the United Nations is required to convene meetings of states (i.e., nation states) to deal with issues arising out of the implementation of its provisions, including the election of members of the bodies established by the convention and other administrative and financial matters. The states that are party to the convention meet to elect the judges of the International Tribunal for the Law of the Sea, elect members of the Commission on the Limits of the Continental Shelf, and deal with various administrative matters relating to those two bodies. There are presently 124 "States Parties" to the convention, which have indicated their consent to be bound by it, in most cases through ratification of the "law." The European Community has also formally confirmed the Law of the Sea, bringing the total number of parties to 125. The United States has been the one major country that has refused to sign.[20]

Today, the LOS Convention's provisions are held to be binding on participating nation states as "international law" (or common law); even though its rules are not enforceable by a world government, the convention establishes "compulsory binding settlements" of ocean disputes based on global agreements among its member states and their IGOs.

International Standards Organizations: A Civil Regime Developing with Tri-Sector Norms

In the United States, business leaders organized uniform standards for products in manufacturing through the American National Standards Institute (ANSI) and other bodies, and now world leaders are working on environmental standards for the global economy. The ANSI is an American "federation of federations" that helps enterprises standardize thousands of products (like nails and shoes) in the market. It is a forum for negotiation as well as a regime that has legitimacy and authority in capitalist markets. It is a body of organizations that base their collaborative work on agreements and standards fixed in custom and by convention and agreement. Its purpose is to create public standards that work for the common good. For ANSI, "standards" are "documented agreements containing technical specifications" to be used consistently as "rules, guidelines, or definitions of characteristics, to ensure that materials, products, processes and services are fit for common use."[21]

The ANSI now works with organizations from other nations on public standards. These INGOs have together created the International Standards Organization (ISO), composed of groups that are "most representative of standardization" in their countries and currently writing standards for environmental protection. By its own count, the ISO represents more than 85% of the world's industrial production, and has more than 200 technical committees and almost 3,000 technical bodies that are developing standards. Governments have an observer status at ISO committee meetings. An environmental management system is being developed to establish third-party certification as a method for monitoring compliance. [22]

The ISO's standard making effort is a tri-sector activity linking the core values of IGOs, IBOs, and NGOs, that is, it integrates different standards and values represented in these three sectors. As competition becomes based upon them, these standards represent an economic advantage for global businesses; indeed, a corporation will be put at an economic disadvantage if it does not accept and abide by them.

Over 260,000 registrations to ISO 9000 (product standards) have been made worldwide thus far, and over 10,000 to ISO 14001 (environmental protection). Over a quarter of a million firms around the world have invested financial and staff resources to improve their quality assurance systems based on these global agreements.[23] Political actors have begun to accept these standards as well. They are being used by national governments in public policies and have become the basis for legal enforcement within certain nations. This process is developing a public commons and a rule of law for world commerce.

CERES Standards: Developing a Voluntary Civil Polity

The Coalition for Environmentally Responsible Economies (CERES) is a confederation of 70 organizations that includes environmental groups, advocacy groups, and global businesses that have committed to "continuous environmental improvement." The CERES Principles is a 10-point code of environmental conduct, which is developing a basis for guiding corporate conduct. Here we see business and Third Sector groups with widely different backgrounds and assumptions searching for specific solutions to environmental problems.

The CERES coalition includes NGOs like Environmental Advocates, Earth Island Institute, Friends of the Earth, Green Seal, the National Wildlife Federation, the Natural Resources Defense Council, the Rocky Mountain Institute, the Sierra Club, the Union of Concerned Scientists, and the World Wildlife Fund. It has investors, advisors, and analysts representing over $300 billion in invested capital. These include the Calvert Group; Friends Ivory & Sime; the Interfaith Center on Corporate Responsibility; Kinder, Lydenberg, Domini & Co.; the New York City Comptroller's Office, the Presbyterian Church (USA); Shorebank; and Trillium Asset Management. Partners also include public interest and community groups such as the AFL-CIO, Alternatives for Community and Environment, the Center for a New American Dream, Co-op America, the Council on Economic Priorities, the Fair Trade Foundation, the New Economics Foundation, and Redefining Progress.

In addition, over 50 companies have endorsed the CERES Principles, which include multinational corporations like American Airlines, Bank of America, Baxter International, Bethlehem Steel, CocaCola USA, Ford Motor Company, General Motors, ITT Industries, Nike, Northeast Utilities, Polaroid, and Sunoco. The coalition also includes small and medium-sized companies like the Aveda Corporation, The Body Shop International, Green Mountain Energy Company, Harwood Products Company, Interface Inc., Timberland, and Wainwright Bank.

CERES Principles include "protecting the biosphere" (making progress in "eliminating the release of any substance that may cause environmental damage"), making sustainable use of renewable natural resources, and reducing waste by recycling through safe methods. The principles emphasize energy conservation, minimizing health and safety risks to employees, eliminating (or reducing) the sale of products that cause environmental damage, correcting conditions that endanger the environment, and more.

The endorsing companies pledge to make "self-evaluations" of their progress in implementing these principles. CERES's staff agrees to not formally rate compliance; instead it asks corporations to enter into dialogue about what "compliance" should entail in the context of their operations.

The CERES Principles are thus a model for business to follow but they are also a corporate commitment for members, hopefully serving as a guide for others in their industry sectors. Certain of them, such as "Protection of the Biosphere," are mainly guideposts to inform the direction of corporate policies through which CERES hopes to make progress on environmental protection "based on a non-bureaucratic, voluntary relationship."

Participating companies agree to submit annual public environmental status reports as part of their contract with the organization; when a company appears to have violated one of the principles it has agreed to abide by, CERES asks for an explanation of that particular event or pattern of conduct. Thus the CERES agreement is an entirely voluntary one, made "in the spirit of ongoing trust-building disclosure and dialogue." The purpose of its inquiries is not to assign blame punitively, but "to identify a way to make progress." This is an agreement to set standards, but it is not a global civil regime in the full sense. It does not have a full-fledged public accountability system that includes monitors and penalties for noncompliance.

Instead CERES has chosen to focus on educational and consulting programs to generate and support standards. For example, CERES promotes initiatives to foster a "market demand for environmentally responsible and sustainable programs," like its "Green Hotel Initiative," which aims to increase "green lodging and meeting options" by catalyzing "market supply and demand." CERES has thus established an intersector (multi-stakeholder) program that involves the business sector with NGOs—the hotel industry, nongovernmental organizations, labor, academia, and environmental advocates—to work together to advance environmental principles in the hotel market. It pushes for "environmentally responsible hotel services" and encourages conference planners and travel buyers to choose "green" alternatives. In this way its standards become part of the etiquette and custom of the hotel service sector of the economy both locally and globally.[24]

The Forest Stewardship Council: A Civil Polity with Global Authority

The Forest Stewardship Council (FSC) is a nonprofit organization founded in 1993 by representatives from environmental and conservation groups, the timber industry, the forestry professions, indigenous peoples' organizations, community forestry groups, and forest product certification organizations from 25 countries. The FSC supports "environmentally appropriate,""socially beneficial," and "economically viable" management of the world's forests. It promotes responsible forest management by encouraging high management standards for national and regional forests, and by evaluating and accrediting assessors. It has a public education program and provides information about independent, third-party certification as a tool for ensuring that the world's forests are protected for future generations.

The FSC works on the premise that forest resources should be managed to meet "the social, economic, ecological, cultural and spiritual needs of present and future generations." Members see a growing public awareness of the ongoing devastation and degradation of forests worldwide. This is a huge and daunting global problem, but the FSC says that consumers are becoming increasingly aware and are demanding that the wood and other forest products they purchase be produced following sound environmental principles. In response to these consumer demands, certification programs have proliferated in this market sector.[25] The FSC works to accredit organizations in a way that "guarantees the authenticity of their claims." Forest owners and managers who request the services of a certification organization must initiate the process of certification voluntarily.[26]

In sum, the goal of the FSC is "to promote environmentally responsible management of the world's forests, by establishing a worldwide standard of recognized and respected Principles of Forest Management." The FSC wants to ensure that all "endorsed forests" are globally managed in an ecologically sound, socially responsible, and economically viable manner. Global "principles" are translated as regional standards, which are adjusted to local conditions. FSC-endorsed regional standards "reflect a balance between the latest science, the best known forest management practices, and current public values."

The Challenges of the Future

Each of the models noted above are "developing." Each has changed capitalist markets by introducing public standards on a global scale, but none is a civil regime in the full sense of the term. For example, there is more work to be done on the Law of the Sea. Nations are eager to claim benefits under customary law (rights permitted by the LOS Convention), but critics note that they have been less inclined to build rules for environmental protection. The "development" of LOS will require integrating more comprehensive rules on environmental protection with "compulsory dispute settlements." The next step in the development of its world authority is to secure support from the United States.

In the International Standards Organization, people are setting environmental standards on products with a high degree of success. The ISO is negotiating agreements on the linking of *universal* standards with *particular* standards, as they say, to fit the uniqueness of each industry. For the ISO to become a civil regime in full measure, it must tighten its measures of accreditation. It must acknowledge stricter standards established in other global agreements, such as Agenda 21, the Montreal Protocol, the Basel Convention, the Convention of Climate Change, and the Convention on Biological Diversity.[27]

In the Coalition for Environmentally Responsible Economies, global business firms are working with Third Sector organizations to create standards for environmental protection. CERES has achieved some public confidence and is becoming a model for civil development in market sectors, but if it is to develop as a civil regime in the full sense of the term, it needs to establish a system of enforcement, which would include public monitoring with procedures to insure member compliance.

The Forest Stewardship Council establishes agreements with business corporations on the protection of timberlands. For the FSC to develop further as a civil regime, it must gain more support from governments. When FSC principles and criteria were first approved, the FSC's voting structure was 75% social and environmental, and 25% commercial organizations. In 1996, this structure was changed to 33% social, 33% environmental, and 33% commercial. When its principles were developed, the commercial interests were a minority and the government sector was excluded. FSC critics today say that this problem with regard to the right proportion for intersector governance has to be resolved. National governments must become more involved in the collaboration.[28]

Conclusion: Developing a New Polity

Capitalist markets, left alone, generate cartels. They produce patterns of domination through globalization and become part of the causes of war and terrorism. The alternative is to build a new polity. A new polity promotes responsible markets, reduces the need for US military forces around the world, and controls the sale of arms and the proliferation of weapons of mass destruction.

The preeminent and immediate task is to stop the spread of weapons of mass destruction. A livable world rests in a democratic (decentralized and effective) system of world governance that sustains civil rights. This means a system of world courts and a multilateral peace force that can deal with terrorism. It does not mean creating a world state.

A livable future means the construction of a global society. This is where markets develop their own regulatory systems with support from intergovernmental organizations. A civil political economy means that intergovernmental organizations collaborate with international business organizations while all parties keep their autonomy. We saw examples of partially civil regimes (LOS, FSC, ISO, and CERES) appearing in world markets. These, we believe, are today's models for building a global market system.

There are thousands of INGOs that have the potential to become competitors, collaborators, and countervailing powers in world markets.[29] Some of those civil society organizations we named in Chapter 8 in the apparel industry, for instance, are available to develop social contracts with IBOs. The Global Compact is another start in this direction, but civil markets could develop better and faster through stronger UN structures.

Trade associations in each market (e.g., pharmaceuticals, chemicals, automobiles, food, jet planes, and computers) need to link with associations in the Third Sector. These links produce a "social density" for global markets. Markets should develop with associations that are setting standards and monitoring compliance. This is, I believe, the best course for world leaders who want to solve social and environmental problems.

The UN has been instrumental in the first phase of the kind of world development we envision, but it cannot work alone. It is an IGO, a political system organized by national governments. It is a government without enforceable law; it is a fragile agreement to work on world peace, not a political federation like the United States, which can reduce violence and regulate markets within its own sphere. The UN depends upon the consent of member nations to advance peace, improve the common welfare, and commerce.

Civil society organizations are trying to gain greater power and influence within the UN. They want more equity in decision making to balance the power of business and nation-states. Civil society leaders want their international associations to become stronger within the UN General Assembly; some even want to organize a parallel governing body—a society of civil associations. This movement is part of the future.

There are thousands of civil associations that would be part of this global society and economy. They are in the educational order, like the International Association of Universities (UNESCO-based), bringing together organizations from some 150 countries for action on common concerns in higher education. They are in the religious order, like the World Council of Churches, which is a fellowship of Christian churches in more than 120 countries on all continents. There are hundreds of scientific associations like the International Union of Geodesy and Geophysics, dedicated to promoting the values of independent inquiry and coordinating studies of the Earth, its resources, and the web of life that sustains us all. There are professional organizations like the International Association of Agricultural Economists (IAAE), a confederation of agricultural economists concerned with problems related to the use of renewable resources and the environment. There are world unions like the International Association of Machinists and Aerospace Workers. There are nonprofit governmental associations like the International Association of Chiefs of Police, and sports and game federations like the World Chess Federation. And so on and on. We cannot forget about even the smallest of these, as we would build civil regimes.[30]

The UN is vital to sustain world peace but it is an intergovernmental organization. It does not represent all the members of the emerging "global society." It is not designed sociologically to represent the whole human community. But the most ideal world community is not what we are talking about as the immediate task. We are talking about a democratic system of world governance organized to stop terrorism and change capitalist markets. Nation states, the Third Sector, and the United Nations should civilize markets through world law and common law.

We have seen some civil models developing in markets—the Law of the Sea and the Forest Stewardship Council, for example—and these systems advance values higher than those in global commerce alone. By supporting these efforts and inventing new institutions and alliances, nations can help construct fair trade inside free trade, a system of exchange grounded in the principle of justice as well as the principle of freedom.

This is a new direction for globalization. It should be called international development, as it builds civil societies. It promises to bring nations closer to a type of governance that people have never seen before, a civil republic based on world federations that advance the deeper values of humankind.[31]

Notes

1. Big corporations develop around the world along with their home nations. A good chunk of the money spent for rebuilding Iraq goes into the pockets of companies like Kellogg, Brown & Root, a subsidiary of Halliburton, Vice President Dick Cheney's former company. This is why terrorists think that global finance is a strategy for the United States to build a world empire, a view not unrelated to the destruction of the World Trade Center and threats to US financial buildings.
2. Richard Barnet and John Cavanaugh, *Global Dreams* (New York: Simon & Schuster, 1994), 14.
3. We noted in Chapter 1 that businessman Peter Peterson warned of the dire consequences of this debt trend. For a view of the total debt at any moment, see Michael Hodges, "Grandfather Economic Report," at http://mwhodges.home .att.net/debt.htm.
4. There is no research currently being done in economics that follows the policies we are suggesting. The European Central Bank encourages research on international monetary policies, but only within its own regional framework. Among its working papers, one finds articles by V. Brouseau and F. Scacciavilani on "A global hazard index for the world foreign exchange markets," and by C. Conticelli and O. Tristani on "What does the single monetary policy do?," but these papers are concerned with regional capitalist markets. Research on international trade and financial takes place under the auspices of the World Bank Group and the European Bank for Reconstruction and Development (EBRD). This is done for the Group of Seven (G-7) industrial countries' economic policy coordination exercises and in the work of the Group of Twenty (G-20), the new forum of the G-7 with other systemically significant economies. In planning a civil world order, we must start thinking about civil markets developing within commerce in a new way.

5. The United States insisted that the Security Council should adopt an omnibus resolution exempting all UN peacekeepers from the jurisdiction of the ICC and threatened to veto all resolutions renewing peacekeeping operations unless the Council agreed to a new language. This US policy has provoked strong opposition from other nations. See the International Criminal Court, at http://www.un.org/News/facts/iccfact.htm.

6. The IPU is a center for parliamentary diplomacy among legislators representing every political system and all the main political leanings in the world. See the IPU website at http://www.ipu.org/english/whatipu.htm. Any conference held in the United States on this issue of world law should include some 25,000 World Federalists and members of Citizens for Global Solutions, and World Parliamentarians as well as the National League of Cities. See http://www.nlc.org/nlc_org/site/inside_nlc/about_nlc.

7. The legal scholar Roscoe Pound (1870–1964) asked, "For what end does the legal order exist? What do we seek to achieve through the political organization? What is the ultimate purpose in lawmaking?" The Law and Society Association, founded in the year of his death, comprises a group of scholars, from many fields and countries, who are interested in this kind of perspective in the law, a philosophy upon which a new legal system for the economy could be formulated. See http://www.lawandsociety.org.

8. Many studies have been done on the power of mores to shape conduct, but here are some examples. People will not eat human flesh (as it is against the mores of society) but will without a qualm go over the speed limit (although this is against the law) to get someplace on time. People will not appear naked at a party but will cheat on their income taxes.

9. Ian Hurd suggests that an actor at some point will "internalize" a rule made by an outsider, whether a friend, a government, or a trade association. Internalization happens, as the actor's own interest is established in concord with the outsider. Compliance then becomes habitual and legitimate. Hurd also suggests that "legitimacy" is a mechanism of social control and should have an economic advantage over political coercion. Non-legal norms have "long-run efficiency." Without enforceable world law, "legitimacy" becomes an essential ingredient for civil order. No international pesticide standard can be adopted in markets, Hurd argues, until it is made legitimate. Pesticide standards become legitimate in only those global regimes that gain "authority."

10. Political scientists also speak of "spheres of influence" and "milieus of standards." Institutional economists have different terms, such as "inter-firm hierarchies," "transaction costs," and "principal agent issues." Analysts who look at the Worldwide Web could define a regime space, as "network communities" in which there is an informal jurisdiction based on codes for communication and rules on how to make an exchange. See Deborah Spar, *The Cooperative Edge: The Internal Politics of International Cartels* (Ithaca, New York: Cornell University Press, 1994).

11. Stephen Krasner, a regime analyst asks, Who are the participants in a regime? They could be a mix of state actors, private actors, non-governmental organizations, or some combination of the three. How then, he asks, does a regime

hold together? See Stephen Krasner, ed., *International Regimes* (Ithaca, New York: Cornell University Press, 1983).

12. See Stephen Krasner, "Structural Causes and Regime Consequences," in Krasner, ed., *International Regimes*.

13. See Richard Hawkins, "Standards for Communication Technologies: Negotiating Institutional Bases for Network Design," in Robin Mansell and Roger Silverstone, eds., Communication by Design (New York: Oxford University Press, 1996); Peter F. and Edward Long, "Testing Theories of Regime Change: Hegemonic Decline or Surplus Capacity," in *International Organization* 37, no. 2, (Spring 1993).

14. Hurd contends that the internalization of global norms can occur on a decentralized, rule-by-rule basis. Decentralized rule making, he says, does not mean "anarchy." A system of decentralized authority is governed by rules that actors conform to out of an internal sense of rightness. Ian Hurd, "Legitimacy and Authority in International Politics," *International Organization*, v.53, n.2, 1999..

15. International Union of Geodesy and Geophysics, http://www.iugg.org/eoverview.html.

16. The term "political" is usually associated with a state. It derives from a family of Greek words relating to the *polis*, or city-state. The words included *politeia* ("constitution"), *polites* ("citizen"), and *politikos* ("statesman"), and they are connected to public concerns, in contrast to what is private or "one's own" (*idion*). Romans called their political regime a *res publica*, which became translated into the sixteenth-century English usage of "commonweal." The core meaning of "political" was "a sharing of what is common"—as expressed by Cicero. Now we are talking about a private economy that is developing a public order apart from government. Hence the term "political" in this case includes NGOs as part of that new public order. And "sharing of what is in common" could include core values.

17. Source: Maritime Transport: The Evolution of International Marine Policy and Shipping Law Lanham, Maryland: Lexington Books, 1981) See also A. Claire Cutler, "Private Authority in International Relations: The Case of Maritime Transport," in A. Cutler, V. Haufler, and T. Porter, eds., *Private Authority and International Affairs* (New York: State University of New York Press,1999), 309. Other global associations began in the nineteenth century to establish customary law, such as the International Law Association in 1873.

18. On July 28, 1994, the 48th UN General Assembly adopted an agreement modifying the LOS Convention's Part XI provisions on deep seabed mining beyond national jurisdiction. This agreement concluded a four-year series of informal consultations convened by the UN Secretary-General to remove impediments to widespread adherence to the convention.

19. United Nations press release, 28 May 28 1999, http://www.un.org/Depts/los/Press/SEA/sea_1617.htm.

20. UN press release, 29 May 1998, http://www.un.org/Depts/los/Press/SEA/sea_1589.htm.

21. On the Internet one can find a plethora of standard making bodies that are local to global. For example, there is a Worldwide Web Consortium of organizations setting standards. Then, some standard making organizations are concerned

about the public use of HTML. HTML is the *lingua franca* for publishing hypertext on the World Wide Web. It is a non-proprietary format based upon SGML and can be created and processed by a wide range of tools, from simple plain text editors. Hundreds of codes and protocols are now being set that will affect global communications for a long time. The National Information Standards Association keeps monitoring the US programs, staying in touch with international standard making organizations.

22. ISO is a global regime that began in 1947 and has become a significant player in the global economy. It is an international federation of standard making bodies from some 130 countries, one from each country. It is an international non-governmental organization (INGO) whose mission is to promote standardization for the exchange of goods and services, and advance intellectual, scientific, technological, and economic activity. ISO's work links with IBOs with IGOs and creates international agreements published as International Standards. International Standards Organization, http://www.iso.ch/iso/en/aboutiso/isomembers/index.html. See also Sandra George, "ISO 1400: Solution to International Crisis or Corporate Window Dressing?" *A Journal of Positions and Possibilities*, vol. 1, 1999, Department of Sociology, Boston College.

23. This organization is now on www.businessstandards.com.

24. CERES, http://www.ceres.org/eventsandnews/index.html.

25. Sociologist Steve Waddell describes a full-system "coproduction" model for such civil markets. The Forestry Stewardship Council is an example of how stakeholders—who were traditionally outside of the production and supply chain—engage in production. These stakeholders include NGOs such as environmentalist and community development organizations, along with government agencies. Steve Waddell, "Societal Learning: Creating Change Strategies for Large Systems Change," Systems Thinker 12, no. 10 (2001), 1; and Steve Waddell, "Core Competencies: A Key Force in Business-Government-Civil Society Collaborations, *Journal of Corporate Citizenship* 7, no. 3 (4) (2003), 19-27.

26. A list of forestry standards can be found on the Internet. Forest Steward Council, http://fscus.org/html/standards_policies/index.html.

27. For example, in Agenda 21, 179 countries made critical decisions on how global corporations should report annually on routine emissions of toxic chemicals. This annual report is one item not included in ISO's agenda. "Agenda 21: A Plain Language Version," Rio de Janeiro, Brazil, June 1992. See http://iisd1.iisd.ca/rio+5/agenda/default.htm.

28. The majority of the earth's forests are managed or owned by government and private industry, and yet they have not been brought (adequately) into the process of developing and enforcing standards for just and sustainable forest management. The FSC is contemplating how this could be done.

The FSC's ten principles are the basis for developing national or regional standards against which companies can be audited. Critics say that the FSC allows some certifications to be done in the absence of FSC-approved standards. They complain that "interim standards" were not developed in a sufficiently transparent multi-stakeholder process. They argue that the FSC is too decentralized and lacks sufficient government participation. For this criticism, see http://www.82.cyberhost.net/fscfacts/third.htm.

29. The Council on Economic Priorities (CEP), for example, serves as an accreditor of corporate responsibility in global markets. It organized the nonprofit Council on Economic Priorities Accreditation Agency (CEPAA), which has developed Social Accountability 8000 (SA8000), a system modeled after ISO 14000 that defines a set of "auditable standards" and an independent auditing process for the protection of workers' rights.

30. See the *Yearbook for International Associations*, at http://www.uia.org. For the IAU, see http://www.unesco.org/iau. *The Directory of Associations* is another comprehensive source of information on professional, business, and trade associations, 501c nonprofit organizations, chambers of commerce, and other charity and community institutions; see http://www.marketingsource.com/associations.

31. Great poets, like the Sufi Mevlana Jalaluddin Rumi, spoke of a higher order life on earth, saying, "I am neither Christian, nor Jew, nor Gabr, nor Moslem." Great philosophers like Martin Buber spoke of a higher order of community, beyond a single religion or nation. See Coleman Barks, *The Essential Rumi* (San Francisco, California: HarperSanFrancisco, 1995; *Paths in Utopia*, translated by R. F. Hull (Syracuse, New York: Syracuse University Press, 1996); and Martin Buber, *I and Thou* (New York: Charles Scribner's Sons, 1970).

10

A Civil Republic
How Do We Get There?

The conclusion must be that the location of decision-making in the economic world has shifted. Ownership ceases to play much decision-making in from two thirds to three fourths of the American economic republic. Instead, that power lies in corporations management, in administrators of savings-gathering institutions and pensions trusts, in the offices of the larger commercial banks, in government agencies, and in an inchoate emerging group which may be called the "scientific community."
— Adolph A. Berle, *The American Economic Republic*

The citizens of the United States could create a type of society that has never existed before. The task would be formidable and the responsibility would be considerable. It would require leaders of great strength, courage, intelligence, and far-reaching vision, like those of the Northern American colonies in the eighteenth century. For the common good, those colonial leaders became convinced, they had to overcome the power of a growing British Empire and create an independent nation. They constructed a new form of democratic government and in doing so fought their way out of the medieval period.

Today, I am suggesting that the government of the United States needs to fight its way out of the modern period. The "capitalist market" is no longer workable and the idea of a fully "independent nation" is history. Capitalism and nationalism were right for their time, but they no longer work for the common good. Great leaders who take on this challenge will start a new era. They will build a civil republic.

In 1963, in his book *The American Economic Republic*, Columbia law professor Adolf Berle argued that the market system is "not a state of nature but a state-created, state-sustained institution," that it is a political phenomenon as much as it is an economic phenomenon. In a "modern republic" like the United States, Berle said approvingly, economic institutions, no matter how powerful, are subservient to political institutions; that is, economic power is subject to check—and in the long run, to control—by the democratic will. Business, labor, government, and "public welfare sectors" interact and counterbalance one another to bring about an "economic republic," he argued, and he concluded that this modern economic republic is the best ever devised because it is guided by political values, not just economic values.[1]

But our argument here is that this type of republic is not working. In his review of Berle's book, Robert Heilbroner came to the same conclusion—that there is much more ahead for the development of society. Heilbroner's view was that Berle had made a superb analysis of some aspects of the relationship between the state and the economy but had failed to describe the market accurately, that his "economic republic" was a "whitewash" covering over a flawed system. Berle had left out facts, Heilbroner wrote, about this market that revealed its faults; in particular Berle had said nothing about the corporate elite it produces or how the market system generates poverty.

> The level of comprehension or compassion to be intuited from the speeches of our business leaders, from the pieties and platitudes of the business press, from the editorials of our mass media, from the congressional testimony of our trade associations—none of this is weighed in the balance. Nor is there mention, in discussing the "successful" operation of our system, of its dependence on an armaments industry huge in size and not easy to excise or replace. Nor did I find in a description of the American economic republic any discussion of the extent to which the "consensus" which supports (and supposedly judges) the business manager is itself constantly pumped up by the deliberate efforts of the managers themselves.

Berle's book claimed that the market economy was propelled by great "political values," but Heilbroner was not convinced. Something was missing in this "economic republic." What other values ought to be compelling and driving modern society? he asked. Two were high on his list. One is known in philosophical language as "truth."

> By this I mean truth in the large, in all aspects, from individual interest in not telling lies and in personal sincerity, to the frontiers of scholarly re-

search. . . A second enduring value is beauty. . . . The constant conflict by the more honorable portion of the American community against sordid murder of the esthetics of an open road by advertisers, or to maintain the dignity of an honorable main street against dollar chasing real-estate schemes, testifies to that fact.[2]

Heilbroner has raised our question. How could the core values of society motivate and propel an economy? The question is whether an economic republic could change into a civil republic.

The Argument

At the beginning of this book we saw how political and civil society leaders in the United States and other nations have defined the problems of globalization, and we detailed their concerns about the potential disasters ahead. A terrorist attack could destroy a whole city or a whole nation anywhere on earth. The state of the economy could worsen and lead to another great depression. A collapse in the world's ecosystem could threaten all life on the planet. We have to work with all our might to stop those things from happening, but while government leaders know what the issues are, so far they have offered only Band-aid solutions, some of which have worsened the situation.

We have argued that this is because the problems we face are not rooted in the political economy alone, and addressing them requires a larger framework that brings the values of civil society into globalization. The traditional outlook on political economy assumes that the state is the foundation of society and the market is the engine of development. But this outlook is inadequate. We need a vision that focuses on a civil society developing inside the nation. All the orders of a civil society are part of the economy, and they are both part of the problem and the key to its solution.

In Part 2 we presented evidence of the American society "decline" in education, religion, and the professions, sciences, and government. We saw the warning signs in the growing power of the market over these orders of society. We asked whether there could be an alternative and proposed a civil market model. We said that a civil market could be advanced in the United States, and likely in the world economy. The implementation of this model could lead to a new nation and a model for all nations—a civil republic.

There are over a million civil associations and federations in the United States of America—religious and educational associations, labor unions, trade federations, professional organizations, and science and scholarly associations. There are federations in sports, the arts, and the humanities, and a multitude that focus on specific issues, from environmental and consumer protection to race and gender equality.[3]

Civil society planners note that all of these associations—organized by lawyers, accountants, teachers, architects, engineers, artists, laborers, librarians, social workers, physicians, clergy, and scientists—subscribe to core values and ideals that are written into their constitutions and nonprofit charters as statements of public purpose. These are self-governing bodies operating in a (relatively) public domain.

Along with civil society leaders who call for a more "participatory polity," we argue that through these nongovernmental associations, citizens and scholars could become revolutionaries: they could organize a civil republic.

What Is a Civil Republic?

In our model, a civil republic is a web of federations that bring society's core values into the economy. It would be a nation in which political and economic interests are brought into balance with the values of ordinary citizens. In a civil republic, economic interests would still operate in the market, but economic values would not dominate society as a whole.

In other words, a civil republic becomes a reality when studies confirm that political and economic interests are not the primary forces governing society and not the main principles explaining the market. Political and economic interests in this new republic would still shape markets but they would not be the outstanding dynamic of society. A civil republic appears when the core values at the heart of society mix resourcefully to guide the market. It materializes as people see a sufficient combination of society's core values represented in the structure of markets.[4]

A civil republic is a dream, but it is also a vision for planners. We have been talking about how to put this vision into reality by fostering the development of a civil market through the engagement of voluntary associations in a tri-sector economy. Such a market is built through the appointment of civil commissions and the construction of "civil polities"; it is developed by "civil investment" and organized through "civil regimes." Civil society planners in government could make this dream come true.

If planners were to seriously implement this plan, a civil republic could become real within this century—just as an economic republic became real in the eighteenth century, after the American Revolution. How does this happen? Let's review what we have said government could do to advance the development of a civil republic in the context of globalization.

Existing Civil Federations: Their Problems and Their Potential

A "federation" is not simply an organization of states that join in a congress to govern themselves. A federation refers to any organization in the private sector whose members gather in a congress, a parliament, or a general assembly. Members vote for representatives to a higher body of authority and a chief officer or president. They choose a governing board and establish a purpose in their field of activity. They set standards and organize a polity based on the consensus of members. We have described these organizations as "associations in the nonprofit sector" but many of them are federations. If we include nonprofit trade associations as federations—as business leaders do (see Chapter 2)—our picture of civil society enlarges. It is not just the Third Sector. Trade associations are also nongovernmental federations, and we consider them "civil" for this moment in the sense that they are outside government. But we also argue that they could become *more* civil (i.e., more just, fair, and democratic). Chartered nonprofit federations in business and the Third Sector together, then, could develop the core values of society.

In the Third Sector, "civil orders" (Chapter 5) have developed more than a million associations. We do not know how many of them are federations, but the number is substantial. In Appendix J (A Republic of Federations) we describe them in more detail for research and as a strategy for societal development.

They include federations in the religious order (Jewish, Christian, Moslem, Hindu, Buddhist), the professional order (medicine, law, engineering, architecture, social work), academic disciplines (physics, chemistry, biology, sociology, history, economics, anthropology), business, (management, accounting, investment), education (private and public schools, colleges, universities, accreditors, administrators), and more. The most controversial among these federations in a theory of societal development are those in the business sector. We are suggesting that part of this strategy for civil development is finding new relationships between trade associations and Third Sector associations. These new (civic) relations would be quite various, including more competition and conflict for the common good. Civil conflict is essential to serious change and development. But development also includes cooperation, which might lead to new alliances, partnerships, and other systems of mutual governance.

Let's look at studies of this business infrastructure. Some business analysts say that the huge array of trade associations (i.e. confederations) is "not significant" to the organization of markets, that is, they are not important in understanding how market competition really works. Many associations are too small and short-lived to make them significant to study, while big federations are "highly fragmented, lacking authority over members." Many firms do not even bother to join trade groups, preferring to be a "free riders" that gain the benefits of their lobbying without contributing time or money.[5]

Other analysts would say that trade associations are too big and powerful, entrenched in government. By their influence on government, they are self-serving, not working on behalf of the public, designed simply to advance the profit of their members; they have no care for the common good and are destroying civic life and democracy in the United States.

All these views are true by some measure. Some trade associations and federations have too much power and others are powerless and fragmented; some operate only to advance the wealth and influence of their members, but others also practice their ideals of "corporate citizenship," "civic duties," and the "public interest." So in this order of society too—perhaps the most responsible for the erosion of society's core values—we see both peril and promise. How can we seize upon the promise that exists in all the associations and federations of society?

Development Strategies: How Do We Get There from Here?

It is our contention that government must work with all of society's nongovernmental associations to build a new, civil republic. All the "processes" for development we have described in earlier chapters are strategies for government planners.

Government's Role in Building a Civil Polity

The word "polity" refers to the ruling structure of an organization. It designates the way people distribute power and authority. It can indicate the way a business or a church or a government is organized based on the dispersal of control.[6]

For our purposes, then, the term can also apply to a market sector where corporations compete for power. In a "capitalist polity"—including an "economic republic" like the United States—corporations use their power to influence government, customers, communities, and the public. Each market has an elite. Their aim is to make money and control a market.

Thus, every market is a political field. A political field exists in manufacturing, where business firms struggle for power (and status) while engaged in the production of goods. There is a political field in education, where colleges and universities struggle for power (and status) while engaged in providing services. It is this idea of a political field of power that helps us understand how markets work. And it also tells us how business markets might be transformed into civil markets.

We have used the term "civil market" to describe a system of exchange in which stakeholders exert a significant measure of control, one in which self-directing groups of business and Third Sector associations set standards and monitor them together. This type of "civil polity" develops when stakeholders create solutions in market sectors, as we saw in the case of JCAHO and the wearing apparel industry. But we also argue that a civil polity advances more quickly and effectively with government support.

Specifically, the federal government could cultivate a civil polity in the American economy. It could encourage social contracts between trade groups and Third Sector federations, with outside monitors and the enforcement of standards inside the market. It would do this by conventional methods—tax breaks, economic incentives, conferences, and jawboning. Trade federations and Third Sector federations can then work to build that civil polity together.

Bringing a new mix of values into the marketplace would be like making good soup—adding the spice of democracy, the flavoring of fairness, and the vital ingredient of transparency. The result should add "real value" to capitalist markets—increased safety, equity, reliability, and creditability—through social contracts, partnerships, and nonprofit accreditors. Let's review what we have said about how this is done and add a few more ideas.

Multiple Strategies: Civic Monitoring, Industry Boards, Social Contracts, and Accreditors of Business

A democratic government would encourage a market toward greater civility in different ways. It would demand more transparency and accountability by contracting with Third Sector groups to act as public monitors. When corporations break the law and endanger the public, the government would add public citizens from appropriate Third Sector associations on corporate boards. When big corporations break the law by setting up accounting systems overseas to avoid taxes, the government can create federal charters for them. With congressional approval, the charters would state their responsibility to account for their expenditures with public responsibility. And if any trade association becomes a monopoly, the government can add competent Third Sector directors as watchdogs on their board. Let's look at examples of these strategies for civil development.

Civic Monitors

Nearly two decades ago, the State of Massachusetts began planning for the massive highway and tunnel construction project that came to be known as the Big Dig, which included replacing an antiquated elevated highway through the heart of downtown Boston with a tunnel that could carry a higher volume of traffic, and a "third harbor tunnel" for access to the airport from the south. The Bechtel Corporation, a huge private engineering firm, was hired to take a major role in oversight and construction of the project, which over the next fifteen years ran into "cost overruns" amounting to more than $1.6 billion. Various "post-Big Dig" inquiries revealed that government officials had approved more than 10,000 overruns and investigated only 335 for a possible refund, recovering only $35,707. These inquiries also led to the discovery that state procedures called for Bechtel "to identify issues of potential cost recovery." This meant that the state had relied on Bechtel to point out flaws in its own designs and management. Is it any wonder that when government gives this kind of power to a private business, citizens will pay for its "mistakes"?

What to do? In light of the civil market model we presented in Chapter 4, we would say first that an engineering federation in the Third Sector could be assigned by contract to keep an eye on a city project with so much impact on the life of citizens. Nonprofit engineering associations like the American Society of Mechanical Engineers (ASME), we propose, could be enlisted as watchdogs and whistleblowers for government. Having committed themselves by charter to act in the public interest, they would be motivated to be diligent in order to protect the reputation of the engineering profession as a whole.

An inquiry into how an overrun by an engineering corporation can be stopped to prevent losses is usually too technical and costly for a government to handle. A government's resources for hiring outside experts are limited. So, how could outside experts monitor this project without charging the city?

Other nonprofit corporations could be called upon. In this case, for instance, the schools of engineering at Boston University, Harvard, and M.I.T. could have participated in an ongoing evaluation. Graduate students and faculty alike could gain from studying what happens when engineering leaves the drawing board and enters the real world. Such matches between government projects and university monitors could reduce city costs. The schools would not charge the city because it is internship project for graduate students who would of course have close faculty supervision.

There are other options as well. As we have pointed out, there is likely to be a difference between oversight by a single professional, like an accountant, who is selected by the corporation in question and oversight provided by a team selected by a federation like the American Institute of Certified Accountants (AICA), which has made a public commitment to certain standards and whose reputation is therefore at stake.[7] Choosing the latter sends a signal. As government bodies enlist Third Sector associations as partners, the word will get around and more corporations will see the necessity (for business reasons) to accept such oversight arrangements as a condition for "doing business" with government—and, by extension, with other businesses and with nonprofit organizations as well.[8]

Each case is different. If large corporations are running afoul of the law, the government could ask the American Bar Association to appoint an overseer to investigate. If a major accounting problem arises, the government could ask the American Accounting Association to appoint a team to look into the matter. If a project runs into architectural problems, the American Institute of Architects or an appropriate engineering association could be consulted.[9] In each case, however, it would be the nonprofit professional association that appoints investigators, not government. And it would be the profession as a whole—not just a single hired lawyer, accountant, or engineer—that would assume responsibility. The association's representative is expected to be fair and impartial.

Corporate and Industry Boards

We also envision the nomination of individuals representing professional associations to corporate boards. They would serve the interests of the firm of course but equally serve the public interest. These would be "public directors" who create a balance between core values and corporate needs in the market. This is another way Third Sector federations could become agents for change in market sectors.

Government could insist on this kind of board "restructuring" when the law has been broken or when the public interest is transgressed. We argue that government at every level must get tougher on transgressions, including professional dishonesty, oligopolies and accounting tricks. Similarly, government might insist that a representative of an independent Third Sector organization be given a seat on the board of an industry trade association whose members have broken the law, and that this representative is given full access to corporate information that applies to the public interest. This "public director" would agree to inform industry CEOs about problems before going public, but with the understanding that if there is no adequate response from the corporation in question, he or she would serve as a whistleblower to bring the case to the attention of the government and the public.

Think back to the case we presented in Chapter 5, in which Willamette Industries was ultimately held to account for polluting the environment, but only after a sustained effort from the outside by Third Sector organizations to "blow the whistle." But if government brings public citizens (e.g., experts representing the Northwest Environmental Defense Council, the Plumbers and Steamfitters Local 290, and others) onto industry boards in such cases, future crises should be headed off at much less cost to all parties.

A civil polity develops in a market through systems of accountability as standards are set, monitored, and enforced by social contract in the private sector. The two nongovernmental parts of this sector—profit and non-profit—become "countervailing powers" and work out the problems together on the job. Bringing Third Sector associations into the market in a selective fashion like this would enable the economy to become increasingly self-governing.[10]

For-profit and Third Sector corporations would, of course, need to keep their distance from one another while working together. And when they differ, private arbitrators and mediation boards would be set up to settle conflicts. The point here is that government can promote cross-sector cooperation and does not need to be the main standard maker, monitor, and regulator. This policy should reduce government expenditures.

Social Contracts

A civil polity is built by social contracts for public monitoring. Where social problems arise in a market, the government can help to write these contracts. We saw how the federal government enabled nonprofit universities to connect with a business (wearing apparel) federation. Together they organized the Fair Labor Association (FLA). It all began when universities and union federations demanded standards—transparency and attention to worker health, safety, and fair wages—in overseas factories. The National Consumers League, the Interfaith Council on Corporate Responsibility, the RFK Memorial Center for Human Rights, the Lawyers Committee for Human Rights, the Union of Needletrades, Industrial, and Textile Employees (UNITE), and the AFL-CIO all became part of the market structure through this business/Third Sector federation, which contracts with a professional corporation to monitor conditions in "sweatshop factories." By taking on this task, the FLA (however incomplete) works toward worldwide standards and equity for workers and reduces the need for more staff in the Labor Department and the Occupational Safety and Health Administration.[11] If governments did more to encourage markets to develop in this way, we should see a more civil economy.

Third Sector Accreditors

The Third Sector's accrediting federations provide another model—and a potential resource—for civil development planners. In Chapter 5 we saw how a Third Sector healthcare federation, the Joint Commission on Accreditation of Healthcare Organizations (JCAHO), monitors standards in business-chartered hospitals and HMOs. In Chapter 6 we described how accreditors like the New England Association of Schools and Colleges (NEASC) establish standards for—and judge the conduct of—for-profit universities. It remains to be seen whether they can "hold the fort," so to speak, against for-profit enterprises in medicine and education, but such Third Sector federations set standards, monitor corporate conduct, and have the clout to publicize and enforce those standards. They become exemplars of a civil market system.

We've also discussed how professional associations like American Society of Mechanical Engineers (ASME) create public standards for business. But when business firms hire individual professional experts to act in their corporate interest, the core values of the profession are not always followed. Hence, in the future we will need to talk about how professional federations (not individuals) could take more responsibility for preventing actions by their members that could undermine the common good.

What builds a civil republic? *Public directors* (members of boards of directors with a special mandate to safeguard the public interest), *social contracts, nonprofit accreditors,* and *cross-sector federations* are the building blocks. These strategies generate accountability systems through which core values evolve to govern the economy. These *public accountability systems*—contracts, standards, monitors, and authorities (judges and enforcers)—are the key. Nongovernmental associations become proportionately more responsible for monitoring conduct in business markets. The government can advance this development by creating civil commissions.

The Role of Civil Commissions

In our model, a civil commission is a democratic public (nonprofit) association set up by government with representatives from government, business, and the Third Sector. Its purpose is to bring substantive values into the economy. In this strategy the government invites leaders in associations to join together to study market problems and search for solutions. Such a civil commission would be advisory to the parties involved, and its main task would be to figure out how the needs and values of all stakeholders can be met in a given market sector, not just those of business. It is not created to coerce, but if "market reorganization" is not successful on a voluntary basis, commissioners might propose legislation for Congress. Let's look at some examples we discussed earlier, and some new ones.

A Commission on the Public Media

In Chapter 7, we set out the arguments of critics that in the mass media the concentration of ownership in the hands of a small number of corporations has led to a situation in which corporate power and profit, not the public good, motivate the media, and that this is one of the causes for a decline of civil society. We described in some detail how a civil commission could be appointed to study the problem and take action. The outcome of our imaginary scenario involved a public debate and the formation of a tri-sector federation for the media.

A Commission on Science and Society

A civil commission on science for the common good would have a decades-long task. As an example of the problem of the increasing privatization of science, we noted that although the scientists who founded the Human Genome Project said they wanted a free exchange of scientific information and organized the effort as "a public project" in which all research findings would be shared through "international collaboration," some left the project to develop a commercial venture with a proprietary database. This turn of events is but one example of hundreds that require national study. Critics (around the world) view this trend toward the commercialization of science as damaging to the public interest and the tradition of openness in science. Science should develop publicly for the common good, they say, not privately for profit.

Just what are the dangers of commercialization? John Rennie, the editor of *Scientific American*, says that today scientists speak of how new technologies in genetics and the physical sciences will change the natural world as we know it. "We will certainly continue to evolve naturally in many small ways, but our technology may exert the greatest influence."[12] If this is true, it's no wonder that many scientists see the marriage of science and business as dangerous, and with good reason.

Of the 3,000 chemicals produced in high quantities in this country today, only 43% have been even minimally tested. Only about 10% have been thoroughly tested to examine their potential effects on children's health and development. Meanwhile, chemicals found in home and garden pesticides are also found in the urine of children, and chemical constituents of termite poisons, toilet deodorizers, and flame-retardants in the milk of nursing mothers. Of all the chemicals we use to kill insects and weeds, clean clothes and carpets, unclog drains, and create lawns, most have not been tested for their toxic effects on the next generation.

It seems obvious that there could be danger as well as promise ahead as geneticists change the structure of organisms and chemists change the structure of molecules.[13] Scientists speak about how nanotechnologists will change the structure of atoms, the foundation of the universe. Nature created atoms and molecules and cells. But all these elements of the natural world are now being altered in the private laboratories of for-profit ventures, which are given patents on scientific discoveries with proprietary rights that allow them to keep the results of their research secret. What will happen? Even a powerful national government like that of the United States cannot monitor all these activities to ensure that they do no harm to people or to the environment.

But government could consult with civil planners and appoint a commission to study science in society. It could call upon the American Association for the Advancement of Science and other scientific federations to address these urgent issues, get the facts, and make public their recommendations for how greater public oversight could be established in the scientific realm to counter the pernicious influence of the profit motive. The latter is a huge and daunting goal, but a civil commission on science and society would be a start.

A Commission on Civil Governance in Industry

At the same time, other commissions could work on the problem of increasing the public domain from the inside, by promoting civil governance among businesses in the marketplace. Let's propose a scenario for how that might happen with regard to labor and environmental practices. We'll use the present tense to help us imagine how the cast of characters might behave as events unfold.

The president of the United States asks the secretaries of commerce and labor, and the EPA administrator, to organize and serve on a new Civil Commission on Industry and Civil Governance, and that they recruit the heads of business federations like the Conference Board, the Chamber of Commerce, and the National Association of Manufacturers to join in the effort.

The first federation mentioned by the president, the Conference Board, was founded in 1916 in response to "declining public confidence in business and rising labor unrest" and has a membership of 3,300 enterprises in 63 countries. Its stated purpose is "to strengthen business performance" and "to better serve society." The secretary of commerce knows that the Conference Board held a global conference in February 2003 on "transparency as a key driver of corporate citizenship."[14] It looks for "ethical leaders" in business and wants to promote "effective stakeholder engagement." A promising place to begin.

In our scenario, the commerce secretary takes the role of point person when she talks in the afternoon with the Conference Board's president about corporate citizenship. This is a familiar subject for both of them, but this conversation becomes more pointed when the secretary asks, How can we create better labor and environmental standards in global markets? What does your board think about professional monitoring and arbitration systems? Later the secretary of labor joins them for dinner, and the discussion proceeds. The two cabinet members praise the Conference Board for its work on global citizenship. Then they talk about what "civil governance" means and the possibility that a new international effort to promote it would include global stakeholders like the International Labour Organisation.

Over the next weeks, the secretaries have similar talks with the International Chamber of Commerce, the National Association of Manufacturers, the International Bar Association, the International Labour Organisation, and social auditing firms. And they ask them all to participate on the new commission.

Themes and crosscurrents develop as these discussions proceed. Let's say that the commerce secretary talks personally with the president of the International Chamber of Commerce, which is a nonprofit federation that includes businesses, trade associations, and the Fortune 500 companies. It has already developed a global code of ethics and modes of arbitration.[15] The secretary asks its president, How could we enforce codes in markets that already have labor and environmental standards? Exploration of this theme will later include the EPA administrator and representatives from grassroots organizations.

And the process includes an acknowledgment of political realities as well as ideals. Business leaders know that the cabinet officials who approach them are doing so at the behest of a president who is also seeking to fulfill campaign promises. These constructive discussions contain hints of what might become a power struggle. The US administration has the power of law enforcement through its agencies, but the Chamber of Commerce and other business associations have a great deal of lobbying power in Congress.

When the commerce secretary talks privately with the president of the National Association of Manufacturing (NAM), she says, "Let's be straight. The president wants more productivity and growth in manufacturing, but he also wants to reduce government costs for monitoring standards in the industry. To achieve these goals he is appointing a civil commission to look into standards and enforcement."

"Yes, and what's a civil commission?" NAM's president asks. Given his position, he may be a bit clever, but he might just be asking for clarification. The secretary chooses to assume the latter. "A civil commission is an organization that represents all the stakeholders in a market," she says. "It advises the government on how to set standards and enforce them. This one would act like ANSI but on a much bigger scale. We need voluntary standards and bodies to enforce them to build civil markets."

NAM's president is of course familiar with ANSI—the venerable American National Standards Institute—as an effective private nonprofit organization that coordinates voluntary manufacturing standards. ANSI is the US representative to the world's leading standards bodies, such as the International Organization for Standardization (ISO). But again he wants clarification. "What exactly do you mean by civil markets?" he asks.

The commerce secretary responds, "By our definition, civil markets are trade sectors, like manufacturing, that have standards monitored by professional parties. We'll talk about the details as we go along, but I can give you a few examples of what we have in mind for the United States. We do not want extra paperwork for you—or for us—but we do want better public safety and health standards in manufacturing.

"The president is proposing a civil commission that would include a representative from your association, if you choose to participate, along with the Labor Department and OSHA, the AFL/CIO, public interest groups, and insurance companies. The purpose would be to increase standards and reduce government costs."

The president of NAM is cautious, but the commerce secretary keeps talking. She turns to the topic of the Occupational Safety and Health Administration, whose regulations some businesses find onerous.

"As you know, OSHA costs the government and taxpayers a lot of money. In spite of its work, thousands of workers are killed and millions injured each year in on-the-job accidents, and the number of injuries and deaths keeps mounting. I'm sure you'll agree this is a problem. The president believes that a civil commission could figure out how to prevent many of these accidents through self-governance within industries. After all, Sweden, for example, doesn't have an OSHA, and it doesn't need one. Why? Because the government brought trade and labor together to solve the problem. This country isn't organized like Sweden, but we can still self-manage this problem in our own way. The commission the president is asking you to look at our records on public safety, health, and environmental protection—industry by industry, market by market. We need you to help us."[16]

"What else do you have in mind?"

"We're also thinking of setting up a commission to study uniform pension funds. We need you in on this one, too, along with the American Bar Association, the Labor Department, pension fund managers, and executors of state government pension funds. We'll stay in touch on that, one step at a time." The NAM president is not particularly enthusiastic, but he agrees to take all of this under advisement and meet with the secretary of commerce again.

This is the end of our quick scenario about how civil commissions start. The government must create its own story. It must play softball in some situations and hardball in others as it lays the foundation for "civilizing" trade with the help of Third Sector associations. Participation in government-organized civil commissions would be optional, but business leaders can be counted upon to know when the government is getting serious and it would be in their best interest to support such efforts.

A Civil Commission on Education

The US Department of Education has 4,800 employees, a budget of $54.5 billion, and a mission to strengthen the federal commitment to "equal opportunity in education" and to improve the quality of American education. It could do much to advance the idea of a civil republic in this key realm.

Let's imagine that at the behest of the president, the secretary of education meets with the heads of the educational federations asks them to participate in a civil commission calling upon them to ask members to study the principles of a civil republic. Assuming that most agree (the secretary has pointed out that serving on the commission will gain them influence), here are some topics each might address according to its own mandate and interests.

- The Association of American Colleges and Universities (AAC&U): *How do the core values of higher education connect (or not connect) with the business economy? Are those core values of excellence in higher education changing?*
- The American Council of Learned Societies (ACLS): *Can the sciences and the humanities initiate studies on the proper role of big business in university life?*[17]
- The Association of American Universities (AAU): *Can university research help solve problems in a corporate economy (e.g., environmental protection, public health and safety, transparency, and accountability)? Can they examine their public responsibilities in negotiating contracts with business corporations?*[18]
- The American Association for Higher Education (AAHE): *Can students be prepared for global citizenship (i.e., being a "citizen of the world" as well as "a citizen of the United States)? Are teachers helping students develop a sense of human rights and ecological sustainability in nations around the world?*[19]
- The American Association of School Administrators (AASCU): *How can we prevent the loss or erosion of small colleges in market competition with large state and for-profit universities?*[20]
- The American Council on Education (ACE): *Is a "culture conflict" developing between for-profit and nonprofit education? If so, how it could be resolved?*[21]
- The American Association of School Administrators (AASA): *Can educational leaders in public schools help communities develop within a civil society?*[22]

The reports of these federations back to the commission and the Department of Education would be invaluable in constructing a philosophy of education and government policies that advance civil society. And, as participants in that planning, the federations would also be allies in their implementation.

A Commission on Corporate Law and Governance in a Global Context

This is a coordinated effort in which the president is also interested in the role that lawyers will play in the development of civil society, both in this country and internationally. He asks his attorney general to speak at the ABA's next annual conference, only a month away, about the profession's stated mission: "serving the public good."

The attorney general calls the president of the ABA to consult about the idea of a civil commission, highlighting the upcoming ABA conference. "First, the President and I would ask the ABA to send a representative to this commission to study corporate charters. Second, we would ask you to appoint a representative to a panel to study uniform pension funds. Third, we would ask for the ABA's ideas on the development of international law and corporate responsibility. Justice Department experts and leading scholars in these fields will also be represented on the commission." The ABA president agrees on to the proposal and sets a thematic section at the conference for the attorney general to speak along with other members of the administration.

At the ABA conference, the attorney general begins by saying "Our commerce secretary is talking with CEOs about corporate citizenship. As lawyers, we have a role to play here. We need to keep a certain distance from corporations to fulfill our public purpose—just as accountants are now required to do by government oversight. The ABA needs to do its part to ensure that big corporations are held accountable for their actions."

He then goes on to talk about how public interest lawyers are changing corporate charters through state legislatures. "There are new codes today in state charters to advance corporate responsibility," he says. "These charters say 'Board directors may not pursue shareholder gain at the expense of employees, the community, and the environment. If stakeholders can demonstrate harm, they have a right to sue under the proposed law.' The president wants your advice. Should state and national charters be written to include corporate responsibility? What does that phrase mean? And who are the "stakeholders?"

As a partial answer to his question, the AG identifies company employees as major stakeholders and asks the ABA to consider how their interests could be better protected under law. Here he focuses on pensions, pointing out that when employees move from one organization to another—and sometimes just between departments within the same organization—whether they do so out of choice or involuntarily, they often lose some or all of any pension benefits they have accrued. Even worse, when firms go bankrupt or misuse their pension funds, employees may lose their life savings. "Could a uniform pension fund system be created in the United States," he asks, "one that ensures pension protection?"

Finally, at a special session of the conference, the attorney general is joined by the secretary of commerce to "chart out" how existing international agreements pertain to corporate practices (see Box 10.1). They propose a discussion of how this body of law might be developed in the future.

Box 10.1. The Development of International Law and Standards[23]

Sovereignty and Development Strategies: UN Charter of Economic Rights and Duties of States, Articles 1 & 2; ILO Tripartite Declaration of Principles Concerning Enterprises and Social Policy 10, 19, 20.

Working Conditions: International Labour Organisation (ILO) Conventions 29, 87, 98, 155, 105, and 138; ILO Tripartite Declaration 34, 33 and ILO Tripartite Declaration 37.

Equality: ILO Conventions 100 and 111.

Consumer Protection: UN Guidelines for Consumer Protection; World Health Organization (WHO) codes on breast milk substitutes and on promoting pharmaceuticals; Food and Agriculture Organization (FAO) convention on pesticides. Food standards of Codex Alimentarius.

Environment: the Rio Declaration,; the UN's Agenda 21; Conventions on Climate Change, Biodiversity, and the Law of the Sea; the Basel Agreement; the Montreal Protocol; the Rotterdam Convention.

Local Communities: ILO Convention 169 on Indigenous and Tribal Peoples 7, 14, 15, 16, 20.

Business Practices: United Nations Conference on Trade and Development (UNCTAD) Rules for the Control of Restrictive Business Practices.

Basic Human Rights: The Universal Declaration of Human Rights, Articles 3 and 5 and Preamble; the UN Code of Conduct for Law Enforcement Officials.

At the end of this presentation, the attorney general says to the ABA assembly, "We are asking you to advise our government on these matters." The president and the civil society advocates he has consulted hope to enlist the help of the country's legal community to address other international issues as well—including laws and treaties to expedite the pursuit, arrest, and trial of terrorists, and to prevent the spread of weapons of mass destruction—but these issues lie outside the scope of the ABA's current mission statement. They are already asking for a stretch, and are pleased when the head of the ABA joins the president of the United States at a news conference to announce his association's cooperation on the civil commission. The president comments quietly, "These are new responsibilities for us, but we will endeavor to fulfill them." Again, this would be a start for civil planners to build upon.

A Commission on Oligarchy and Democracy

We must remind ourselves that, like the ABA, the nonprofit federations and associations that these proposed civil commissions would rely upon are not perfect. As we noted in Chapter 2, all organizations are to some extent oligarchies. They may be chartered to be democratic but the larger they grow the more they become oligarchies in reality by some measure.

The American Society of Mechanical Engineers (ASME), to cite another example, serves a global membership of 125,000. A member-elected board of governors oversees five councils, 44 subsidiary boards, and hundreds of committees in 13 regions around the world. It has developed 400 sections or subgroups to serve its members in particular markets. This is a democratic federation with professional goals that intends to work for the common good, but who, in the end, runs it? Most large organizations have a very modest participation of members. A "select number of leaders" run them, and the percentage of members who vote for these officers and board members is generally quite low.

Governments are no exception. Every "democratic government" is also a command bureaucracy put into place mostly by party elite. Heads of state and other officials get elected by a low percentage of potential voters. In United States, even when the franchise was restricted to white, property-owning men, the percentage of eligible voters participating rarely reached 50%. In fact, from a world perspective, the United States ranks 139th out of 172 countries in voter turnout.[24]

Hence, although civil planners would speak of associations in education, religion, and the professions as being like "sleeping giants" in a business economy, they would seek a new republic based on a decentralized system of organization—the creation of federations of small associations, so that more members participate. Each association is designed to advance a special interest but by choice can develop through confederations for the common good. Organizers would aim for greater civic engagement from the local to the national level across all major civil orders of society.

New Institutions

To coordinate these efforts and others, a US government that aims for a civil republic would also include a Council of Social Advisers (CSA) to work in tandem with the existing Council of Economic Advisors, as we proposed in Chapter 5. The CSA would conduct research on the comparative success of financial investments and social investments, and offer guidelines for allocating capital for the common good. It would also study the development of new institutions for a civil economy, and gather statistics on the well-being of people and the environment and use them to develop *social indicators* on the nation's health, education, and welfare to guide public policy. It would monitor changing economic trends and provide guidelines on how to respond to them for the common good.

Advancing Civil Investment

The nonprofit Council of Institutional Investors (CII) seeks to promote social responsibility and accountability in the realm of finance. Founded in 1985 in response to corporate takeover activities that threatened the financial interests of pension fund beneficiaries, it is now a large and influential organization with over 130 pension fund members whose assets exceed $2 trillion, and more than 125 honorary international participants and educational sustainers. It has taken a significant role in opposing excessive CEO salaries, and in pressuring business for more transparency and more accurate accounting. It provides an extensive guide to corporations on civil governance.[25]

But as much of a leap forward as voluntary social investment is—including screened portfolios offered by investment brokers of all kinds—we would argue that it is only a beginning. With government support it could evolve into a professional practice of civil investment that works in accord with the strategies we have been proposing, seeking to develop a civil polity in local to global markets, a balanced system that involves public standards and neutral monitors. Ultimately, such a system could have the power to insist on public directors for corporations that violate the law or do not perform according to the standards of a civil society.

When, on September 17, 2003, the New York Stock Exchange's board of directors announced the resignation of chairman and chief executive officer Richard Grasso, many analysts believed that the Securities Exchange Commission should require the NYSE to have public rather than private directors. The problem was not simply Grasso's $140 million paycheck—out of bounds for someone who was supposed to function as a regulator—it was the board's whole structure, the conflicts of interest that had developed, and the fact that the NYSE had become an insider club, not the public institution it purported to be.[26]

This could be a case study for our Council of Social Advisers, which would examine how to build a civil economy, including the monitoring of enforceable standards set in the public interest, as the next stage for correcting the practices of major corporations that violate the public trust. Its focus would be on matching and balancing many different criteria, such as social benefits vs. economic benefits, individual beneficiaries vs. the common good, and the corporate interest vs. the common good.

Civil investment is a new paradigm that takes into account the development of polities in market sectors and regimes in global markets. Its agenda links local to global development for the common good. It evolves through associations affiliated with the UN and scientific, economic, and social research on how to allocate capital in a global context.[27]

Organizing Civil Regimes

A "civil regime" is a system of authority with public norms to which international organizations give consent. It is a space where business, governments, and Third Sector groups develop standard making agreements. Civil regimes in global markets are a frontier, which we illustrated in the Law of the Seas, the International Standards Association, and the Forestry Stewardship Council. They are different from either political or business-dominated regimes in the global economy.

We have proposed a mode of civil governance based on the collaboration of *intergovernmental* organizations (IGOs), international business organizations (IBOs), and international *nongovernmental* organizations (INGOs). These organizations are already beginning to work together, but the goal of a global civil republic will be achieved much sooner if collaboration is done well and more systematically.

The World Trade Organization (WTO) is developing a world constitution for trade. It has a set of rules to guide markets and it is having a profound effect on governments. Some analysts tout the WTO as "the first effective world government" in history, but others say the same thing with grave concern. They see the WTO as a means by which global corporations are gaining power over national governments. What is missing is the countervailing power of those Third Sector associations representing the interests of the people and the planet.

In truth there is no world government to keep markets from destroying the environment, no world authority to regulate stock sales, arms sales, or insist on public service in telecommunications. Hence we speak of the need for civil regimes and a republic of world federations that can develop fair standards while sustaining free markets, and argue that this is the foundation for a global republic.

Today, organizing global corporations, private cartels, and political regimes is the name of the game. We gave examples of political regimes, such as the European Community (EC), the Organization of Petroleum Exporting Countries (OPEC), and the North American Free Trade Agreement (NAFTA). But their goals are economic and political, based on capitalism and nationalism. A civil regime is different. Its goals emphasize the principles of equity and justice for the common good. This develops with the aid of IGOs promoting "common law" and a system of jurisprudence administered by tri-sector tribunals.

A civil regime develops through common agreements between business and Third Sector organizations grounded in localities and backed by intergovernmental agreements. It develops as people see local to global standards essential to their well being and survival. The UN has a role to play in advancing civil regimes by supporting social contracts between global firms, civil society organizations, and local community corporations.

In this type of global development, federations create systems of public accountability. Business and the Third Sector associations keep their distance, but work together as countervailing powers, like the congress and the judiciary or like political parties. They emphasize cooperation in the midst of their countervailing positions and work for the overall good. They promote transparency markets while preserving appropriate proprietary rights. They negotiate with the UN to create global charters; they cultivate social and cultural resources along with material resources.[28]

Conclusion

A civil market is advanced inside a capitalist market by public policies that also advance a civil republic. These two aims of development—a civil market and a civil republic—go hand in hand. The United States could take the first step. It could advance civil polities in market sectors, support civil investment, organize civil commissions, provide support to civil federations, and encourage civil regimes in world markets. In this way the United States could evolve beyond what Adolph Berle once called an economic republic.

Will this plan for a civil republic work?[29] Looking back at the amazing accomplishment of the early North American colonists as they broke with

Britain, the historian Daniel Boorstin wrote, "They were not obliged to construct a whole theory of institutions." His point was that they simply tried to solve the practical problems at hand; in the meantime, their vision of a new republic grew as they kept debating differences and finding agreements.[30]

If we, too, look back, we see that the American colonies were a loose alliance in the seventeenth and early eighteenth centuries. They fought one other and competed with one another as each colony tried to advance its own interests. Many influential colonists resisted a higher union. They argued against federation and did not imagine how it could promote the general welfare. But leaders like Jefferson, Jay, Madison, Monroe, Washington, Franklin, and Hamilton brought them to realize a higher purpose in a union for the common good.

A civil republic is based on a higher union of associations and a more elevated purpose for markets and the nation. This is today's Fertile Verge. In civil commissions, citizens would study democracy in society, not just democracy in government. They would promote self-governance in business, not just the state. Citizens with an eye on their civic responsibility could bring forth a civil republic, a new way of life and a new level of governance for the nation. New forms of self-governance will be forged in the heat of debate about how to create a stronger and more humane union for the common good. It could begin with a struggle for a new media system. It could start with protests about corporate malfeasance or about government foreign policy. It could begin with people at any level of society.

One thing is clear. It will be fight to build a society of federations. It would be a bit of luck to have a set of leaders who are willing to live dangerously and construct a new nation. But if this is done, and done well, citizens will create a new order of democracy, one that could make this country once again a model for the world. When—and if—the work were finished, this new kind of nation would be called a civil republic.

Notes

1. Adolf A. Berle, *The American Economic Republic* (New York: Harcourt, Brace & World, 1963). Berle is not alone in this concept of the nation as an economic republic. It was implied in the work done by the "institutional economists," beginning in the late 1880s in the United States. The German "historical school" and some English historicists influenced these thinkers, and they made great advances in economic theory. They included Thorstein Veblen (1857–1929), John R. Commons (1862–1945), John Maurice Clark (1884–1963), Clarence E. Ayres (1890–1972), Gardiner C. Means (1896–1988), and Arthur R. Burns (1895–1981). In *The Modern Corporation and Private Property* (1933), Adolf Berle and Gardiner Means discussed how the concept of property was changing as a different concentration of economic power was developing at that time.

2. Ibid.
3. The use of "federation" replaces "association" here for our purposes. The term "learned society" is more common than "scholarly federation." For a list of federations of scholarly societies, see http://www.scholarly-societies.org/federations.html. The number and variety of federations has yet to be carefully researched.
4. Put another way, a civil republic will have replaced the (current) economic republic when people see that those values represented in the major orders of society inspire the market as a system. A civil republic then evolves with international law and civil regimes that develop prominently to shape markets.
5. These trade associations are very controversial. Here are four other outlooks, all contrary, yet, true by some degree. First, the business order is composed of corporate command systems that organize their power through trade associations. Second, the business order is a democracy of self-governing associations. Third, trade associations could destroy civil society. Fourth, trade associations can contribute to the development of society. Social scientists have explored the characteristics of trade associations. Mancur Olson, for example, describes the bargaining methods and monitoring costs among them. Other scholars have shown how associations check on cheating (i.e. self-monitor) each other. Others show how a sense of community ("cohesion") among members can be high or low, finding that a strong community is more likely among those associations with small memberships. Lane and Bachmann have suggested that a "culture of support" is needed to create a greater effectiveness among associations. Mancur Olson, *The Logic of Collective Action* (Cambridge, Massachusetts: Harvard University Press, 1971); C. Lane and R. Bachmann, "Cooperation in Inter-Firm Relations in Britain and Germany," *British Journal of Sociology* 42: 226–254; W. Streeck and P.C. Schmittrer (eds), *Private Interest Government* (London: Sage Publications,1985); Robert J. Bennett, "The Logic of Membership of Sectoral Business Associations."
6. According to *The New Fowler's Modern English Usage* (Oxford University Press, 1968), "A polity is (1) a form or process of civil government or constitution; (2) a society or country as a political entity." According to the Penguin *Dictionary of Sociology* (1994), "polity" refers to a set of political institutions within society. The term *polity* refers to power that is not just in the state and business but also equally in society. The development of a *civil polity* for our purposes refers to how organizations exercise responsible authority. A *civil market* develops through an increased participation of organizations that are not political or economic at the core.
7. The AICPA mailed ballot packages containing proposals about how to address issues of professional responsibility in light of corporate accounting failures to its more than 340,000 members. One proposal would allow the AICPA to sanction members without investigation if they have been sanctioned by governmental agencies such as the Securities and Exchange Commission, or by other organizations that have the authority to regulate accountants, such as the Public Company Accounting Oversight Board. A second proposal would give the AICPA the flexibility to disclose more information about an investigation, subject to the review and approval of its governing council; this proposal would

also allow the AICPA to disclose the results of a case to the individual or a body filing a formal complaint with the institute. Currently, remedial actions taken against AICPA members are not disclosed other than to specific government agencies that have referred matters to its Professional Ethics Executive Committee. AICPA, http://www.aicpa.org/news/2003/p030819.asp. The Sarbanes-Oxley Act of July 30, 2002, represents a push to reform corporate accountability in the United States but we are saying that accounting federations should take stronger stands when their members fail to enforce this act. The Act creates a Public Company Accounting Oversight Board (PCAOB) to oversee the accounting profession, protects the objectivity of research analysts, but the AICP could do more than the law requires.

8. At this writing, the state is seeking to sue Bechtel but its own laws forbid it from recovering costs on overruns that took place more than three or six years previous to its suit, depending upon "negligence" or "breach of contract." *The Boston Globe* reports that two-thirds of the $1.6 billion in overruns could be "off limits." The state governor, Mitt Romney, appointed a committee to investigate. Rick Klein, "Romney to Hire Firm to Recoup Big Dig Funds," *Boston Globe*, 11 February 2003, A-12.

9. The American Accounting Association is a federation that promotes "excellence in accounting education, research, and practice." The association emphasizes "integrity, objectivity, a sense of community, open communications, respect for others, high ethical values and behaviors, an increasingly global perspective, and an obligation to serve important stakeholders, including the broader society within which we operate." See the American Accounting Association, http://aaahq.org/about.cfm. The American Institute of Architects (AIA) comprises some 300 organizations—across the United States and around the world. AIA promulgates "a code of ethics and professional conduct outlines canons, ethical standards, and rules of conduct." AIA at http://www.aia.org/institute/ default.asp.

10. A government would strategize the development of civil markets based on the principle of countervailing powers. See John K. Galbraith, *American Capitalism: The Concept of Countervailing Powers* (Cambridge: Houghton Mifflin Company, 1956).

11. The Fair Labor Association (FLA) is a US federation with representatives from the apparel industry and from the Third Sector. This is "development" in its initial stage. The apparel industry is worldwide. A government agency in any single nation (e.g., OSHA) cannot set standards for American firms overseas. The next logical step is to write a contract with the International Labour Organisation.

12. John Rennie, "The Future of Human Evolution," *Scientific American*, March 2001, 8.

13. When "engineers" alter a genetic code, its new code-combination begins to affect both the internal and external life of organisms. Altering this chemical composition modifies every cell in the organism. A genetically engineered organism then evolves and interacts with its environment and with other living organisms. Generation after generation it passes on its mutant characteristics to its offspring as well as to other related and unrelated organisms. When

genetically engineered organisms (GMOs) are released unmonitored into the environment they become a permanent part of the earth and its biosphere. They cannot be recalled back into the laboratory, nor contained within a fenced pasture or a special marine environment. These organisms are self-propagating. Genetic engineering is, in the minds of many scientists, an unpredictable new technology. Scientists agree that genetically engineered (GE) foods are not adequately safety-tested for possible damage to human health. GMOs and GE foods may present serious hazards to human health and the environment. Ronnie Cummins and Ben Lilliston, *Genetically Engineered Food* (New York: Marlowe & Co., 2000), 3.

14. The Conference Board was born out of a crisis in industry in 1916. See http://www.conference-board.org/aboutus/history.cfm. The Conference Board held its "2003 Leadership Conference on Global Corporate Citizenship," with the subtitle "Transparency: The New Rules of the Game," on February 10–11, 2003, at the Waldorf-Astoria in New York.

15. See the Chamber's International Court of Arbitration, http://www.iccwbo.org/index_court.asp.

16. OSHA says "6,371 job-related injury deaths, 13.3 million nonfatal injuries, 60,300 disease deaths, and 1,184,000 illnesses occurred in the US workplace" in the year 2000. The total direct and indirect costs associated with these injuries and illnesses were estimated to be $155.5 billion, or nearly 3% of gross domestic product (GDP). Direct costs included medical expenses for hospitals, physicians, and drugs, as well as health insurance administration costs, and were estimated to be $51.8 billion. The indirect costs included loss of wages, costs of fringe benefits, and loss of home production (e.g., child care provided by parent and home repairs), as well as employer retraining and workplace disruption costs, and were estimated to be $103.7 billion. J. Paul Leigh, et al., *Costs of Occupational Injuries and Illnesses* (University of Michigan Press, 2000), See http://www.pbs.org/wgbh/pages/frontline/shows/workplace/etc/cost.html, excerpted with Permission on *Frontline*, "A Dangerous Business." details on civil alternatives to OSHA, see Severyn T. Bruyn, *A Future for the American Economy* (Stanford, California: Stanford University Press, 1991), 255ff. For an example of how OSHA is now working in this direction, see Trade News Release, 12 December 2002, "The US Department of Labor: OSHA and the Washington Group International." This is an alliance to advance "a culture of accident prevention" in the engineering and construction industries. See http://www.osha.gov/pls/oshaweb/owadisp.show_document?p_table=NEWS_RELEASES&p_id=9934&p_text_version=FALSE.

17. For more on this educational direction, see Wendell Berry, *Life is a Miracle* (Washington, D.C., Counterpoint, Perseus Books, 2000); David Korten, *The Post-Corporate World* (West Hartford, Conn.: Berrett-Koehler, 2000); and natural historian R. C. Lewinton, *Biology as Ideology* (New York: HarperCollins, 1992). In our scenario the secretary would quote Henry David Thoreau "the universe is wider than our views of it."

18. All American universities vie for position on rankings issued by assessors (e.g., the National Research Council and *U.S News & World Report*). For information on assessors, see The Center, http://thecenter.ufl.edu/index.html. They also

compete for government funding, but Irwin Feller, an economics professor at Pennsylvania State University, says that pumping money into "marquis pro-grams" in market-oriented science could drain money from the arts and the humanities, leaving "steeples of excellence" surrounded by "tenements of mediocrity." Feller is quoted in Michael Arnone, "The Wannabes: More Public Universities Are Striving to Squeeze into the Top Tier," *Chronicle of Higher Education*, 3 January 2003, A 18. The question here is, How can we advance sci-ence and the humanities and the arts together?

19. See A. Sachs, *Eco-Justice: Linking Human Rights and the Environment*, (Washington, D.C.: Worldwatch Institute, 1995), 1–2, 11. For a rationale from Great Britain on the importance of teaching global citizenship, see also, "Citizen Education: The Global Dimension," at http://www.citizenship-global. org.uk/faqs.html. Also see, in the US, the College of Education and Social Services, University of Vermont, http://www.uvm.edu/~dewey/mono-graphs/ glomono.html.

20. Some argue that for-profit educational institutions promote a free market ide-ology. Yorktownuniversity.com., for example, is chartered to promote "a con-servative ideology" and challenge the "liberal agenda." It seeks to hire faculty and admit students who believe liberal colleges "do not welcome free-market views." Courses at this new university include "Virtue and Business," "Adam Smith and His World," and "Entrepreneurial History of the US". Yorktown, based in Virginia, says that it emphasizes, "business oriented courses." It has approval from the state to enroll students in bachelor's degree programs in government and in managerial economics. Goldie Blumenstyk, "An Online University Plans to Present a Conservative View of the World," *Chronicle of Higher Education*, 15 December 2000, A 49.

21. Accreditation of educational programs offered on the Internet would be a major issue here. The North Central Association of Colleges and Schools has accred-ited some "all-online" institutions, but the Southern Association of Colleges and Schools has refused to do so. Meanwhile, many traditional universities are moving into this arena. New York University, for example, has organized a for-profit online-education subsidiary. "Teaching" at its for-profit company, NYUonline, is broken down into separate components. First one professor gen-erates a syllabus, then an "instructional designer" works to put the content on-line, then a different instructor interacts with students in "real-time chat sessions." In fact, in this case, actual faculty *may or may not* be involved in the design, development, content expertise, delivery, and distribution of courses. Some educators have commented that NYUonline is like Adam Smith's "pin factory all over again." Although supporters argue that this "division of labor" increases "productivity," William Scheuerman, president of the faculty union United University Professions, says, "We are concerned about a disassembling and de-skilling of the profession. "Sarah Carr, "A Day in the Life of a New Type of Professor," *Chronicle of Higher Education*, 47.

22. See AASA "Comprehensive School Reform," http://www.aasa.org/ issues_and_insights/ESEA/ESEA_best_of_web_index.htm.

23. This chart has many sources. See Simon Zadeck, *The Civil Corporation* (London: Earthscan, 2001), 19; Zadeck's chart was drawn from World

Development Movement, *Making Investment Work for People* (WDM, London), and adapted from Annex. In addition, see Severyn T. Bruyn, *A Civil Economy* (Ann Arbor: University of Michigan, 2000), 223–229; and "Organizations Advocating World Government," at http://www.williamcooper.com/ wrldgov.htm.

24. These figures are drawn from cumulative results of all elections held from 1945 through 1998; See PBS's *NOW* program archive, at http://www.pbs.org/ now/politics/votestats.html.

25. On guidelines for the civil governance of corporations in which their members invest, for example, the CII expects that all board directors should be elected annually by confidential ballots counted by independent tabulators. "Confidentiality should be automatic and permanent and apply to all ballot items. Rules and practices concerning the casting, counting and verifying of shareholder votes should be clearly disclosed. At least two-thirds of a corporation's directors should be independent. A director is deemed independent if his or her only non-trivial professional, familial or financial connection to the corporation, its chairman, CEO or any other executive officer is his or her directorship. . . . A corporation should disclose information necessary for shareholders to determine whether each director qualifies as independent, whether or not the disclosure is required by state or federal law . . . [and] corporations should disclose all financial or business relationships with and payments to directors and their families and all significant payments to companies, non-profits, foundations and other organizations where company directors serve as employees, officers or directors." See the Council of Institutional Investors, at http://www.cii.org/corp_governance.asp.

26. The announcement that Grasso would receive $139.5 million in accrued benefits touched off the fury. Grasso sat on the board of Computer Associates, a company with a reputation for excessive executive compensation whose stock traded on his own exchange. He also sat on the board of Home Depot Inc., another company that traded on his exchange. Meg Richards, "Stock Exchange Is Back to Business, But Many Questions Remain," AP Business Writer, http://www.newsday.com/ news/local/wire/ny-bc-nyse-grasso0918sep18,0,2830927.story?coll=ny-ap- regional-wire.

27. Social investors today sponsor shareholder resolutions, meet with management, screen their investments, divest stock, conduct public hearings and investigations, publish special reports, and sponsor actions such as vigils, letter writing campaigns, and consumer boycotts. They promote economic development in low-income and minority communities. But as this practice evolves, we should see it based on more social scientific research and a larger framework for deciding the allocation of capital. Each year, for instance, the member investors of the Interfaith Center for Corporate Responsibility sponsor over 100 shareholder resolutions on major social and environmental issues. They are concerned with eliminating sweatshops, increasing human rights, stopping corporate abuses, reversing global warming, halting the proliferation of genetically modified foods until their safety is proven. They want to guarantee equal employment opportunity for all, end the use of racially offensive images as logos and ads, and make pharmaceuticals and healthcare safe, avail-

able, and affordable to all. They want to end tobacco product advertising, foreign military sales, prevent the "militarization" of outer space, and make capital available to all on an equal opportunity basis. Social investors say that they want to achieve "more than an acceptable financial return" while at the same time using their "resources" to stop harmful corporate policies. They "work for peace," "economic justice," and "stewardship of the Earth." See ICCR at http://www.iccr.org/about/index.htm.

28. The UN has begun work toward a global civil republic. The first 20 articles of the UN 1948 Declaration of Universal Human Rights lays out the course. Charles Derber, *People Before Profits* (New York: St. Martin's Press, 2002), 110.

29. The late Norman Cousins, writer, literary editor, and president of the world federalists, said to me in the 1960s that we (Americans) might have to face a devastating WWIII before we learn how to share power with other nations. It may take a terrible nuclear war to force us to study the history of fallen empires. See Norman Cousins, *In Place of Folly*, (NY. Harpers, 1961.

30. Daniel Boorstin, *Hidden History* (New York: Vintage Books, 1989), 108.

Glossary of Key Terms

Capitalist markets

Capitalist markets are systems of exchange that cultivate economic values with attributes such as efficiency, productivity, profit making, competition, freedom, and self-interest. They are defined for our purposes as an "ideal type" for research and as a "planning model" for public policy. These markets never fully achieve their ideals; markets are never totally free and it seems that there is always room for more efficiency and competition. Economists explain markets by concepts of scarcity and calculable utilities, but this is not the whole story. They are also bound up quietly with the social and cultural values of society.

Civil association

A civil association is a voluntary organization that has a predominantly democratic structure and core social values as part of its constitution and purpose. For example, the American Medical Association (AMA) would promote the core value of public health, and the American Bar Association (ABA) would promote justice. If this type of association were an ideal type, it would have measurable levels of transparency, fairness, cooperation, equity, self-management, and self-financing.

Civil federation

A civil federation is a voluntary organization in which members elect representatives to a general assembly and make decisions on a democratic basis. It expresses society's core ideals, which have the potential to develop more effectively for members of the organization. For example, federations might express some level of democracy, equity, fairness, honesty, and transparency, but these values can usually be further developed and refined for the common good of their constituencies.

Civil commission

A civil commission is a nonprofit corporation of stakeholders in the economy. The government appoints stakeholders to this commission to study solutions to a market's social problems, such as consumer safety, environmental damage, and debilitating externalities. A commission can recommend changing the structure of a market to work more effectively in the public interest. It might propose that market competitors bring public standards into the bylaws of their trade association. It might suggest that a trade group contract with a Third Sector organization for monitoring its industry. If the recommendations are not advanced voluntarily, the commission can propose corrective legislation to government.

Civil development

Civil development is a process whereby people bring public standards to the interior structure of markets. For example, nonprofit accreditors today promote standards of excellence in the competitive market of universities, or raise standards of health care in the market of hospitals and HMOs. Civil development is a process in which business leaders set up public accountability systems for their industry. Accountability systems require corporations to integrate their traditional economic values (e.g., private profits, competition, productivity, and efficiency) with social values (e.g., public honesty, fairness, cooperation, and transparency).

Civil economy

A civil economy in its ideal form is a private (nongovernmental) system of production, distribution, and services that has an ample number of public accountability systems. In a civil economy, people develop stakeholder contracts with business. Stakeholder contracts help make a competitive market more profitable, equitable, fair, reliable, free, and transparent for the common good.

Civil governance

Civil governance refers to the democratic management of an organization with measurable levels of transparency and egalitarian values. The core values of democratic management are usually *latent* (not fully developed) within the life of major organizations, but with good planning they become more *manifest* (developed). Corporations, as organizations, are usually based on a command system or an oligarchy, but there is generally room to make latent values (such as equity, fairness, and transparency) more real.

Civil investment

Civil investment develops from the profession of social investment. Civil investors work on societal development within the context of the economy. They support *civil polities* in domestic markets and *civil regimes* in world markets. They seek the best possible synthesis between opposing criteria for allocating capital, such as "ethical norms vs. economic norms," and "corporate interest vs. public interest," and "national development vs. international development."

Civil markets

Civil markets are systems of exchange that cultivate social and cultural values with economic and financial values. They are defined for our purposes as an "ideal type" for research and as a planning model for policymakers. They are "economically oriented" (prudent) more than they are "economically determined" (profit-driven). Their values are advanced through three sectors: business, government and the Third Sector. They develop when business leaders augment the level of self-management within their corporation and bring public standards into the bylaws of their trade association. They develop when government brings the concept of fair trade into free trade and promotes transparency in markets. Most important, they develop through public accountability systems in private markets.

Civil orders

Civil orders are ways of life that represent the most critical values and institutions in a nation. These orders include the broad fields of religion, government, business, art, science, and the professions. Each civil order has its own associations, institutions, and a culture that emphasizes substantive values. Civic leaders in these orders become agents for change when they translate their key values into public standards in the economy.

Civil republic

A civil republic is a society of federations that brings core values into a market economy. It is not an economic republic. Political and economic interests are not the main forces driving a civil republic, or the main determinant of national policies. Profit making still drives the market, and political interests are still part of national policy, but they are not the single or primary motifs. Public policy in this model encourages a creative mix of society's most basic values.

Put another way, a civil republic is a prototype (model) for public planning. Following this prototype, government planners would help capitalist markets develop into civil markets. This requires supporting strong "civic engagement" of Third Sector organizations in the economy, and the development of civil federations in the market system.

This prototype of a civil republic is a planning strategy for nations, but it is equally important to see it as a model for planning global governance. In a competitive world of nations, fraught with the dangers of new technology and terrorism, the concept of a *global civil republic* is a frontier for world leaders to explore. Developing a decentralized democratic republic of nations with the participation of civil society organizations will call for the promotion of international law. It will require a system of world courts and a multilateral global peace force. All this planning takes place in the context of a market organized by civil regimes.

Civil trade

Civil trade is a type of economic exchange that in theory combines the values of freedom and justice. Government policy in this case would support the principles of equity and fairness along with the principles of a free market economy. It is done with the help of international nongovernmental organizations (INGOs) and intergovernmental organizations (IGOs). Nations that engage in civil trade bring social issues into the market, such as safety, health, probity, and transparency. Global institutions for conflict resolution and arbitration help settle these issues.

The common good

Citizens and stakeholders define the common good within different levels of corporate and market organization as well as within government. At the national level, it is equivalent to "the public interest" and defined by law. It develops a meaning in markets through national and international agreements. In a global market plan, civil regime leaders (stakeholders) negotiate a common good in the context of nations.

Core value

A core value is a principle of great worth and concern to citizens. Citizens and stakeholders define it in different ways. A core value could be an ideal, like freedom. It could be an exemplary idea, such as "human safety for all." It could be an abstract concept, like justice. It could be a sought-after principle, like truth. It could be an aesthetic value, like "beauty."

Core values are not all rational. They are connected with human feelings such as "compassion," "understanding," and "appreciation," and are thus not entirely calculable. They inspire people to improve the world and generate public standards in the economy. Core values can be translated into market standards and be measured, like "restaurant cleanliness" or "consumer product safety."

Economic development

Economic development refers to raising the gross domestic product and income per capita in a nation. Economists see capital investment as significant in this development because it enlarges a nation's capacity to produce goods and services. It raises the productivity of resources, creates multiplier effects, and increases aggregate demand as well as the national income. An increase in the national income in theory raises the level of savings and provides financing for more capital accumulation. Economic development thus refers to advancing the material output of society and profits for business.

Global Regimes

A global regime is a system of authority in the private economy based on norms to which international organizations give consent. We discuss two types.

A *capitalist* global regime is based in the business sector with government approval, implicit or explicit. It could be a cartel of global corporations or a set of enforceable trade agreements among nations.

A *civil* global regime, by contrast, is rooted in common law and develops through international bodies of authority. Examples are the Forestry Stewardship Council, the International Standards Organization (ISO), and the Law of the Sea. Stakeholders in civil regimes develop a public domain through uniform standards and systems of accountability. This type of regime is normally organized with trisector stakeholders such as international business organizations (IBOs), international governmental organizations (IGOs), and nongovernmental organizations (NGOs).

Ideal Type

An ideal type for our purposes is a scientific construct and a planning construct at the same time. As a scientific construct, it depicts the features of a social institution that would be present if it were a logically consistent whole, not affected by other institutions and interests. Max Weber described such constructs as "bureaucracy" and noted how its attributes never correspond perfectly to reality. An ideal type is composed of a list of attributes against which observers can compare actual cases.

The ideal type for a capitalist market or a civil market can also be seen as a model for planning. All organizations and institutions—like bureaucracy and markets—deviate from their ideal construct in reality. A civil-market ideal type in this sense can guide both planners and researchers on the degree to which its attributes fit reality.

Manifest and latent

The adjective *manifest* refers to the attributes of a social phenomenon (e.g., an institution or organization) that are most evident to observers. The term *latent* refers to attributes that are not so evident. Manifest can equally refer to "developed attributes" and latent to "undeveloped attributes" in an institution.

In our ideal type of capitalist markets, manifest and latent attributes can both be seen at the same time (see Chapter 5). In capitalist markets, for example, competition is manifest (most obvious) whereas cooperation is latent (not so obvious). We propose that cooperation can be developed, become manifest selectively, and advance a system of civil markets.

Markets

Markets are systems of exchange in which people trade things that have value to them. Economists define markets as exchange systems based on scarcity, that is, where there is a demand for goods in limited supply. Markets are institutional arrangements for trading goods, services, and rights based on the measure of money. Prices allow people to weigh the importance of things traded, to assess how something that is gained is worth more than what is being given up. Sociologists, on the other hand, see markets as "organizational fields" in which people compete and take account of each other in making decisions. Markets have social meanings and are institutions that change their attributes over time.

Market polity

Polity refers to the ruling structure of an organization, that is, the way people distribute power and authority. A market in this case is a political field of exchange. A "market polity" indicates how an economic exchange is organized on the basis of equity vs. hierarchy. A market can include partnerships, proprietorships, and corporations, but its polity is about power relationships. The market is where people compete for control, authority, and money. Every market is a political field where power exists, not just profit making. Two types of market polity are relevant here.

A *capitalist* polity is found in the business sector where corporations use money and power to influence stakeholders, such as buyers, sellers, workers, government, customers, communities, and the public. The powerful influence of this capitalist polity on government is real. These markets are not just a system designed to make profits and create wealth.

A *civil* polity describes how democratic associations develop public standards. The ideal in this case is a (relatively) self-regulating market of competitors who agree on standards for the common good. A civil polity develops when nonprofit (e.g., trade, professional, and union) federations introduce core standards—like safety, health, transparency, fairness, and equity—into the market. Setting public standards and monitoring them helps to resolve stakeholder conflicts, as is done with such associations as the Joint Commission on Accreditation of Healthcare Organizations (JCAHO), the American National Standards Institute (ANSI), and accrediting associations in the field of education.

Political investment

Political investment is the allocation of capital based on the strategic interest of an organization, such as a trade union, a bank, or a government. A political interest can be as important as a financial interest in making an investment. For example, a trade union may invest its pension funds only in "union-friendly" companies; a bank may invest its money in a company just to keep it financially stable for its own protection; a state like New Jersey may invest its pension funds to encourage jobs inside its political boundaries; the World Bank may invest in a nation for ideological reasons, not purely financial reasons.

A public domain

A public domain is a field of exchange where stakeholders (e.g., employees, buyers, and sellers) are free to talk and trade openly. Stakeholders in this domain would observe transparency in their transactions and compete according to community standards. They aim at best to reconcile society's values with market values. They seek a common ground in the midst of their differences and have the opportunity of expressing opinions freely and honestly. They are able to dissent from convention and negotiate without government reprisal.

A public media

A public media for our purposes is a societal system of mass communication. This is different from a business system of mass communication that is designed mainly for profit. It is where people entertain, debate, and address common problems through all three sectors, business, government, and the Third Sector. It is where people express opinions openly and widely, as in a city or a nation. It is where organizations compete but also organize for the common good. In our ideal model of a public media system, a board of directors from the whole society—representing their constituencies—would govern it. (Chapter 7).

A public standard

A public standard is a societal (core) value that is translated into a practical norm and introduced into the market. The core value of truth, for example, is translated into standards for honesty in corporate accounting; it sustains integrity in bookkeeping. The core value of human health is a societal (core) value that is translated into standards of hygiene in factories.

Rationality

Rationality is a type of thinking that balances the means and ends of action and is based on agreed-upon rules. It is a type of thinking that is considered logical and rooted in reality. It is not seen as grounded in emotion or some absolute principle. For our purposes, there are two special types of rationality relevant to a market economy.

Formal rationality is based on calculations that increase the chance of reaching a goal, like making a profit. It applies technical criteria to measure success. It is emphasized in the business sector but also operates throughout the culture of modern nations.

Substantive rationality cannot be measured and it does not assess the outcome of a decision. For our purposes, it includes the core values of society. Rationality develops around substantive (core) values that are based on the appeal of them as principles of humanity. There is rationality in the sense of logical consistency that develops in their defense. Core values like freedom, justice, democracy, and truth then translate into standards as part of the economy—like *sovereign* choice, *fair* competition, and *honest* accounting.

Max Weber argued that formal rationality could replace substantive rationality in a market society because modern institutions emphasize a technical orientation that would match means to ends. We propose that civil development can mitigate that market tendency to lose the substance of core values. This proposal is based on the notion that there are links to be found between formal and substantive rationality in the public standards set in a market. They are more than abstract constructs; they are connected in reality.

Social investment

Social investment is a strategy for allocating capital based on a combination (or the best synthesis) of financial and ethical principles. It is different from ordinary financial investment, which is designed to increase monetary returns alone. Its purpose is to blend social-cultural values with economic-financial values in the interest of stakeholders.

Societal development

Societal development refers to the cultivation of core values in the major orders of society. It is different from business development and economic development. It is a creative mix of values that are drawn from various civil orders. For example, societal development occurs when government officials develop efficiency and productivity (normally practiced in the business order) to reduce state bureaucracy. It happens when business leaders see "justice" and "democracy" (normally concerns of the state order) as important to markets and business. It happens by the expansion of different core values together, such as individuality and community.

Put another way, it happens through a creative blend of different broad-scale interests and values. It is an original combination of competing core values that could be classified as economic, political, governmental, educational, artistic, recreational, religious, scientific, and professional. It is a synthesizing of contrary values to reach a higher order of thought. It occurs often through the mutual influence of people working in different cultures of a nation. We noted, for example, that a new field of finance developed in the last century owing to the reciprocal influence of people working in business and the Third Sector. It is called *social investment*, a confluence of very different sets of values.

Stakeholders

Stakeholders are people who are affected substantially by a corporation or a market. They could include owners, employees, competitors, investors, customers, buyers, suppliers, governments, and communities. In a civil market plan, concerned stakeholders specify the meaning of public standards for them. For example, "transparency" is a market standard with a commonsense meaning, but stakeholders must define it precisely in their concern about a specific market.

Synthesis

Synthesis is the resolution of two or more contradictory outlooks. It results in a new outlook (sometimes a new structure) that includes the essential values in the prior (contradictory) outlooks. It can be a linking of opposite interests, norms, or values and then a resolution based on some higher ground of rationality. Stakeholders with conflicting outlooks, for example, negotiate solutions all the time in the market. When representatives of a factory and a union negotiate a contract, they typically bring opposing views together to form a new outlook, a higher purpose, and a more elevated cause to work for toward their common good. Stakeholders in a process of civil development link and integrate opposing values and bring them into a more advanced level of market organization.

Systems of public accountability

Stakeholders create a system of public accountability by: 1) *agreements* (contracts, deals, covenants, compacts, pacts, and documents), 2) *standards* (norms, rules, principles, criteria, measures, guidelines, codes, and regulations), 3) *monitors* (observers, witnesses, critics, advisors, directors, counselors, informants, and whistleblowers) and 4) *authorities* (judges, courts, tribunals, enforcers, arbiters, adjudicators, and mediators). An example would be the American National Standards Institute.

Third sector values

Third Sector values are mainly social/cultural as distinguished from being political/economic, although both types of values coexist. They are ideals embodied in the major orders of a modern nation. For example, Third Sector values are embedded in the professions, in medicine (e.g., public health and physical well-being) and law (e.g., civil justice and fairness); in religious life (e.g., spiritual compassion and human kindness); family life (e.g., caring and nurturing); and education (e.g., truth and reasoning). For our purposes, the Third Sector is notable for posing a countervailing power to the market at the same time it maintains its ability to work effectively with business. The Third Sector, business, and government together have the potential to create a civil republic.

Index

About the Author

Severyn Bruyn is an emeritus professor in the Department of Sociology at Boston College. He has published numerous books and articles on the economy, has served as director of the graduate Program in Social Economy and Social Justice at Boston College, and has been given various awards for his work.

Also from Kumarian Press...

International Development and Civil Society

Creating a Better World: Interpreting Global Civil Society
Edited by Rupert Taylor

Global Civil Society: Dimensions of the Nonprofit Sector, Volume One
Lester M. Salamon, Helmut K. Anheier, Regina List, Stefan Toepler, S. Wojciech Sokolowski and Associates

Global Civil Society: Dimensions of the Nonprofit Sector, Volume Two
Lester M. Salamon, S. Wojciech Sokolowski, and Associates

Globalization and Social Exclusion: A Transformationalist Perspective
Ronaldo Munck

The Charity of Nations: Humanitarian Action in a Calculating World
Ian Smillie and Larry Minear

When Corporations Rule the World, Second Edition
David C. Korten

Worlds Apart: Civil Society and the Battle for Ethical Globalization
John Clark

International Development, Humanitarianism, Peacebuilding

Ethics and Global Politics: The Active Learning Sourcebook
Edited by April Morgan, Lucinda Joy Peach, and Colette Mazzucelli

Human Rights and Development
Peter Uvin

Nation-Building Unraveled? Aid, Peace and Justice in Afghanistan
Edited by Antonio Donini, Norah Niland and Karin Wermester

Ritual and Symbol in Peacebuilding
Lisa Schirch

Southern Exposure
International Development and the Global South in the Twenty-First Century
Barbara P. Thomas-Slayter

War and Intervention: Issues for Contemporary Peace Operations
Michael V. Bhatia

Visit Kumarian Press at **www.kpbooks.com** or call **toll-free 800.289.2664** for a complete catalog.